ON THE COMMONWEALTH

The Library of Liberal Arts
OSKAR PIEST, FOUNDER

ON THE COMMONWEALTH

MARCUS TULLIUS CICERO

Translated, with an Introduction, by

GEORGE HOLLAND SABINE
and
STANLEY BARNEY SMITH

Macmillan Publishing Company
New York
Collier Macmillan Publishers
London

Marcus Tullius Cicero: 106-43 B.C.

First Edition
Nineteenth Printing — 1989

ISBN 0-02-404980-8

CONTENTS

· · · · · · · · · · · · · · · ·

PREFACE

The present volume offers an English version of Cicero's work on the *Commonwealth*. In addition, we have accompanied the translation with an introduction setting forth in some detail his theory of the state and the sources of that theory, and with such commentary as we thought necessary if the text, especially in its fragmentary shape, was to have any meaning for the general reader. The task was not inconsiderable, because of the lack of technical literature on the subject. It would have been more difficult still, had it not been for the generosity of numerous friends, who gave time and labor to criticizing our manuscript. Accordingly, we take this opportunity to thank those who have read the manuscript in whole or in part and who have made valuable suggestions: Professors A. R. Chandler, F. W. Coker, J. A. O. Larsen, and Dean W. J. Shepard, of the Ohio State University; Dean Paul Nixon of Bowdoin College; and particularly Miss Mabel C. Hawes of the Eastern High School, Washington, D. C.; Professor M. B. Ogle of the Ohio State University; and Professor W. S. Ferguson of Harvard University.

January 1, 1929.

LIST OF ABBREVIATIONS

The following is a list of the abbreviations of those works of Cicero to which we have most frequently referred in the notes of the Introduction and translation. In referring to the *Commonwealth*, we cite book and chapter, while in the case of all other works we give book, chapter, and section.

acad.................. *academica posteriora* or *priora* (as in Reid's ed.)

ad Att................ *epistulae ad Atticum*

ad fam............... *epistulae ad familiares*

ad Q. fr.............. *epistulae ad Quintum fratrem*

Brut. .... *de claris oratoribus liber qui dicitur Brutus*

de am................ *Laelius sive de amicitia dialogus*

de fin................ *de finibus bonorum et malorum libri quinque*

de leg................ *de legibus libri tres*

de leg. ag............. *de lege agraria contra P. Servilium Rullum tribunum plebis in senatu oratio prima* or *secuna* (as further indicated by ref.)

de n. d............... *de natura deorum libri tres*

de off................ *de officiis ad Marcum filium libri tres*

de opt. gen. orat....... *de optimo genere oratorum*

de or................. *de oratore libri tres*

de sen............... *Cato maior sive de senectute ad T. Pomponium Atticum*

in Cat................ *in L. Catilinam oratio prima*, etc.

in Pis................ *in L. Calpurnium Pisonem oratio*

parad. .... *paradoxa ad M. Brutum*

pro Arch.............. *pro A. Licinio Archia poeta oratio*

pro Caec............. *pro A. Caecina oratio*

pro Cluent............ *pro A. Cluentio Avito oratio*

pro Planc............. *pro Gn. Plancio oratio*

pro Rosc............. *pro Q. Roscio comoedo oratio*

top. .... *ad C. Trebatium topica*

Tusc................. *Tusculanarum disputationum libri quinque*

PART I

ON THE COMMONWEALTH

INTRODUCTION

CHAPTER I

THE COMMONWEALTH
AND ITS AUTHOR

THE VATICAN PALIMPSEST OF THE COMMONWEALTH

The text of Cicero's *Commonwealth*, with the exception of such excerpts from it as were made by later writers, especially Lactantius, Augustine, and Macrobius, depends wholly upon one manuscript in the Vatican Library. This consists of one hundred and fifty-one leaves, and was written probably in the fourth or fifth century of the Christian Era. At some later period an attempt, fortunately careless, was made to obliterate the Ciceronian text; and Augustine's commentary on the Psalms was copied over the imperfectly erased words of Cicero. The large letters of the *Commonwealth* are thus visible beneath the smaller but sharper letters of Augustine. Angelo Mai, the librarian of the Vatican, discovered this palimpsest and published it in 1822. It is generally thought that the extant portions of the *Commonwealth* constitute about one-third of the work as it left Cicero's hands.

LIFE OF CICERO

Marcus Tullius Cicero was born on January 3, 106 B. C., at Arpinum, a small town located about sixty miles to the southeast of Rome. Moving to this latter city during his youth, he devoted himself to the studies which prepared a young man for the legal profession. While still in his twenties, Cicero began to appear before the courts in the capacity of advocate. But he was not satisfied with his early training, and desired to supplement it by further study in Greece. Accordingly, he left Rome in 79 B. C. for a period of two years in the East, where he attended philosophical lectures in Athens, traveled over various parts of Asia Minor, and was a pupil in the famous school of rhetoric conducted by Molo at Rhodes.

In 77 B. C. Cicero returned to Rome and speedily became the leading figure of the Roman bar. His prominence opened the way to public life. By winning the office of quaestor in 75 B. C. he began the political career which carried him successively to the curule aedileship in 69 B. C., to the praetorship in 66 B. C., and finally to the consulate in 63 B. C.

The chief event which marked Cicero's term of office was the outbreak of the Catilinarian conspiracy. In suppressing the treasonable designs of Catiline and his faction Cicero acted with great vigor. He sponsored the motion which the senate passed in the form of the *senatus consultum ultimum*. This practically created a state of martial law. It is a much disputed question whether Cicero acted illegally in summarily putting to death the conspirators. At all events, the course which he followed made it possible for his political foes to allege that, by refusing to allow the accused conspirators to appeal to the *comitia centuriata*, he had disregarded or infringed upon a venerated right of Roman citizens. Hence, at the termination of his consulate, when, in accordance with the usual action of a retiring consul, he was to take public oath that he had not violated the laws, he was forbidden to do so by Metellus Nepos. Accordingly, he declared instead that he had saved the state.

After the formation of the so-called first triumvirate in 60 B. C. Cicero ceased to play a major rôle upon the stage of Roman politics. In 58 B. C., due to the antipathy which he had aroused by his action in the Catilinarian conspiracy, he was exiled through a proposal sponsored by the tribune Publius Clodius Pulcher. In the following year he was recalled, and on his journey from Brundisium to Rome was accorded a most fervid welcome. However hopeful he may have been of regaining his former position in political life, the conference of Luca in 56 B. C., at which the triumvirs renewed their powers, completely quenched his aspirations.

During the period which lasted from 55 to 51 B. C. Cicero sought relief from disillusionment and despair in literary work. While at no time did he cease his duties as an advocate, it was at this time of discouragement that he began the long series of rhetorical and philosophical works which perhaps give him his chief claim to immortality.[1] He finished the work entitled *De oratore* in 55 B. C. and devoted the four years which followed to the composition of the *Commonwealth*.

In 51 B. C. he began his belated proconsulate in Cilicia where his rule was characterized by efficiency and honesty, virtues none too common in Roman provincial administrators at any time. After his return to Rome in the following year Cicero took no share in political life, unwilling to compromise his own convictions by taking sides either with Caesar or with Pompey or, after the latter's defeat at Pharsalus in 48 B. C., to approve the measures which Caesar put into effect. Profoundly depressed because of the condition of the Roman state, Cicero was thrown into still deeper sorrow by the loss of his daughter Tullia in February, 45 B. C. Seeking consolation where he might find it, he turned again to literary composition and in the two years before his death wrote a very large number of philosophical works, some of them hardly more than elegant paraphrases of Greek originals, others marked by a distinctively Roman touch. In spite of the fact that Cicero's brilliant style is rarely accompanied by originality of thought, it is perhaps not too much to say that there is no body of ancient literature which is equally important in bringing before us the intellectual history of the past, since it is to these works that we owe most of our knowledge of the Hellenistic philosophies.

After the assassination of Caesar on March 15, 44 B. C., Cicero became the leader of the party in Rome which opposed Antonius. This was in some respects the most heroic moment of his life. In a series of speeches, which became known as the *Philippics* because of a general similarity to the orations in which Demosthenes had attacked Philip of Macedon, he assailed Antonius and gained his relentless hostility. In the

---

[1] Schantz: *Gesch d. röm. Lit.* 1. 2 (1909), pp. 339 ff.

proscriptions which followed the establishment of the second triumvirate between Antonius, Octavius, and Lepidus in 43 B. C., Cicero was marked for death. He was killed by Antonius' soldiers on December 7, 43 B. C. in his sixty-third year.

PERSONS OF THE DIALOGUE

PUBLIUS CORNELIUS SCIPIO AFRICANUS MINOR, who is the chief interlocutor in the *Commonwealth,* was born about 185 B. C. He was the son of Aemilius Paulus, who defeated Perseus at Pydna in 168 B. C., and from him derived the alternative cognomen of Aemilianus. Displaying great promise in his youth, he was adopted as son by the elder son of the Africanus who had vanquished Hannibal at Zama in 202 B. C. His wife was the daughter of Tiberius Sempronius Gracchus, and thus he was the brother-in-law of the famous tribunes. He died in 129 B. C. under circumstances of the deepest mystery.

Scipio was the most distinguished Roman of his time. He was connected by blood, marriage, or adoption with three notable Roman families, the Cornelii, the Aemilii, and the Sempronii. His character was above all vulgar reproach. In the course of a long and glorious military career, he fought at Pydna in 168 B. C.; in 151 he went to Spain as military tribune; as consul in 146 he brought about the capture and destruction of Carthage; and in 133, again as consul, he ended with victory the difficult and protracted struggle which the Romans had carried on against the Spanish stronghold Numantia. His political career was hardly less remarkable. He was elevated to the censorship in 142 and vigorously attacked the luxurious and immoral tendencies of his age. In the following year he conducted an embassy to the East for the purpose of fortifying the Roman interests in those countries. In his political attitude he was a moderate, satisfied neither with the unintelligent conservatism of the senatorial faction at Rome nor with the radical aims of the Gracchan party.

Scipio's position in history is due quite as much to other qualities as it is to those of the general or statesman. He was imbued with a deep but discriminating love of Greek civilization, and he appreciated the society of scholars and literary men. Around him gathered the most famous group of literati in Roman history, including the comic poet Terence, the satirist Lucilius, the philosopher Panaetius, and the historian Polybius. The influence of this circle can hardly be exaggerated. Through them was developed a purer sense of form in literature, a wider and more generous attitude toward law and government, and an interest, however superficial, in philosophy. With eminent propriety, therefore, was Scipio made the leading figure in Cicero's discussion of the state.

GAIUS LAELIUS, who after Scipio is the chief participant in the *Commonwealth*, was born about 186 B. C. He combined distinction as a soldier with ability as a statesman and with liberality as a patron of literature. In the Third Punic War he was an able officer under Scipio. He became tribune of the plebs in 151, praetor in 145, and, after an unsuccessful campaign in 141, gained the office of consul in 140. Laelius was one of the chief members of the Scipionic Circle. In addition to his interest in liberal studies, and especially in the Stoic philosophy, he was himself a speaker and writer of elegant and forceful Latin. His friendship with Scipio was very noted in antiquity, and is commemorated in Cicero's work entitled *Friendship*. In Cicero's eyes Laelius is the embodiment of the ideal Roman who engrafts upon the sturdy Roman virtues the liberalizing influence of Hellenism.

LUCIUS FURIUS PHILUS was born probably about 180 B. C. In 136 he was elected consul and surrendered to the Numantines the consul Mancinus who had made a treaty with them without consulting the senate and people at Rome.[2] He was interested in literature and was an orator of marked excellence.

MANIUS MANILIUS was born about 193 B. C. and became consul in 149. He was known in antiquity for his ability as a speaker, but he owes his fame to his legal studies. He wrote two works, one, named *monumenta*, on the laws of Numa, the other, called *actiones*, on the forms of legal procedure.

SPURIUS MUMMIUS, the brother of the general who sacked

---

[2] For this episode see *de rep.* 3. 18, below, and note.

Corinth, is noted, not for any attainments in the political sphere, but for the eagerness with which he espoused the cause of aristocracy and for the skill with which he composed epistles of an ethical and satirical character.

QUINTUS AELIUS TUBERO was the grandson of Aemilius Paulus. At some time before 129 B. C. he was elected tribune of the plebs, and in some year after that date he was an unsuccessful candidate for the office of praetor. His stern and uncompromising character made the Stoic philosophy congenial, and he became the pupil of Panaetius. His manner of speaking was rough and unpleasant, but he partly compensated for this defect by his knowledge of law.

PUBLIUS RUTILIUS RUFUS had a distinquished career as soldier and statesman. In 134 B. C. he served under Scipio in the Numantine War. In 111 he was urban praetor and seems to have introduced rules of procedure which improved the legal status of freedmen. In 95 he was *legatus* attached to Quintus Mucius Scaevola, the proconsul of Asia. By his inflexible honesty in this office he gained the hatred of the equestrian order, and in 92 was banished on the wholly unjust charge of peculation. The rest of his days he spent at Smyrna, highly honored by the people whom he was accused of having robbed. His devotion to Stoicism seems to have given a gloomy cast to his character, and to have prevented his marked gifts as a lawyer from receiving due public recognition.

QUINTUS MUCIUS SCAEVOLA THE AUGUR was the son-in-law of Laelius. In 128 B. C. he was plebeian tribune, and three years later was plebeian aedile. When Gaius Gracchus was murdered in 122, Scaevola was praetor and was governing the province of Asia. On his return from the province in 120 he was arraigned by Titus Albucius on the charge of extortion but was acquitted. He was famed for his knowledge of law. Cicero tells us that in his youth he closely attended Scaevola in order to profit by his discourse.

GAIUS FANNIUS STRABO was also a son-in-law of Laelius. He was consul in 122 B. C. He is known to us as a distinguished orator, a writer of history, and a Stoic philosopher.

CHAPTER II

THE POLITICAL THEORY
OF THE STOICS

The period of political thought between the death of Aristotle in 323 B. C. and the time of Cicero's literary activity in the middle of the first century B. C. is at once important and obscure. It is obscure because no great and outstanding personalities dominate the period as Plato and Aristotle dominate the classical age of Greek philosophy. Large numbers of works on political philosophy were written, but they have come down to us only in the briefest fragments. On the other hand, the period is important because it includes the transition between two great social and political ideals. The political vision of Plato and Aristotle is bounded by the city-state; their political philosophy is throughout a statement of the ideals and problems of that type of political organization. And yet, when Aristotle died, the city-state had already ceased to hold a place of first-rate importance in the political development of European society, which was destined henceforth to govern itself in larger units and to pursue other ideals. The city-state gave place to the world-wide empire, and the political ideals of the compact and self-centered urban community had to be reconstructed to fit the ideal of a universal community as broad as humanity itself. In one form or another, the conception of a single humanity governed political philosophy for upwards of fifteen hundred years, until the appearance of modern nationalism, and so ingrained itself in the consciousness of western Europe that even national sentiment could not displace it. Between the appearance of the ideal of world empire and the ideal of the city-state a sharp line seems to be drawn; if there is any point in its history where the continuity of political philosophy is broken, that point is at the death of

Aristotle.[1] From the beginnings of the theory of natural law in the Stoic school to Cicero and Seneca, from the latter to the Fathers of the Church, and from them through medieval political philosophy to the modern doctrine of the rights of man, we have a continuous and unbroken development. It is in the period between Aristotle and Cicero that the transition took place which prepared for this majestic march of thought.

Only complete historical ineptitude would belittle the political achievement of the city-state, or the intellectual achievement of those thinkers who strove to state its principles.[2] Here for the first time in human history we find the reality and the theory of constitutional rule, of free citizenship, and of government conducted by the forms of law. The genius of the Greeks displayed itself in their political life and philosophy no less than in their literature and art, in history, in science, and in metaphysics. And all western civilizations after them, in law and government as in literature and science, owed them a debt which can scarcely be appraised. "The problems of Greek citizenship touch us today because they are ours; and they are ours because the experience of the Greeks has passed into our substance and merged into our being."[3] Again and again, in the nineteenth century as in the Middle Ages, political philosophy has drawn vitality from the perennial freshness of Plato and Aristotle and has found both clarity and depth in the incomparable humanity of their ethical and social philosophy. Never perhaps in western civilization has social life so completely met the spiritual needs of the individual, or individual life been so perfectly socialized, as in the Athenian state at its best.[4]

---

[1] Carlyle: *History of Mediaeval Political Theory*, 1 (1903), p. 2.

[2] The political theories of Plato and Aristotle fall outside the scope of this Introduction. See especially Barker: *Greek Political Theory, Plato and his Predecessors* (1918) and *The Political Thought of Plato and Aristotle* (1906); other books are listed in Gettell: *History of Political Thought* (1924), p. 62.

[3] Barker: *Greek Political Theory, Plato and his Predecessors* (1918), p. 16.

[4] See the well-nigh perfect statement of the Athenian political and social ideal which Thucydides puts into the mouth of Pericles in the Funeral Oration, 2.35 ff.; translated in Zimmern: *Greek Commonwealth* (1915), pt. 2, ch. 8; Ferguson: *Greek Imperialism* (1913), pp. 43 ff.

Nevertheless, there is another side to the picture, and in many respects the life of the city-state is extremely remote from our own political experience.[5] The civic life of Athens was intense precisely because every interest and activity of its citizens centered in the city. Dramatic art was an incident in the celebration of civic festivals; the plastic arts found their highest use in the adornment of public monuments; religion was a civic duty directed by the officers of the state. The highest ethical good which the Athenian could conceive was the distinguished performance of public service. And even from an economic point of view, considerable numbers of Athenians drew a not insignificant part of their maintenance from the pay which they received for public employments. This very intensity and pervasiveness of civic life, which gave the city-state its unique significance and was responsible for much that was politically and ethically most valuable in its life and organization, can never be duplicated in any larger kind of political unit. In no small degree the problem of political philosophy after Aristotle was to transmute political and ethical values created within the city-state into a form in which they might survive in a world where the city-state had become little more than an administrative unit.

Inevitably something must be lost from the intensity of the older political life. And yet there was the possibility also that something might be gained, not only in actual politics, but also in political philosophy. For, despite the brilliance of its political achievement, the city-state possessed the defects of its virtues. If it created once for all the ideal of constitutional government, it realized that ideal only on a very narrow scale; in foreign affairs the city-state failed conspicuously in the maintenance of peace and order throughout the Greek world. If it created the ideal of free citizenship and of government by law rather than by arbitrary will, it realized this ideal also for only a part of its inhabitants; the slave and the metic were as much a part of the city-state economy as the

[5] The value which the Hegelian school derived from a renewed study of Plato and Aristotle was partly offset by a failure to appreciate the great differences between the ancient and modern state. See MacIver: *Community* (1920), Appendix A.

9

citizen. And if it realized the ideal of government by discussion and under the forms of law, it rarely succeeded in attaining the orderliness and stability which larger states have achieved; factionalism and civil strife were curses from which Greek politics never escaped. Even the moral self-sufficiency of the city-state—its dominance over all the material and spiritual interests of its citizens—brought loss as well as gain. When we reflect upon the many values, both ethical and political, which have grown from the separation of church and state into distinct social bodies, with distinct institutions and organizations, we perceive how far removed is the life of the city-state from the condition of personal privacy and independence which we should deem essential to a good life. The political theory of the city-state approached its problem from the point of view of the citizens' functions, and this is clearly the normal conception in a society where all private associations and groupings are included in the single system of the state. The conception of private rights as a chief value to be conserved by political institutions is correspondingly absent, for personal liberty is largely meaningless where a single organization overlaps all the interests of life.

It was a natural consequence that the theory of the city-state emphasized education more than politics, as we understand the latter term, and that it tended to neglect the legal aspect of the state. In Plato this tendency is carried to the point of denying all need for law in a perfect state, an exaggeration which falsified one of the most significant political aspects of the city-state itself. Even in Aristotle, who corrected Plato's one-sided emphasis on education, the constitution is conceived for the most part as an ethical relationship between citizens, "a mode of life," rather than as a legal organization of institutions and governing agencies.[6] The notion that the state is peculiarly a legal institution belongs necessarily to a less intimate type of political organization.

---

[6] In fact, both views are to be found in Aristotle. The phrase quoted is in the *Politics*, 1295 a 40 ff.; the constitution is defined as an arrangement of magistracies, *ibid.* 1278 b 8 ff. A good summary of Aristotle's political theory will be found in Ross: *Aristotle* (1924), ch. 8.

State

It belongs also to an age which distinguishes clearly between law and morals and which has become conscious that the relations between the two form a special problem. The stimulus to thought in this direction is given when men become conscious of the variety in local practice and when they institute comparisons between the customs of different peoples and states; such a process began far back in the history of Greek political thought. But the problem becomes pressing when closer relations force them to seek for common principles in divergent customs, when it becomes practically necessary for them to define justice and good faith and fair dealing as general forms of human relationship behind the particular duties imposed by the customary law. The necessity which gives force to this attempt is not philosophical curiosity but the clash of local practices in a society which has become more than local.

If it is true, as Mr. Barker says, that the political "experience of the Greeks has passed into our substance," it is equally true that much besides the conceptions proper to the city-state has found lodgment in the political ideals of later citizenship and statecraft. The conceptions of political freedom and self-government had to be made to play a part upon a stage vastly larger than the political theory of the fourth century could conceive. They had to be transformed to meet a situation in which, at the most, but a small number of citizens could hold political office and in which the performance of political functions held a diminishing part in the serious personal concerns of the average citizen. They had to allow for a degree and a kind of personal privacy and self-centered individualism which the citizen of the city-state could contemplate only with despair and abhorrence. Viewed from the standpoint of the classical political philosophy, the political situation which prevailed at any time after the death of Aristotle meant that free government had perished and the worth of citizenship had vanished.

It is a mark of the profound vitality of Greek political philosophy that despair did not win the day, but rather that it was able to strike out a new and permanently significant point

11

of view for the ethical criticism of political institutions, on which political idealism depends. The ideal of a universal justice which of right ought to be realized in the civil law of every community, the conception that every human being embodies an element of value which law and political institutions are morally bound to respect, and the conviction that right and reason should prevail over the prescriptions of established use and wont have passed into the substance of European political civilization. In no small degree the beginnings of these ideals belong to the age with which we are dealing. In what follows we shall seek to point out the main stages in the rise of these conceptions.

THE EARLY CRITICISM OF THE CITY-STATE

Considered purely as a political institution, the city-state had shown its worst defects long before the time when Plato and Aristotle embodied its principles in classical political theory. Both in foreign affairs and in the preservation of internal stability and order it showed itself no more than a qualified success. The fact is that from an early date in its history the city-state was faced with a dilemma which in the end proved insoluble. It could attain political and economic self-sufficiency only at the cost of isolation, and isolation, if possible at all, meant stagnation in culture and the reduction of internal politics to the level of petty dissension between interests too bitterly opposed to permit a stable balance. If, on the other hand, it chose not to isolate itself, it was faced at once with the necessity of seeking alliances with other cities.[7] By the middle of the fourth century B. C. such federations were the prevailing form of government in the Greek world,[8] but they had failed in their foreign policy before they were well tried. The treaty of Antalcidas (387-6 B. C.) had established Persian suzerainty over the Greek world in matters of war and peace, and this Persian overlordship was lifted only when it passed into the possession of Macedon.[9] The battle of Chae-

---

[7] Ferguson: *Hellenistic Athens* (1911), pp. 1 ff.
[8] Beloch: *Gr. Gesch.* 3.1 (1922), p. 519.
[9] Ferguson: *op. cit.* p. 6.

ronea (338 B. C.) established the power of Philip over the
Greek cities and unified Greek military power at least long
enough to permit the conquest of Asia and to effect the mix-
ture of Greek and oriental civilizations upon which all the
later history of European culture depended.[10] Alexander's demand that he be enrolled among the gods of the city-states
marked the victory of a new political principle, the world-wide
empire, which required the consideration of philosophers no
less than the city-state and which continued to dominate the
imagination of Europe down to the emergence of the national
state in modern times.[11]

Strictures such as these upon the foreign policy of the city-
state are by no means the property of the modern historian;
they belong quite as much to the Greeks themselves, who were
not at all blind to the dangers of their own particularism.
Even as early as the Peloponnesian War, the urgent need of
presenting a unified front to the Persian menace was clearly
perceived,[12] and Plato himself, despite the fact that his political theory is bounded by the city-state, is no stranger to this
need.[13] As a group it was the orators who were mainly
responsible for the currency of this criticism. The Sophist
Gorgias of Leontini had led the way in an oration delivered
at Olympia, on the occasion of the national games, in which he
urged all Hellenes to unite against the barbarians.[14] The
orator Lysias on a similar occasion in 388 had urged the cause
of the endangered Greeks both of Ionia and Sicily. But most
significant of all in this respect was the orator and teacher
Isocrates, who made the policy of a unified Greece the life-
long theme of his oratory and teaching.[15] Isocrates sees in the
rising power of Macedon the consummation of his hopes for

---

[10] Beloch: *op. cit.* pp. 576 ff.
[11] Barker: "The Conception of the Empire" in *The Legacy of Rome*
(1923), pp. 45 ff.
[12] On the whole subject see Beloch: *op. cit.* pp. 520 ff.
[13] *Republic*, 470; Barker: *Greek Political Theory, Plato and his Predecessors* (1918), pp. 264 ff.
[14] Beloch (*op. cit.* p. 521) places the date at 392 B. C.; Wilamowitz
(*Aristoteles und Athen*, 1893, 1, p. 172) at 408.
[15] Jebb: *Attic Orators from Antiphon to Isaeos* (1876), 1, p. 155
(Lysias); p. 203 ff. (Gorgias); 2, pp. 13 ff. (Isocrates).

Greek unity.[16]   But what we find in the orators is not a political theory, or even a criticism of the principles of the city-state; they stand merely for the policy of concerted action in foreign affairs.

While the orators were thus exposing the weakness of Greek foreign policy, the social distinctions and practices of the city's internal life by no means escaped criticism.   The skepticism which enveloped traditional religious belief in the second half of the fifth century turned no less upon the social order. The traces which we find in Athenian literature, especially in Euripides, enable us to guess how eagerly social questions must have been canvassed in Athens in the years before and after the turn of the fourth century.   Thus we find Euripides [17] looking with skeptical eyes both at the top and bottom of the social scale, at the nobleman with his claim of inherited excellence and at the slave, who for no intrinsic reason is degraded below the true status of man.   The interest which the same author shows in the social position of women is likewise significant, and when Aristophanes can make a comedy out of women's rights and the abolition of marriage, it is obvious that such questions were not unknown to considerable numbers of Athenians.   The communism which Plato seriously proposes in the *Republic* was certainly not a wholly novel idea.[18]   Even the distinction of Greek and barbarian did not go unquestioned: "We all breathe the air through our mouth and nostrils," as the Sophist Antiphon ironically remarks.

Behind this skepticism regarding the value of traditional social distinctions lay the germ of an important philosophical idea, viz., the contrast of the natural or permanent with the conventional or merely local and traditional.   This contrast

---

[16] The *Panegyricus* (380) and the *Philippus* (346) are his most important works for this purpose. See Barker: *op. cit.* pp. 100 ff.; on Isocrates and Plato see Burnet: *Greek Philosophy*, 1 (1914), pp. 215 ff.

[17] For references on this subject see Barker: *op. cit.* pp. 75 ff.; the whole chapter on the Sophists is relevant.

[18] Whether Aristophanes' *Ecclesiazusae* preceded the composition of the part of the *Republic* which deals with the status of women is uncertain. A comedy could hardly be based upon an idea that was unfamiliar to any considerable part of the audience, and the teaching of Plato's school would hardly have been notorious enough by itself to make the idea current.

was an adaptation of the distinction, made long before by
physical philosophers, between an underlying and permanent
substance of which everyday things are made and the manifold
of things themselves. About the middle of the fifth century
B. C. a humanistic reaction took place in Greek philosophy
which had the effect of directing interest toward ethical and
political problems, and this change of interest led to a trans-
formation of the distinction between nature and convention.
It now pointed to the difference between that which has permanent and universal human interest and that which has
merely external and superficial importance, or between the unchanging principles of human conduct, moral or naturalistic,
and the varying practices of customary morals, law, and religion. In this sense the distinction was made current by the
Sophists. Its effect was to render conscious a radical contrast
between some sort of ideal mode of life and the requirements
of established law and morals, and such a contrast is a powerful solvent of traditional morality.

Greek political and ethical theory was largely concerned
from this time forward with the distinction of the natural
and conventional. The distinction was capable of being developed in two broadly different ways, according as nature was
interpreted ethically or, as we should say, naturalistically.
In contrast with the rules of traditional morality, nature
might be identified with the power or advantage or pleasure
of the individual; thus the true or natural rule of life would
be the pursuit of self-interest. This, in the mature opinion of
Plato, was the logical upshot of the Sophist teaching, though
not, of course, the doctrine taught by every Sophist.[19] From
this point of view, a regard for the interests of others, if it

[19] This view is expressed in the *Laws*, 889 e. The most important con-
temporary document for the Sophists is the fragment "On Truth" by the
Sophist Antiphon. Text and translation are in the *Oxyrhynchus Papyri*,
11 (1915), no. 1364, pp. 92 ff.; it is translated also in Barker: *Greek
Political Theory, Plato and his Predecessors* (1918), pp. 83 ff. Plato
represents this aspect of the Sophist teaching in *Gorgias*, 482 c ff.;
Republic, 338 b ff., 358 e ff. With these compare the discourse of the
Athenian ambassadors to the Melians as given by Thucydides: 5. 85 ff.
On the distinction of nature and convention see Burnet: *Greek Philoso-
phy*, 1 (1914), ch. 7; Barker: *op. cit.* ch. 4.

were more than sheer stupidity, could be justified only as contributing to self-interest. Government and law, accordingly, depend upon a tacit contract by which men accept a limit upon the untrammeled pursuit of their own good in order to avoid the aggression of others. It is an evil, indeed, but a less evil than "the war of all against all" which follows inevitably from a life according to natural, selfish impulse. It is against this extrinsic theory of the moral virtues and social obligations that Socrates and his great followers Plato and Aristotle contended, but in spite of their efforts a purely egoistic theory of the state persisted throughout antiquity in the Epicurean and Skeptic schools.

On the other hand, it was possible to place an ethical interpretation upon the dictates of nature, as was done in fact by all the schools except those last mentioned. The conflict between convention and nature would thus be transformed into a contrast between two ethical ideals, the ideal of obedience to the laws and established practices of existing communities on the one hand, and the ideal of loyalty to some higher and more reasonable code of conduct on the other. Nature itself, both human and cosmic, must be conceived as embodying moral principles which establish a law to be followed in the pursuit of a happy life. The requirements of morality and law must be conceived to flow from the essential qualities of human nature itself. They are therefore not imposed on men by an outside force but are requisite to the complete development of human nature. With this view of human nature will go normally the conception that the forces of nature at large are ruled by principles of intelligence and right akin to those which work in human nature at its best. In short, against unreasoning custom transmitted by blind tradition and enforced by unreflecting use this type of ethics sets the ideal morals of the wise man, discovered by intelligence and enforced by the inherent reasonableness of the ethical standard itself.

From this exposition it is apparent that a criticism of the city-state and its institutions was implicit in Greek political theory from the start. That Socrates was no admirer of Athenian democracy is obvious, and that Plato and Aristotle

1 6

developed their political philosophy with a disapproving eye upon certain practices of all existing city-states may be read between the lines, even when it is not clearly expressed. But this criticism was not destructive in its purpose. In Plato and Aristotle it is kept within limits by the assumption that a perfected society will conform at least to the main principles of the city-state; they cannot envisage a good life in any other form of community. Their criticism is, so to speak, from the inside; it is designed to improve the city-state itself.

It remained, therefore, for another of the Socratic schools, the Cynics, to show that Socrates' ethics might be worked out to a much more revolutionary and subversive conclusion. The main importance of this school lies in the fact that it was the first to abandon altogether the ideal of the city-state. They show us the seamy side of its excellences, as they appeared not to the citizen but to the foreigner and the exile.[20] The theoretical basis for the Cynic philosophy is the assumption that the wise man, of whom Socrates is supposed to be the type, is completely self-sufficing. Only that which is fully within his power, that is, the world of his own thought and character, can be necessary to make a happy life. Everything except moral character is indifferent, and in this wide circle of the indifferent the Cynic includes not only the amenities and even the decencies of life, but also property and marriage, family and citizenship, learning and good repute, and all the practices and conventions and pieties of civilization. For the wise man is ruled by the law of virtue and not by the law of any city.[21] He will not desire even the independence of his native city.[22]

---

[20] Antisthenes, who founded the school, was the son of an Athenian father and a Thracian mother (Diog. L. 6.1; 2.31). Diogenes of Sinope, its most famous member, lived at Athens after his exile from his native city (*ibid.* 6.20). Crates appears to have chosen voluntarily a life of poverty and exile (*ibid.* 6. 87 ff.; 93). Both Antisthenes and Diogenes are said to have written on the state (*ibid.* 6.16; 80). The important period of the school was contemporary with Plato and Aristotle. For a general account of the Cynics see Zeller: *Phil. d. Griech.* 2. 1 (1922), pp. 280 ff.; Eng. trans., *Socrates and the Socratic Schools* (1885), ch. 13; for their political theory see Barker: *Greek Political Theory, Plato and his Predecessors* (1918), pp. 105 ff.

[21] The saying is attributed to Antisthenes; Diog. L. 6.11.

[22] See the story related of Crates; Diog. L. 6.93; many other citations to a similar effect will be found in the reference to Zeller above.

It follows that for the Cynic the only true social relation is that between wise men, and, as wisdom is universal in its nature, the relation has nothing to do with the local limits of earthly cities. All wise men everywhere form a single community, the city of the world, which is the only true state. To the wise man no local custom is foreign or strange, for he is a citizen of the world.[23] He stands out as intrinsically superior to all the conventional and customary stratifications of society and to the vast mass of stupid and foolish humanity.[24] All the customary distinctions of Greek social life could thus be subjected to an annihilating criticism. Rich and poor, Greek and barbarian, citizen and foreigner, freeman and slave, well-born and base-born are reduced at a stroke to a common level.[25]

In the Cynic school, then, we see the first appearance of cosmopolitanism, and not without reason did the ancients themselves perceive a relation between this philosophy and the rise of the Macedonian empire. Nevertheless, there was little that was positively significant in the cosmopolitanism of the Cynics; it is a leveling attack upon the city-state and all its typical social institutions. It looks not so much to the setting up of a new social principle as to the destruction of all civic ties and the abolition of all social restrictions. It aims at a return to nature in a sense which makes nature the negation of civilization. The Cynic philosopher, dirty, witty, contemptuous, shameless, a master of billingsgate, is the earliest example of the philosophical proletarian.

THE EARLIER STOICS

To impart a positive content to the ideal of world citizenship was the work of the Stoics, but this was a work of time; in

---

[23] Diog. L. 6. 11; 12; 63; 72; 98.
[24] Diog. L. 6. 27; 33; 35; 41; 86.
[25] For rich and poor, see Xenophon: *Symposium*, 4.35; Diog. L. 6.11; 50; 72; 104. For Greek and barbarian, see references on cosmopolitanism above. For citizen and foreigner, see Diog. L. 6.93. For freeman and slave, see *ibid.* 6.4; 29; 30; 74; Aristotle: *Politics*, 1253 b 20 ff., which probably refers to the Cynics. For good birth and social position, see Diog. L. 6.10; 60; 72; 92; 104.

fact, ideas derived from the Cynics strongly marked the philosophy of the early Stoics and there were outcroppings of these
ideas throughout the history of the school. The founder of
the Stoic school, Zeno of Citium in Cyprus, was a pupil of the
Cynic Crates, and his work on the state is said to have been
written while he was still a Cynic.[26] So far as can be judged
from the very scanty remains, it must have been essentially
similar to the work on the same subject by Diogenes of
Sinope.[27] In the ideal state all men should live as in a herd,
without distinctions of family and nationality, and without
courts or money—in short, in a state of nature. Similar views
persisted also in the work of Chrysippus on the state.[28] At
the start, therefore, it would appear that Zeno changed the
spirit more than the substance of the Cynic political teachings.
It is certain that he could not stomach the indecencies of the
Cynics, and, if Professor Ferguson is right in supposing that
the opening of the school coincides in date with the overhauling
of the educational scheme for the Athenian ephebes,[29] it is
highly probable that instruction in political subjects was a
part of its purpose from the start. This does not mean that it
had a popular or democratic tendency. On the contrary, the
ideal of the wise man, who alone is fit to rule, would predis-
pose it toward monarchy or aristocracy.[30] Zeno was on inti-

[26] Diog. L. 7.2; 4. Like the Cynics the Stoics were recruited from non-
Athenians; in fact, most of them came from outside Greece and many
were probably not wholly Greek by birth. Zeno himself is called a
"Phoenician" (*ibid.* 7.3), which presumably means that one of his parents
was Semitic. The more important of the early Stoics, after Zeno, with
their birthplaces, are as follows: Cleanthes of Assos in the Troad,
Aristo of Chios, Herillus of Carthage, Chrysippus of Soli in Cilicia, Zeno
of Tarsus, Diogenes of Seleucia on the Tigris (or of Babylon), Antipater
of Tarsus, and Panaetius of Rhodes. It was not until after the death
of Panaetius (c. 110 B. C.) that the Stoic school in Athens was headed by
an Athenian. See the table of scholarchs in Ueberweg: *Grundr. d. Gesch.
d. Phil.*, 1 (1909, ed. Praechter), pp. 355 ff. For the little that is known
of their lives see Zeller: *Phil. d. Griech.* 3. 1 (1923), pp. 27 ff.; Eng.
trans., *Stoics, Epicureans, and Skeptics* (1880), ch. 3.
[27] The fragments are given in von Arnim: *Stoicorum veterum fragmenta,* 1 (1921), nos. 222, 248, 252, 259-270. See especially no. 262 (Plut.
Alex. virt. 1. 6); Diog. L. 7. 33.
[28] Diog. L. 7. 131; 188.
[29] *Hellenistic Athens* (1911), p. 129.
[30] The Stoics in general favored the mixed constitution (Diog. L. 7.
131), but whether this was true of all the Stoics from the start is not
clear.

mate terms with Antigonus II of Macedon, who was his pupil, and had sent one of the members of his school to be the teacher of Antigonus' son.[31]   Accordingly, at the beginning the Stoa is to be conceived as attached to the Macedonian interest. The practical application of its political philosophy was perhaps enlightened despotism.[32]

With the passing of the Macedonian overlordship and the recovery of a qualified independence by Athens in 229 B. C. the Stoic philosophy received a somewhat different political complexion.   By this time the Stoa had become the most important of the Athenian schools, a position which was secured for it by the vigor and industry and ability of Chrysippus of Soli, who was its head from 232 until about 206.   The honor in which Chrysippus was held at Athens surpassed that which the city accorded to any other of her great teachers.[33]   He it was who gave the Stoic philosophy the systematic form which it retained throughout antiquity; he is rightly known as the second founder of the school.   At the same time, despite a forbidding literary style, he made some attempt to popularize and liberalize the political teaching of the school.   In the hands of Chrysippus the Stoic philosophy assumed a form which made it throughout antiquity "the intellectual support of men of political, moral, and religious convictions."[34]   It gave a positive moral significance to the conception of a world-wide society and of a universal human law.

The general formula of the Stoic ethics is that the good consists in a life according to nature.   This in itself means little until we answer the question, What is natural?   The Cynics, as we have seen, taught a return to nature which was pure nihilism, and Stoicism retained elements of a similar sort. But in principle Stoicism was different.   It contained from the start a germ of religious feeling which cannot be wholly neglected in studying its political philosophy.   The nature to

---

[31] Diog. L. 7. 6; 36.

[32] See Ferguson: *op. cit.* p. 176, especially the quotation from Wilamowitz: *Antigonus*, pp. 217 ff.   For a case in which Zeno's pupil Persaeus used his influence against democracy see Diog. L. 2. 143.

[33] Ferguson: *op. cit.* pp. 259 ff.; Pauly-Wissowa: *Realencyclopädie*, s. v. Chrysippus.

[34] Ferguson: *op. cit.* p. 261.

which human life must conform is fundamentally rational.
It is governed throughout by a universal meaning and purpose
to which its parts, including man, must conform. The order of
nature is like a work of art, a dramatic composition, in which
each man, like an actor, is assigned his proper part. His duty,
and indeeed his highest right, is to perform well the part to
which he has been assigned, but the part is always subordinate
to the purpose of the whole composition. Perhaps the clearest
note in the early Stoics is a sentiment of religious pantheism,
a feeling for the oneness and perfection of nature and a conviction that the world constitutes a true moral order, whatever
may be the apparent reality of physical and moral evil. Life
according to nature connotes to the Stoic perfect resignation
to the purposes of divine Providence, cooperation with all
good ends in so far as a man may understand what ends are
really good, a sense of dependence upon a power above men
which makes for righteousness, and the composure of mind
which comes from the faith that no evil can befall a good man,
whether in life or death.

The Stoic conception of human nature is closely related to
this view of universal nature. Man is indeed a part of nature
and subject to nature's law, but because he possesses reason he
is more than a mere tool. His reason places him in a special
relation to the divine being, because the soul which animates
man is one with the soul which animates nature. Human
nature is unique among the creations of the world-soul. It
includes the spark of divinity which makes it akin to God.
And for this reason the relations which arise between rational
beings are likewise unique. The animals are endowed by
nature with the impulses and powers which are needed to preserve them according to their different kinds. Man, being
endowed with reason as his peculiar attribute, lives his life
most completely in so far as he lives according to reason.[35]
And a life according to reason is essentially a moral and social
life. Only rational beings are capable of morality, and to
them a life of moral association is necessary, for man is by

---

[35] Diog. L. 7. 85 ff.; see also the other references in von Arnim; *op. cit.*
3 (1923), pp. 43 ff.

nature a social creature.[36] To live in accord with nature means, first, to live as part of a moral world-order and, second, to develop fully a human endowment which is fundamentally rational and social.

It follows that justice and law, upon which the social life depends, exist by nature and not by convention.[37] They are natural not only in the sense that an inborn social impulse has brought men together, but also in the more important sense that the development of reason, which is the specifically human capacity, issues inevitably in a life according to justice and law. The fundamental principle of the Stoic ethics and politics is the existence of a universal and world-wide law, which is one with reason both in nature and in human nature and which accordingly knits together in a common social bond every being which possesses reason, whether god or man. "Law is the ruler over all the acts both of gods and men. Law must be the director and governor and guide with respect to what is honorable and base, and therefore the standard of the just and unjust; for all beings that are social by nature, it directs what must be done and forbids what must not be done."[38] Hence men and gods taken together form a single community. The world is their city, which nature has given them to be possessed in common, "as children are said to share a city with their fathers, being citizens by nature,"[39] and right reason, by which the universe is governed, is their constitution.[40]

In the world-state the extraneous social distinctions which prevail in human states have no meaning. So far as the wise are concerned, Stoicism is a doctrine of perfect human equality; in this respect it carries forward the tradition begun by the Cynics. As we have already seen, Zeno and Chrysippus

---

[36] For the view that moral relations are confined to man, see von Arnim: *op. cit.*, pp. 89 ff.; for the view that they are essential, see pp. 83 ff.

[37] Diog. L. 7. 128; see also von Arnim: *op. cit.* 3 (1923), pp. 76 f.

[38] These are the opening words of Chrysippus' book *On Law*; von Arnim: *op. cit.* 3 (1923), p. 77, no. 314; cf. Cic. *de rep.* 3. 22. This definition of law is echoed over and over again in the remains of Stoic literature; see, for example, nos. 323; 332; 613; 2. no. 1003. Cic. *de n. d.* 1. 14. 36 attributes the idea to Zeno.

[39] Von Arnim: *op. cit.* 3 (1923), p. 82, no. 334.

[40] *Ibid.* no. 337.

continued to deny, in the Cynic fashion, that a state composed of wise men required any institutions at all. Accordingly, we find among the Stoics the same criticism of the traditional divisions and classes of the city-state as among the Cynics. Distinctions between Greek and barbarian, between ruling class and artizan, between well-born and common, slave and free, are for the Stoics indifferent and insignificant compared with the intrinsic moral distinction between the wise man and the fool. "No man is by nature a slave," for only folly and badness can make him one.[41] This doctrine was used by Chrysippus to mitigate the evils of actual slavery, for he enjoins that the slave is to be treated as a perpetual wage-earner.[42] Gentle birth without true gentility is "as useless as dross and filings," for only the wise and good are truly noble.[43]

The Stoic conception of the world-state is not primarily political. It is partly ethical, emphasizing reason as a bond of union extending throughout the whole race, and partly religious, emphasizing the common dependence of men upon divine Providence and their common affinity with the divine nature. Indeed, the political importance of Stoicism lay precisely in the reaction of its ethical and religious principles upon political thinking, not in a specific theory of the state. Though the school preferred the mixed constitution, there was nothing peculiar or especially important in that fact. For Stoicism forms of government and the details of political administration are included among things that are indifferent. Its valuable element was the conception of an ethical norm, above the state and law, which might be made the principle for a criticism of positive law and actual institutions.

THE SKEPTICAL ATTACK ON EARLY STOICISM

Unfortunately, the ethical theory of the early Stoa was in certain respects very ill-qualified to become a vehicle of philosophical enlightenment. Its conception of a universal moral law and a common humanity made it, indeed, in the third cen-

---

[41] Von Arnim: *op. cit.* 3 (1923), p. 86, nos. 352; 355.
[42] *Ibid.* no. 351.
[43] *Ibid.* no. 350.

tury the chief ancient expression of ethical idealism, but its dogmatism, its aloofness from common concerns, and its indifference to the realities of everyday moral and political life made it no less a legitimate prey for the attacks of the Skeptics. Stoicism had assumed such proportions that it could furnish the material for a life-time of skeptical criticism, witness the jocular gratitude of the Skeptic Carneades: "Except for Chrysippus, where should I be?"[44] But on the other hand, the attack became so sharp that in the end the criticism of Carneades exerted no small influence in changing the temper and spirit of Stoicism, if not the systematic form of its teaching. We shall first note some serious defects in early Stoicism which laid it open to the attack of the Skeptics and then point out briefly the character of Carneades' criticism, in so far as the latter affected the political philosophy of the school. In the next section we shall point out some important changes which this criticism produced in the so-called Middle Stoa.

We have already indicated that the early Stoics carried over in many respects the moral and political teaching of the Cynics, and in particular that they tended to set the wise man quite apart from the world of ordinary humanity. All men belong to one or other of the two classes, wise men or fools. Wisdom is a condition of grace which, if attained, is perfect and complete; the man who has not attained it is still a fool. There are no degrees of good or bad and no middle ground between wisdom and folly,[45] though with this paradoxical doctrine the founders of the school united the notion of progress toward virture and the belief that even indifferent acts are of varying degrees of value. The last proposition is the chief divergence between Zeno and the Cynics.[46] In a similar

---

[44] Diog. L. 4. 62.

[45] Diog. L. 7. 120; 127; see also von Arnim: *op. cit.* 3 (1923), pp. 140 ff.

[46] For obvious reasons the problem of making consistent these two positions—the denial of degrees of goodness and the assertion of progress toward the good—has caused no little difficulty to the critics. Zeller considers them inconsistent and regards the notion of progress as a concession to practical needs; see *Phil. d. Griech.* 3.1 (1923), pp. 263 ff.; Eng. trans., *Stoics, Epicureans, and Sceptics* (1892), pp. 278 ff. Hicks believes a sweeping charge of inconsistency unwarranted but admits the difficulty; see *Stoic and Epicurean* (1910), pp. 89 ff.

fashion, the world-state, composed only of wise men, is the only true state; in this none of the ordinary institutions and customs of civilized life is required.[47] Actual societies, on the contrary, are not really states at all, since they are composed of fools incapable of entering into truly ethical relations.

Accordingly, Stoic ethics and politics tend to fall into a radical dualism. On the one hand, there is the impossible ideal of the wise man who has achieved complete moral perfection and has altogether put aside the weaknesses and passions of ordinary human nature. On the other, there is humanity as it is, sunk in unfathomable folly, and falling altogether short of a virtue which, to be attained at all, must be realized in its entirety. Corresponding to this in their political theory we have the perfect society of wise men, without institutions or organization, a pure ideal having no apparent relation to any society of actual human beings. It is clear that a separation of the ideal and the actual so complete and absolute affords only the most precarious grounds for making its ideal effective by a fruitful criticism of existing institutions. It is accordingly ill-adapted to be an instrument of enlightenment. It was a fundamental defect of early Stoicism that it was in principle capable of almost complete indifference to the realities of ordinary moral and political life, though it would be unjust to assert that the founders of the school actually were thus indifferent.

Closely related to this indifference is a conception of human nature which may perhaps be described with the phrase "barren intellectualism." This phase of Stoicism is due in part to a tendency of all the Greek schools to become more highly professionalized with the decline of active political life in the city-state and after the contact of the schools with civic life had become less important than in the days of Plato and Aristotle.[48] At the same time, the highly dialectical nature of

---

[47] Diog. L. 7. 32-33; 131; 188.
[48] The tendency toward professionalism, in turn, was an illustration of a broader change going on throughout Greek society, viz., the tendency to form private associations apart from civic life, not only in religion but in all departments of human interest. Philosophy aimed at a higher standard of technical excellence, which it paid for by becoming more scholastic. See Ferguson: *Hellenistic Athens* (1911), pp. 214 ff., 226 ff.

Chrysippus' method perhaps tended to give Stoicism a special twist toward intellectualism.[49] At all events, it is a fact that the psychology of the early Stoa runs to an extreme in this direction. The principle that reason is the typical human faculty is pushed to the conclusion that the mind is exclusively rational.[50] All the so-called faculties of the mind are forms of reason, and from this it follows that the virtues are forms of knowledge, while the vices are errors in the perception of truth. The passions and emotions are imperfect and fallacious forms of judgment which the wise man must exclude as contrary to reason. It is largely because of this psychology that the self-sufficiency of the wise man is often hard to distinguish from sheer callousness and lack of all human feeling. The ideal is not only impossible to realize but, if realized, would create a monstrosity out of all relation to human nature.

We may turn now to the criticisms of the great Skeptic Carneades,[51] who was mainly instrumental in forcing home, even to the Stoics themselves, the difficulties which we have noted in their theory of the wise man and of natural law. The greater part of his criticisms, which deal with their meta-

---

[49] Cf. the remark by Philus in Cic. *de rep.* 3. 8, and note.

[50] Cf. Hicks: *op. cit.* p. 62. This interpretation is contrary to that given by Zeller: *Phil. d. Griech.* 3. 1 (1923), p. 229; Eng. trans., *Stoics, Epicureans, and Sceptics* (1892), p. 243. Zeller supposes the position of the early Stoa to be that men have both rational and irrational impulses. In general, Zeller fails to distinguish between the different periods in the history of the school. According to Schmekel: *Phil. d. mittleren Stoa* (1892), pp. 327 ff., the distinction between the rational and the irrational was an element of Platonism introduced into Stoicism by Panaetius.

[51] Carneades of Cyrene (214-12—129-8 B. C.) was the founder of the third or New Academy. Since he was already head of the school in 155 B. C., the date of the embassy mentioned in Cic. *de rep.* 3. 6, he was probably teaching at the time when Panaetius came to Athens as a student. Starting from the principle that there is no sure criterion of truth, Carneades submits to a searching criticism the chief bodies of supposed scientific knowledge taught by the Stoics. He examines with great keenness the proofs of the existence of God, of final causes in nature, and the Stoic attempts to impart philosophical meaning to divination and popular religious belief. On the positive side, Carneades goes farther than the earlier Skeptics in developing his account of probability. See Ueberweg: *Grundr. d. Gesch. d. Phil.* 1 (1909, ed. Praechter), pp. 289 ff.; Hicks: *Stoic and Epicurean* (1910), ch. 8; Zeller: *Phil. d. Griech.* 3. 1 (1923), pp. 514 ff.; Eng. trans., *Stoics, Epicureans, and Sceptics* (1892), pp. 535 ff.; Schmekel: *Phil. d. mittleren Stoa* (1892), pp. 304 ff.

physics and religious beliefs, we need not discuss. Though not much is known of Carneades' ethical theories, it seems clear that he demonstrated the artificial and inhuman nature of the wise man and the impossibility of extirpating the emotions and passions. Apparently his argument turned upon the inconsistency of asserting that the good life is in accordance with nature and at the same time denying all goodness to the natural desires and impulses.[52] The ambiguities of such a word as nature offered unlimited possibilities to a critic with the acumen of Carneades. We shall see presently the effect upon the Middle Stoa of this attack upon the wise man.

The main weight of Carneades' attack, however, was directed against the wholly ideological character of the Stoic theory of natural law. As we see from Philus' presentation of Carneades' philosophy in Book III of Cicero's *Commonwealth*, he denied outright the existence of natural justice, traced all conduct back to the pursuit of self-interest, and explained society by a contract resting upon mutual advantage. This position, of course, was derived from earlier Skepticism, going back as far as some of the Sophists. As Carneades presented it, the main burden of the argument was that the natural law of the Stoics corresponded to nothing in the realities of politics and social life. Everywhere we find variety of law and custom determined by the principle of individual or national self-interest, but nowhere a generally recognized moral principle of rendering to each his own. A criticism so thoroughgoing, and backed withal by so great an array of fact, left Stoicism no recourse but to consider anew the relation of its "true law" to the multiform positive law and practice of existing states. We must turn, then, to the effort to deal with these questions in the Middle Stoa.

THE MIDDLE STOA

To the more erudite scholars of antiquity the pure and classic form of Stoicism remained that which Chrysippus had

---

[52] Cf. the influence which Cicero attributes to Carneades' criticism of the Stoic view that a good reputation is indifferent; *de fin.* 3. 17. 57.

given it.[53]   For Cicero and Roman Stoicism, and indeed for our own understanding of the total significance of Stoicism, a special importance attaches to the modifications introduced into the system by Panaetius, who was head of the school at Athens about a century after Chrysippus and who was the last great representative of Stoicism to hold that place.[54]

Panaetius was the first of all the Stoics who achieved fame for the excellence of his literary style. His writing aimed to strike a note of urbanity and enlightenment which would appeal to the intelligent man of the world. He was therefore well qualified for what was certainly his greatest work, the introduction of Greek thought and culture at Rome, and especially to the influential group of Roman nobles who were the intimates of Scipio Aemilianus. These men had no possible interest in or aptitude for the technicalities of Greek philosophy, and the implicit Cynicism of the Stoic wise man was for them at most only a reminder of traditional Roman frugality and self-control. As Romans of the aristocratic class they were inevitably men of affairs; but as the best of the Romans in their generation, they were susceptible to instruction in the responsibilities of their newly won position as the masters of European civilization. None of the schools was so well qualified as the Stoic to undertake this task of education, for no philosophical ideal could so readily appeal to a conscientious Roman as the hope that Roman dominion, by including all races and all nations and by developing world-wide legal and political institutions, might realize in some degree the universal state of Stoic speculation. It was to this work of edu-

---

[53] Von Arnim in Pauly-Wissowa: *Realencyclopädie*, s. v. Chrysippus.
[54] Panaetius (185-0—110-9 B. C.) was a member of a distinguished Rhodian family; he became head of the Stoic School in 129. He lived for a while (probably 144-2) at Rome in the house of Scipio Aemilianus, whom he accompanied on the embassy mentioned by Cicero in *de rep.* 6. 11. During his residence at Rome must have occurred the discussions on politics with Polybius mentioned in *de rep.* 1. 21. He was the friend and teacher of the group of well-born Romans who made up the Scipionic Circle. Even after he became head of the school he continued to live at intervals in Rome. The standard work on this period of the Stoic philosophy is Schmekel: *Phil. d. mittleren Stoa* (1892); for the life of Panaetius see pp. 1 ff.; for the relation of Panaetius' ethics and political philosophy to that of the older Stoics see pp. 356 ff.

cating a ruling aristocracy in the responsibility of wielding an imperial authority that Panaetius addressed himself.[55]

In common with all the philosophy of the Hellenistic-Roman period, the philosophy of Panaetius [56] shows a definite tendency toward eclecticism. This characteristic, which is in part an indication that its appeal is meant to be popular rather than professional, is also a sign of the success with which Carneades had done his work; for the tendency to take ideas wherever they may be found and to put them together without too much regard for systematic unity shows that skepticism has sapped the dogmatic belief in any single philosophical principle. On its positive side, however, eclecticism doubtless signified a consciousness of the need for finding a unified intellectual basis for a culture grown world-wide and all inclusive; opposed schools tended to draw closer together and technical differences were deemed of slight importance compared with a presumed agreement in essential meaning. In the case of Panaetius eclecticism takes the form especially of a return to the ethical and political writings of Plato and Aristotle. Cicero states that Panaetius felt and continually expressed the liveliest admiration for these philosophers both in his teaching and in his writing.[57] The Middle Stoa is the first of the many cases in the history of philosophy in which a return to the great thinkers of the fourth century was the means to a broader and more humane view of life and social relations.

---

[55] Ferguson: *Hellenistic Athens* (1911), p. 341.

[56] The philosophy of Panaetius is known almost wholly through Cicero. Books I and II of *de officiis* are stated by Cicero himself to be based upon a work by Panaetius (*de off.* 3. 2. 7; *ad Att.* 16. 11. 4). For a full discussion of this and other sources, see Schmekel: *Phil. d. mittleren Stoa* (1892), pp. 18 ff. According to Schmekel's conclusions, Book I of Cicero's *Laws* and Book III of the *Commonwealth* have a common Stoic source which was almost certainly a work of Panaetius. He further concludes that Polybius: 6. 3-10 represents essentially the views of Panaetius. On the basis of the similarity between Polybius and Books I and II of the *Commonwealth*, and also because these books presuppose the argument in Book III, he concludes that the philosophical parts of Books I and II also depend upon Panaetius, with certain changes introduced to make them accord with Cicero's account of Roman history.

[57] *De fin.* 4. 28. 79. Numerous passages in the *Commonwealth* which show the influence of Aristotle's *Politics* probably mark the influence of Aristotle on Cicero's source. See Hinze: *Quos scriptores Graecos Cicero in libris de re publica componendis adhibuerit* (1900), pp. 13 ff.

We have already pointed out that a very damaging part of Carneades' criticism of the older Stoa had dealt with the character of the wise man and the psychological preconceptions on which the ideal of apathy had been based. The effect of this was to cause Panaetius to abandon the traditional psychology of the school, which had traced all the mental faculties back to reason, and to adopt the Platonic distinction between a rational and an irrational part of the soul.[58] In line with this change in psychology, Panaetius held the ideal of perfect apathy to be unnatural and accepted as good such external things as health and property, which the older Stoics had held to be indifferent.[59] Self-love is allowed to be justifiable within limits — a clear concession to Carneades — and the desire for honor and reputation is accepted as a normal and, if properly guarded, as a justifiable motive for the wise man to follow. It is significant that Panaetius addressed his book *On Duty* not to the wise man, but to the man of good sense and good will who has set himself the task of growing in wisdom.[60] His ethical ideal is not to extirpate the passions or to attain a state of apathy, but to rationalize all the impulses and inclinations which form a normal part of human nature, as well as those which form the special endowment of each individual. In short, Panaetius makes the Stoic ideal milder and more humane; he modifies the impossible ideal of self-sufficiency in the direction of kindness and sympathy, while at the same time he seeks to retain the strength of will and the self-mastery which had formed from the start the main objects of Stoic discipline.

In a similar fashion Panaetius aims to close the chasm which the older Stoicism had left between the world-state, composed of wise men, and ordinary communities, composed mostly of fools. The paradox of the Stoic theory had been that it made a monism of reason and law the basis for a radical dualism of society and politics. All men are by nature rational, and reason is the law not only of human nature but of the

---

[58] The change appears in Cicero also: see *de rep.* 2. 41; *Tusc.* 4. 5. 10.
[59] Diog. L. 7. 128; Schmekel: *op. cit.* pp. 364 ff.
[60] Cic. *de off.* 3. 3. 13 ff.

universe as well; and yet morality is described on the supposition that conduct is either absolutely virtuous or not virtuous at all and that human beings are either wise or foolish. Panaetius softens this contrast by changing both extremes. Just as he abandons the dogma of absolute rationality in human nature, so he denies the antithesis between the ideal community of wise men and ordinary social relationships. Reason is the law for all men, not merely for the wise. Despite differences of rank or position, race and nationality, even despite differences of natural endowment and moral character, there is a sense in which all men are equal. They are equal at least in the possession of a common humanity, a common affinity to the divine reason, and a common subjection to the eternal principles of right and justice.[61] Thus interpreted the principle of natural law becomes a recognition of intrinsic worth in human personality, with the necessary implication of equality and universal brotherhood. The effect of this conception may be perceived in the increasing humanitarianism of the later Roman Stoics.[62]

As we saw above, the objection which Carneades urged against the law of nature was its lack of connection with the facts of politics and government. This discrepancy Panaetius seeks to meet by showing that, as reason furnishes a law for all men, so the law of nature must be the basis for the positive law of the state. Government ought to be in accordance with the general principles of justice,[63] both in respect to the treatment of citizens and in respect to the external relations between states. Justice, therefore, is the bond which holds the

---

[61] See Cic. de leg. 1. 10. 29 ff. and de rep. 3. 22, both of which presumably go back to a common source in Panaetius.

[62] "The unity of the human race, the equality of man, the equal worth of men and women, respect for the rights of wives and children, benevolence, love, purity in the family, tolerance and charity toward our fellows, humanity in all cases, even in the terrible necessity of punishing criminals with death—these are the fundamental ideas which fill the books of the later Stoics." Denis: Histoire des doctrines morales de l'antiquité; quoted by Janet: Histoire de la science politique (1887), 1, pp. 249 ff. The later Stoics do not fall within this Introduction. A number of the more important passages are cited in Zeller: Phil. d. Griech. 3. 1 (1923), pp. 293, n. 3; 307 f.; 750 ff. (Seneca); 764 f. (Musonius); 780 f. (Epictetus); 790 f. (Marcus Aurelius).

[63] See Cic. de rep. 2. 44.

state together. It is of course true that states are often unjust, as individuals often act in defiance of the moral law. The compulsion of the natural law is a moral and not a physical compulsion. It can be defied, but only at the cost of alienating one's own better nature. In the same way the state which defies the law may continue to exist, but it loses by just so much the ground of harmony which makes it a state.

In short, for Panaetius, the law of nature is not merely the bond of a hypothetical community of wise men; it is rather an ideal more or less implicit in existing states and therefore a ground for the criticism and correction of positive law and actual institutions of government. The variation of laws and institutions from time to time and from place to place may be accepted as diverse means, applicable to varying situations, for realizing essential justice. But whatever the diversity of means, that which alone justifies the existence of political power is the substantial justice of its exercise, and that which distinguishes the state from mere organized force is the essential rightness of its aims and purposes. Thus it became impossible to believe that law might fly in the face of justice and right without losing the essential moral character which, as law, it ought to possess; there is a minimum of right and justice which government cannot deny without losing the moral claim to the loyalty of its subjects. This belief that law and government are rightly subject to ethical criticism has been and still is the greatest agency of enlightenment and liberalism that civilization has known.

The more strictly political part of Panaetius' philosophy consisted in the development of the theory of the mixed constitution which belonged to the tradition of the Stoic school. The idea of a constitution blended of monarchical, aristocratic, and democratic elements, and the perception of its advantages, were at least as old as Plato.[64] In the time of Panaetius it was a commonplace of Greek political theory. There were special

---

[64] See the form of government sketched in the *Laws*, 754 d ff., which is described as a mean between monarchy and democracy (756 e). This government is criticized by Aristotle: *Politics*, 1266 b 33 ff. The polity or middle-class government is said to be a fusion of oligarchy and democracy; *ibid.* 1293 b 33 ff.; 1294 a 32 ff.

reasons, however, which commended the theory of the mixed state to the minds of Panaetius' Roman auditors, especially after the disturbances which attended the reforms of Tiberius Gracchus. The purposes of the Gracchi had the approval of certain Stoics, indeed, but the methods used aroused the alarm of some who, like Tubero, had favored the end sought.[65] For the policy of the Gracchan party was manifestly an appeal to divergent class-interests, the object being to weaken the senatorial group by extending the influence and privileges of the equestrian order.[66] It was perfectly natural, therefore, that an attempt to set ranks and classes in opposition should be met by an appeal to a *concordia ordinum* as the basis of security and good order in the state, and it was appropriate that the claims of concord should be voiced by the more moderate and more philosophically minded of the aristocratic group. In the long run, however, the theory of the mixed state, with its aristocratic implications, had only a passing importance in the history of later Stoicism, though it bulked large in the political philosophy of the later republican era, which Cicero represents. The greater egalitarianism of the Empire was more truly in accord with Stoic principles.[67]

In the meantime, as the Romans were content to adopt the traditional Stoic theory of the mixed state, so the Stoics were filled with admiration for the Roman constitution. This is apparent from the famous account of Roman government in Polybius, whose theory of the mixed constitution doubtless represents the views of Panaetius as well as his own.[68] It is

---

[65] Cic. *de am.* 11. 37.

[66] Greenidge: *History of Rome*, 1 (1904), pp. 134 ff.; Ferguson: "The *Lex Calpurnia* of 149 B.C." in *Journal of Roman Studies*, 11 (1921), pp. 86 ff.

[67] Arnold: *Roman Stoicism* (1911), p. 280.

[68] Polybius of Megalopolis (c. 204-122 B.C.) was one of the thousand hostages brought to Italy in 168 B.C. as sureties for the good behavior of the Achaean cities. He became the life-long friend of Scipio Aemilianus and the intimate of many members of the Roman aristocracy. The sixth book of his history is the earliest extant analysis of Roman government. That Polybius was acquainted with Panaetius is shown by Cicero: *de rep.* 1. 21, but Panaetius is not mentioned in any extant portion of the history. For a full statement of the reasons for believing that Polybius: 6. 3-10 represents substantially the view of Panaetius see Schmekel: *Phil. d. mittleren Stoa* (1892), pp. 64 ff.

the balance of powers—the mutual checking of consuls, senate, and people[69]—which forms the secret of Roman stability and strength. Each of the simple forms of constitution has its own natural principle of growth and in particular its own inherent tendency to decay.[70] For this reason there is a natural cycle of constitutions.[71] After primitive despotism, which is based merely on brute force, the rise of civilization produces monarchy. This tends to decay into tyranny; the expulsion of the tyrant by the best men of the state gives rise to aristocracy; a similar decay of the aristocrats leads to oligarchy; the downfall of the oligarchs produces democracy; and this in turn is corrupted into ochlocracy or mob rule, which reverts to tyranny. Accordingly, if stability is to be secured, the various tendencies to decay must be so balanced that one naturally checks and retards another. Each interest in the state may be kept in its place by the pressure of the others. This was the arrangement consciously devised by Lycurgus at Sparta and unconsciously produced by the circumstances of Roman history; it is the reason for the permanence and power of these two governments, respects in which they have surpassed all other states.[72]

THE SCIPIONIC CIRCLE

We have had occasion already to mention the group of well-born Romans who formed the personal circle of Scipio Aemilianus and who were especially influenced by the friendship and

---

[69] The mixed constitution in Plato and Aristotle is formed by a balance of social classes, especially rich and poor. Polybius describes a more definitely political balance between organs of government and is therefore the predecessor of Montesquieu in modern times. It is of course true that Polybius regards each of the organs mentioned as representing a social interest.

[70] Polybius: 6. 10. 2 ff.

[71] *Ibid*. 6. 4. 7 ff.; 6. 5. 4 ff. Compare the natural succession of constitutions described by Plato: *Republic*, 545 ff.; the six-fold classification of forms of government in *Statesman*, 302 c ff., and in Aristotle: *Politics*, 1279 a 22 ff.; and Aristotle's theory of the causes of revolution, *ibid*. 1301 a 20 ff.

[72] Polybius: 6. 10. 12 ff. With Polybius should be compared especially Cicero: *de rep*. 1. 42 ff. On the changes which Cicero introduces into his account of the cycle of constitutions see this Introduction, pp. 56 ff.

teaching of Panaetius and Polybius.[73]   The group was united
by a common enthusiasm for Greek letters and learning and
by a common acceptance, at least in a general way, of the
modified Stoicism taught by Panaetius.   Already well trained
in Greek studies by the care of his father Paulus, who had
turned over to the education of his sons the library of King
Perseus captured at Pydna, Scipio Aemilianus was well qualified to form the center of such a group.   His friendship with
Polybius and Panaetius gave a permanent direction to his
youthful interest and made the Scipionic Circle the focus of
Roman enlightenment in the third quarter of the second century.   Its very existence marked a profound change in Roman
society and a new period in Roman history.   With the ever
closer relations of Rome and the East which followed the
Second Punic War had come ideas and influences which were
destined to change ancient Roman manners and customs both
for good and evil.   The first impulse of patriotic Romans like
Cato had been to exclude and forbid foreign ideas, but the
forces at work were too strong.   The next generation welcomed Greek studies and especially Stoicism, which seemed
to offer the possibility of preserving the best of the older
Roman ideals, enlightened by the cultivation of art and literature and humanized by a broader sympathy, good will, and
gentleness.   This ideal, which the Romans named *humanitas*,
was intended to be the remedy both for native Roman crudity
and for the spreading luxury of an aristocracy drunk with
power and unenlightened by taste or ideas.   The nature of this
ethical ideal has been sufficiently presented in the account
given of Panaetius' philosophy.

   To gauge the influence of this ideal, however, we should note
that the scholarly activities of the Scipionic Circle included, or

---

[73] The members of the group included all whom Cicero represents
as being present at the discussion of the *Commonwealth*; see the account
of the persons of the dialogue, pp. 4 ff.   Numerous others were included
as well, of whom the most important were the poets Terence (see Schanz:
Gesch. d. röm. Lit. 1. 1, 1907, pp. 133 ff.) and Lucilius (*ibid.* pp. 203
ff.).   The most complete account of the philosophy of the Scipionic Circle
is given by Schmekel: *Phil. d. mittleren Stoa* (1892), pp. 439 ff.; the
literary activities and purposes of the group are described by Fiske:
Lucilius and Horace (1920), ch. 2; see also Arnold: *Roman Stoicism*
(1911), pp. 380 ff.

at least affected, the earliest systematic study of Roman law.[74]
There can be no doubt that the beginnings of legal study,
which developed some two centuries later into scientific jurisprudence, were made by men strongly under the influence of
Stoicism. In fact, the conception of natural law could readily
unite with conceptions already existing in Roman law itself.
A century or more before the time of the Scipionic Circle the
presence of foreigners at Rome had made it necessary to
appoint a special praetor to handle cases involving those who
were not Roman citizens. The fact that these foreigners
represented every variety of local law and ceremonial practice
forced upon this court the necessity of transacting business on
the basis of common ideas as to what constituted fair-dealing.
Under the pressure of this need there had already developed
the conception of *ius gentium,* or law common to peoples of
different cities. The process was essentially similar to that
by which the law merchant was formed and later incorporated
with the English common law. It was practically inevitable
that men who were familiar both with the legal notion of the
ius gentium and with the Stoic conception of natural law
should unite the two. And this is in fact what happened. The
two terms are used almost in the same sense by the great lawyers of the second century of the Christian era,[75] to indicate a

---

[74] M. Brutus, Manius Manilius, and P. Mucius Scaevola are mentioned
by Pomponius as the founders of the study of the civil law (*dig.* 1. 2.
2. 39). Manilius was certainly a member of the Scipionic Circle and
Scaevola was at least related to it through his brother Q. Mucius
Scaevola, the augur. The son of Publius, Q. Mucius Scaevola, the
pontifex (cos. 95), was the author of the first systematic work on the
civil law (Pompon. *dig.* 1. 2. 2. 41). See Schanz: *Gesch. d. röm. Lit.*
1. 1 (1907), pp. 338 ff. In the next generation, and contemporary with
Cicero, were C. Aquilius Gallus (praetor with Cicero in 66), who is
mentioned by Cicero as guiding his exposition of the law by the principle
of equity (*Caec.* 27. 78), and Servius Sulpicius Rufus (cos. 51), whom
Cicero praises as the most philosophical of the jurists and who was
certainly subject to Stoic influence if not himself a Stoic (*Brut.* 41. 151;
42. 153). See Schanz: *op. cit.* 1. 2 (1909), pp. 481 ff.
[75] Gaius: *dig.* 1. 1. 9. Ulpian's definition of natural law as an animal
instinct (*dig.* 1. 1. 3) stands apart from the Stoic tradition but seems
to have no influence on the conception. Ulpian (*dig.* 1. 1. 4), Tryphonius
(*dig.* 12. 6. 64), and Florentinus (*dig.* 1. 5. 4.) make a distinction between
ius gentium and *ius naturale* in a few respects, for example, slavery,
which is not natural, though it is universal. See James Bryce: "The
Law of Nature" in *Studies in History and Jurisprudence,* 2 (1901), pp.

body of legal principles which are at once in general use and also represent the dictates of equity, reason, and justice.

The union of these two ideas was a decisive step in bringing together the ideal law of the Stoics and the positive law of states. It brings intelligence and enlightenment to bear upon customary right and traditional practice. It throws into the background the ceremonial and religious character of ancient law and makes it possible gradually to substitute common sense and fairness for the exact performance of ritual and the mechanical use of formulas. It tends to break down distinctions of class and privilege, which are inseparable from forms of law that are in part religious mysteries, and lays the foundation for the equality of all men before the law. It brings into the view of law the internal factor of intent — always an essential part of the Stoic standard of good conduct — as qualifying the external act. It mitigates the unreasoning harshness of law which has never been judged in the light of equity. In all these respects the Roman law actually did pass through a process of enlightenment, and in this process ethical criticism was an indispensable factor, though not, of course, the sole cause of the process. Such criticism consisted largely in the judgment of established use and wont in the light of ideals like the just, the fair, and the reasonable, all essential parts of the Stoic's "true law."

It is against the background of an achievement such as this —accomplished, it is true, only long after the period with which we are dealing—that we must estimate the significance of Cicero's assertion: "I declare that no importance is to be attached to anything which, as we suppose, has hitherto been established about the state, and that no further advance is possible, unless we shall prove both the falsity of the view which regards injustice as a necessary part of government, and the truth of the view which regards a high degree of justice as essential if the state is to function at all."[76] That the ideal never was fully realized, either in the ancient or the modern

556 ff.; Pollock: "History of the Law of Nature" in *Columbia Law Review*, 1 (1901), pp. 11 ff.; Carlyle: *Mediaeval Political Theory*, 1 (1903), ch. 3.

[76] Cic. *de rep.* 2. 44.

world, is not to the point. That justice never "triumphed" over the sinister forces of privilege, class interest, or imperialist *Realpolitik* is not a valid indictment of the ideal. For ideals are not important solely because they triumph, but rather because they furnish some principle of rational guidance, some factor of intelligent control, in a society which, lacking them, would scarcely rise above the instinctive, the habitual, and the brutal. When we compare the political society in which Cicero wrote with the society reflected in Aristotle's *Politics,* we are forced to marvel at the vitality and power of thought which enabled Greek philosophy to bridge a chasm so wide and to adapt itself to a change so stupendous. Starting from the conception of citizenship as a type of political activity in a circumscribed local community, it had formulated the ideal of a world-wide humanity involving a measure of human dignity and moral personality for all men, without respect to differences of race, of rank, or of wealth. It had set before the world an ideal of personal value and individual rights which a state is morally bound to respect and even to secure by its institutions and its law. It had held up the conception of rational moral principles which even the most powerful state is obliged to approximate in its legislation, and it had laid down in substance the requirement that even world-wide empire must lay a moral claim upon the loyalty of its subjects, rather than impose its rule by an overmastering force. These fundamental moral conceptions, which lie at the foundation of all political liberalism and idealism, had been built into the structure of European political thought and had been made an unescapable part of any later conception of a rational political order.

CHAPTER III

CICERO'S POLITICAL
THEORY

The art of government, in its practical aspect, must be placed among the crowning achievements of ancient Rome. But that rare combination of aggression and compromise which carried the Roman arms from the city on the Tiber to the Euphrates and to Hadrian's Wall produced no corresponding genius in the realm of political theory — no scholar or statesman who sought to explain the social order in the light of the political experience that had grown with the growth of the Roman dominion. It is, in fact, clear that, except in so far as concerned the nature of law, the Romans possessed neither enthusiasm nor aptitude for a theoretical discussion of the state.[1] In politics they were essentially realists. It is accordingly important for us to consider any attempt made by them at philosophical inquiry into the origin and nature of political society, and any effort made to determine what form and what instruments of government will enable man to realize, in the highest degree, the fundamental end of a happy and honorable life.[2]

The only Roman discussions of the state which have survived from antiquity are from the pen of Cicero.[3] The uniqueness of these works, irrespective of their merit, would claim a measure of attention; and their authorship entitles them to even more. By this statement we do not mean to imply that there is necessarily a large element of originality in Cicero's

---

[1] See Dunning: *A History of Political Theories Ancient and Mediaeval* (1902), p. 119; Boissier: *Cicéron et ses amis* (1865), p. 39.

[2] Cic. *de rep.* 4. 3; 5. 6.

[3] It should be remarked that the political theories of Polybius, as embodied especially in the sixth book of his history, are undoubtedly influenced by Roman conceptions.

speculation.[4] On the contrary, it may be admitted at once that Cicero is not to be numbered among the greatest writers on politics. He did not, for example, possess the profound insight of Thucydides, the imagination and moral fervor of Plato, the analytical and comparative faculty of Aristotle, or the broad experience of Polybius. Nor is he to be numbered among the great luminaries of Roman jurisprudence. And yet in some ways Cicero's view of the state is as important as any which they set forth. He reflects, perhaps with exceptional liberalism, the scope and character of the political ideals which prevailed in senatorial and literary circles at Rome during the half century before Augustus. From the popularity of his work *On the Commonwealth*[5] we may infer the degree to which Cicero's speculations found adherents; we can thus recreate in part the intellectual interests of that important period.

But the significance of Cicero's political theory does not rest alone on the relationship of his ideas to the first century B. C. We have stated above that if there is any break in the evolution of political philosophy, that break occurs with the death of Aristotle.[6] All that was accomplished in the way of speculative advance after that time survives only in fragments or in tradition. Thus it is that Cicero's works are important: they are the repository for much of Greek political theory which accumulated during the Hellenistic age and which otherwise would be lost to us. They furnish, accordingly, some notion, incomplete to be sure but nevertheless valuable, of the ideas about government which passed from Greece to Rome in the three centuries before the Christian era and produced such profound effects upon Roman law.[7] We find, moreover, in Cicero's works the germ of certain theories which were developed during the imperial age by the great jurists,[8] and

---

[4] Carlyle: *Mediaeval Political Theory*, 1 (1903), 3 ff.

[5] Cic. *ad fam.* 8. 1. 4, dated 51 B. C.

[6] See Introduction, p. 8, above.

[7] Moyle: *Imperatoris Iustiniani Institutionum Libri Quattuor* (1912), pp. 37 ff.; Gaius: *inst.*, ed. Poste (1904), pp. xxxvi ff.; Arnold: *Roman Stoicism* (1911), pp. 384 ff.; Introduction, pp. 36 f., above.

[8] Carlyle: *Mediaeval Political Theory*, 1 (1903), pp. 3; 55; 57; 61.

which appear even later in the teachings of the Roman lawyers of Bologna and in the political theories of the Middle Ages.[9]

CICERO'S POLITICAL WORKS AND THEIR COMPOSITION

The deliberate and formal presentation of Cicero's theory of the state is found in the two extant works devoted expressly to that topic, the dialogues entitled the *Commonwealth* and the *Laws*.[10] The former of these works, which is here presented in translation, is a Heraclidean dialogue, that is, one in which the speakers are not contemporaries of the writer.[11] Cicero, with great skill, has chosen to place the scene of the discussion at the time of the Latin Holidays in 129 B. C.[12] There was no period in the history of the Roman Republic in which such a discussion could be placed with greater dramatic propriety than the years following the tribunate of Tiberius and before the tribunate of Gaius Gracchus. The chief speaker in the dialogue is Scipio Africanus the Younger, who is surrounded by a group of the most distinguished men of the day.[13] Scipio, who in all probability represents Cicero's own views,[14] con-

---

[9] Carlyle: *Mediaeval Political Theory*, 2 (1909), pp. 8; 10; 29; 52; 99. It does not fall within the scope of the present book to deal with the history and influence of Cicero's views upon the thinkers of the imperial age or of subsequent times. We have attempted only to trace in a general way the post-Aristotelian sources of Cicero's theories and to state in detail Cicero's own views.

[10] It should be noted that there are a few insignificant fragments extant of Cicero's work entitled *de iure civili in artem redigendo*; see Schanz: *Gesch. d. röm. Lit.* 1. 2 (1909), pp. 380 ff. We should perhaps indicate at this point the system which we have followed in showing Cicero's views. As is well known, Cicero is an eclectic; and we have accordingly decided to consider the view set forth in the *Commonwealth* and the *Laws* as the expression of his mature judgment, and have sought to supplement it, when necessary, by evidence drawn from his other philosophical works.

[11] For a definition of the two kinds of dialogue employed by Cicero see Pease: *M. Tulli Ciceronis de divinatione liber primus* (1920), p. 16.

[12] Cic. *de rep.* 1. 9; *ad Q. fr.* 3. 5. 1.

[13] For the characters in the dialogue see Introduction, pp. 4 ff., above.

[14] This assumption is an important element in determining Cicero's views. We are led to it chiefly by the following facts: (1) In the *de leg.* Cicero, who is the principal speaker, does not hold views essentially different from those attributed to Scipio; and the work is regarded as completing the *de rep.*; (2) When Sallustius, Cicero's friend, suggested that Cicero himself should take the chief rôle in the discussion (*ad Q. fr.* 3. 5. 1 ff.), Cicero does not suggest that such a change would require any modification in the theory set forth.

ducts an inquiry into what constitutes the best form of government and what is the nature and function of the ideal statesman.[15] The solution of the former problem Scipio finds in the composite state;[16] and he claims that this ideal has never been so perfectly realized as by the Roman commonwealth.[17] If we are unable to come to any definite conclusion as to the character and constitutional position of the perfect statesman, it is because of the extremely fragmentary condition in which the fifth and sixth books of the *Commonwealth* have survived.[18]

The *Commonwealth* is composed of six books. In the first of them, after an introduction in which Cicero speaks in his own person, Scipio attempts to show that the composite state is the best form of government. In the second book he traces the various steps by which the Roman state had attained the perfection inherent in the composite form. In the third book, after prefatory remarks by Cicero, the question of justice is discussed, Philus trying to show that justice is solely a convention based upon expediency, and Laelius striving to prove that justice is the true and eternal principle behind all law. At the end of the extant portions of the book, Scipio resumes the lead in the discussion, and argues that, if justice is not present in a government, such a government is not in any true sense a commonwealth. The fourth book apparently concerned education. In the fifth book, which like the first and third Cicero introduces with remarks of his own, and in the sixth book, there is an account of the ideal statesman and an eloquent description of the rewards in the after life which await all who have wisely and honorably administered the state. It is probable that the work was dedicated to Quintus Cicero, the brother of the author.[19]

Because of the preservation of a large part of Cicero's correspondence, we are able to reconstruct the history of the composition of the *Commonwealth*. Cicero returned from exile

---

[15] Cic. *de rep.* 1. 20; 1. 46; *de leg.* 2. 10. 23; *ad Q. fr.* 3. 5. 1.
[16] Cic. *de rep.* 1. 29; 35; 45.
[17] Cic. *de rep.* 1. 21; 46.
[18] See Introduction, pp. 93 ff., below.
[19] See Schanz: *Gesch. d. röm. Lit.* 1. 2 (1909), p. 344.

in August, 57 B. C.[20] In May, 54 B. C., when he felt that he still occupied an important position in public life,[21] he writes his brother Quintus that he is composing a treatise on politics.[22] The work, he adds, is on a large scale and will require considerable labor; and he is not at all certain that he will be satisfied with it when it is finished. By the end of June or the beginning of July in the same year the composition had progressed.[23] In a letter to Atticus Cicero refers to the fact that he is writing a work on the commonwealth, and mentions as its characters practically the same persons who participate in the dialogue which he finally published.[24] In the version upon which he is working, he has written an introduction to each book, imitating in this way the plan which Aristotle had followed in his popular works.[25] At the end of October or the beginning of November, 54 B. C., Cicero addresses to Quintus a letter in which he sets forth at some length the difficulties which he had encountered in writing the work.[26] The *Commonwealth* was read, at least in part, to Sallustius, who suggested that the treatment would carry greater weight if Cicero adopted the Aristotelian form of dialogue in which the writer spoke in his own person. Cicero asserts that he is greatly interested in the criticism, since there are certain political developments of his own time which he would like to discuss. At the time, moreover, when Sallustius made his suggestions, the dialogue was in the form of nine books, each covering the discussion of a single day. After this date we hear no more of the work until the month of July, 51 B. C., when Cicero, who has reached Cilicia, his province, but is again on the high seas, mentions the fact that Atticus is now reading the dialogue.[27] Before he arrived in Cilicia, if we may trust the date and

---

[20] Cic. *ad Att.* 4. 1. 4 ff.; E. Meyer: *Caesars Monarchie und das Principat des Pompejus* (1922), p. 113.
[21] Cic. *de div.* 2. 1. 3, with Pease's note.
[22] Cic. *ad Q. fr.* 2. 12[14]. 1. It should be stated that the chief *testimonia* as to the history of composition are collected in Ziegler's edition, praefatio, pp. xxx ff.
[23] Cic. *ad Att.* 4. 16. 2.
[24] Mummius is not mentioned by Cicero.
[25] This design was not retained; see Introduction, p. 42, above.
[26] Cic. *ad Q. fr.* 3. 5. 1 ff.
[27] Cic. *ad Att.* 5. 12. 2.

reference in a letter of Caelius, the *Commonwealth* had been published and was finding an eager and favorable audience.[28] There are several allusions to the work in letters written to Atticus in 50 B. C., before Cicero returned to Rome from his province,[29] and we know that by the beginning of March of that year Atticus had read and approved it.[30]

The *Commonwealth* was accordingly written during some of the most critical years of Roman history. Nothing, in fact, could be more natural than that a political situation such as prevailed then at Rome should have occupied the attention of Cicero. It was a period in which he might well feel discouraged about the future of Rome, and might naturally seek for some means whereby its vigor could be regained and perpetually secured. In 60 B. C. Caesar, Pompey, and Crassus formed the first triumvirate.[31] In the following year Caesar was elected consul,[32] and immediately secured, through the aid of a friendly tribune Vatinius, the province of Cisalpine Gaul, as a field in which he could create a military power to offset the reputation acquired by Pompey in the East.[33] In 58 B. C., as has been noted, Cicero was exiled and remained in banishment until August of 57 B. C. In 56 B. C. occurred the famous conference of Luca, at which the coalition renewed its powers for five years more, Caesar receiving a continuation of his power in Gaul, Pompey the control of the two Spains and Africa, and Crassus the rule over Syria.[34] Pompey and Crassus were elected consuls in 55 B. C. The defeat and death of Crassus at Carrhae in the summer of 53 B. C. reduced the triumvirate to two members.[35] Meanwhile conditions at Rome

---

[28] Cic. *ad fam.* 8. 1. 4; see also Petersson: *Cicero, A Biography* (1920), p. 462.

[29] Cic. *ad Att.* 6. 1. 8; 6. 2. 3; 6. 3. 3.

[30] Cic. *ad Att.* 6. 1. 8.

[31] The chief modern historical work on this period is E. Meyer: *Caesars Monarchie und das Principat des Pompejus* (1922); see pp. 55 ff. of this work; Mommsen: *Röm. Gesch.* 3, pp. 207 ff. (Eng. trans. 4, pp. 184 ff.).

[32] E. Meyer: *op. cit.* pp. 62 ff.; Mommsen: *op. cit.* p. 211 (Eng. trans. 4, p. 188).

[33] E. Meyer: *op. cit.* pp. 91 ff.

[34] E. Meyer: *op. cit.* pp. 140 ff.

[35] E. Meyer: *op. cit.* p. 211; Mommsen: *Röm. Gesch.* 3, pp. 347 ff. (Eng. trans. 4, pp. 314 ff.).

were steadily growing worse: there were numerous breaches
of public order, and Pompey and Caesar were gradually becoming estranged.[36] The disorder in Rome increased, until,
perhaps because of a demand for some person having dicta-
torial powers,[37] Pompey was chosen sole consul in 52 B. C.,[38]
and became the leader of that party in the senate which aimed
to check the political and military activities of Caesar.[39]

Such were the circumstances amid which Cicero composed
his work upon the commonwealth. We shall have occasion to
note the possible effect of these political developments upon
his theories.[40] For the present, it will be sufficient to indicate
that the necessity of compromise between the various elements
of the actual Roman state before his eyes suggested with great
force the expediency, if not the necessity, of balance and compromise in a perfect state. In the position then occupied by
Pompey we perhaps see a source of that conception of a
"philosophical director" which Cicero developed at some
length in the fifth and sixth books of the *Commonwealth*.

Cicero's other surviving treatise on politics is the Aristotelian dialogue in three books, entitled the *Laws*. This work
also, in its present form, is only a fragment of a larger whole,
if we are correctly informed by Macrobius who implies that
it contained at least five books.[41] The interlocutors are Cicero
himself, his brother Quintus, and his friend Atticus. In the
first book Cicero, who at all times leads the discussion, explains
at length the nature of law. In the second and third books he
attempts to supply the statutes of a religious and secular character which are necessary if the composite state approved in
the *Commonwealth* is to be made effective.[42]

---

[36] Mommsen: *Röm. Gesch.* 3, pp. 305 ff. (Eng. trans. 4, pp. 275 ff.).
[37] Cic. *ad Q. fr.* 3. 8. 4; Plutarch: *Pompey*, 54.
[38] E. Meyer: *op. cit.* pp. 229 ff.; Mommsen: *op. cit.* 3, pp. 337 ff. (Eng. trans. 4, pp. 304 ff.).
[39] E. Meyer: *op. cit.* pp. 241 ff.; Mommsen: *op. cit.* 3, pp. 358 ff. (Eng. trans. 4, pp. 324 ff.).
[40] See Introduction, pp. 96 f., below.
[41] Macrobius: *sat.* 6. 4. 8, where the fifth book is mentioned. In the conclusion of Book III of the *de leg.* we get some idea of the subjects treated in the lost books: they seem to have dealt with legal processes and with the rights of inferior magistrates (*potestates*).
[42] Cic. *de leg.* 1. 5. 15; 1. 6. 20; 2. 10. 23; 3. 2. 4; 3. 5. 12.

We are unfortunately not able to determine with precision the date or the circumstances surrounding the composition of the *Laws*.[43] If there are some indications that portions of the work were written as early as 52 B. C., it is none the less clear that it had not been published in 44 B. C., since the *Laws* is not mentioned in the list of writings which Cicero incorporated in the second book of his treatise on divination.[44] Probably Cicero never finished the work, and the portions found among his papers were published after his death.[45]

In some ways the *Laws* is a more interesting dialogue than the *Commonwealth*. If, so far as we can judge, it covered a somewhat narrower range than the earlier work, it seems to have been less dependent upon Greek sources. While the first book of the *Laws* is probably derived from either Panaetius or Antiochus,[46] in the second and third books Cicero derives his ideas chiefly from Posidonius or from Roman sources, such as Lucius Aelius Stilo, Scaevola, and Varro, and from his own experiences. The quaint and archaic phraseology of early Roman law he revives with no little success in his "constitutions."[47] There is a genuinely Roman touch in the *Laws*.

GENERAL CONCEPTIONS UNDERLYING CICERO'S
POLITICAL THEORY

We have, therefore, in these two works what is essentially a connected treatment of the state, patterned after the more famous discussion of the same topic by Plato in the *Republic* and the *Laws*.[48] It is a treatment designed to persuade good and honorable men to participate actively in public life.[49] It

---

[43] Schanz: *Gesch. d. röm. Lit.* 1. 2 (1909), pp. 347 ff., where will be found the evidence and a full discussion of the whole question.

[44] Cic. *de div.* 2. 1. 1 ff.

[45] This is implied by Schanz: *op. cit.* pp. 346 ff.

[46] See Introduction, p. 29, above; Schanz: *op. cit.* p. 349.

[47] Cic. *de leg.* 2. 8. 19 ff.; 3. 3. 6 ff.

[48] Cic. *de leg.* 1. 5. 15.

[49] Cic. *de rep.* 1. 1 ff., esp. 1. 7; see also Petersson: *Cicero, A Biography* (1920), pp. 455 ff., where the view is presented that Cicero's sole aim was to stimulate unselfish interest in public affairs. Duff (*Literary History of Rome*, 1914, p. 384) holds that "the value of the *De Republica* lies not in any constitutional scheme or political panacea, but in its application of ethical ideas to politics" and in its emphasis on "the social duty of interesting oneself in questions of government."

is further designed to set before the eyes of Roman men
of affairs, especially Julius Caesar and Gnaeus Pompey, a
model on which to reconstruct the Roman state. For the ac-
complishment of such a needed change, Cicero does not hold
that it is necessary to introduce strange or unused forms of
government. On the contrary, what he proposes is, in essence, a return to the Roman constitution as it existed in the
period after the centuriate reform of the third century and
before the revolutionary tribunate of Tiberius Gracchus.[50]
For this was the epoch in which the Romans had defeated
Hannibal and in which flourished the Scipionic Circle, one of
the most significant and liberalizing influences in Roman
history. Cicero looked back to these years as to the Golden
Age.

The theory of the state which Cicero presents derives its
origin and much of its force from the presupposition that
political life is the highest expression of human achievement,
and that a political career is the most honorable of all professions.[51] Of all men the statesman naturally merits most
praise, since his devotion to the public weal has benefited
society more even than the teachings of philosophers. He is
the author of our moral code, for he secures the enactment of
the laws and the development of the customs which determine
our feeling for right and wrong. His career is the highest
employment of excellence; it is the criterion by which the good
and wise are judged; it is the nearest approach to divinity of
which man is capable.

A conviction so intense arose from more than Cicero's

[50] Cic. *de rep.* 2. 22; 3. 29; *de leg.* 2. 10. 23; 3. 5. 12. The dating
which we have suggested for the period in which Cicero placed the acme
of the Roman state is chiefly an inference from the evident and emphatic
approval which he, through the person of Scipio, bestows on the reformed
Servian constitution, and from the desire which Scipio expresses and
which Cicero also feels for the return of the ways of their fathers; in
addition to the Ciceronian references cited above, see Cauer: *Ciceros
politisches Denken* (1903), pp. 32 ff.; Boissier: *Cicéron et ses Amis*
(1865), pp. 43 ff. The interpretation which we have given differs sharply
from the view of E. Meyer (*Caesars Monarchie und das Principat des
Pompejus*, 1922, pp. 184 ff.) who believes that Cicero set forth a
theory of state founded on the constitutional position of Pompey in
52 B.C. See Introduction, pp. 96 ff., below.
[51] Cic. *de rep.* 1. 2; 1. 7; 1. 20; 1, fr. 5.

natural desire to enhance the part which he himself had played upon the political stage. His belief in the worth and dignity of public service was that widely prevalent in antiquity.[52] It springs in part from a deep appreciation of the blessings which an orderly political society had brought to man. In part, also, it springs from a view that the social order is a sacred institution.[53] The foundation of all government rests, as we shall see, upon a divine sanction; and nothing among the achievements of man is more pleasing to this divine power than associations of human beings united by law and denominated states.

This relationship between God and man is of great significance, since between them there exists the natural bond of reason.[54] Nature is ruled by reason, which God possesses in perfection, and in which man also shares.[55] This natural reason results in a natural law which, binding all rational beings together, includes all human society within its ambit.[56] As this law has no beginning, so it knows no end, and it can never be altered or its operation suspended.[57] Transcending all the national boundaries established by man, the true law *(vera lex)* is a universal canon, separating good and evil, impelling men toward rectitude, and recalling them from wrong.[58] By an implicit identification of reason with God, Cicero declares in a striking phrase that the true law is an expression of the purpose and rule of God.[59] It is at once the criterion by which human legislation should be judged, and the source from which it springs.[60]

[52] See, e. g., Thucydides: 2. 40. 2; Aristotle: *Nic. Eth.* 1094 a 24 ff.

[53] Cic. *de rep.* 1. 36; 6. 13. It is one of the statesman's duties to instil this belief; see *de leg.* 2. 7. 15.

[54] Cic. *de leg.* 1. 7. 22 ff.; *de n. d.* 2. 31. 78 ff.; 2. 53. 133. In his treatment of the state Cicero adopts in general all of the important positions developed by the Stoics; see Introduction, pp. 22 ff., above.

[55] Cic. *de leg.* 1. 7. 22; 1. 10. 28 ff.; *de n. d.* 2. 12. 32; 34 ff.; *de off.* 1. 4. 11; *prior. acad.* 2. 7. 21; *de fin.* 5. 13. 38 ff.

[56] Cic. *de rep.* 3. 22; *de leg.* 1. 6. 18; 1. 15. 42.

[57] Cic. *de rep. loc. cit.; de leg.* 1. 16. 43 ff.; 2. 4. 8 ff.; 2. 6. 14.

[58] Cic. *de rep. loc. cit.; de leg.* 1. 6. 18 ff.; 1. 12. 33; 1. 14. 40 ff.; 2. 4. 10.; 2. 5. 13.

[59] Carlyle: *Mediaeval Political Theory,* 1 (1903), p. 6; see note on Cic. *de rep.* 1. 36, below.

[60] Cic. *de leg.* 1. 16. 44; 2. 4. 8; 2. 5. 13; 2. 24. 61.

If, then, law arises from universal reason, so also does justice, that feeling for fair and impartial dealing which satisfies a natural and human instinct to love our fellow-beings.[61] "We are born for justice,"[62] and men naturally seek to live justly.[63] To assert, as Carneades says and as Philus repeats, that justice is simply a convention based upon human experience and the teachings of self-interest, is a complete failure to understand its nature.[64] Justice, indeed, is essentially unselfish, since it bids us consider the interests of all men,[65] and for this reason should be sought for its own sake.[66] Since justice exists in nature its demands are not satisfied by a formal compliance with written statutes and inherited customs.[67] As an attribute of an individual, it is a state of mind which issues in upright conduct;[68] as an element in the government of society, it is the broad principle in accordance with which a state grants to individuals the treatment that is their due.[69].

Moreover, justice must be considered in connection with two other qualities, *aequitas* and *fides,* which also are implicit in the true law, although it is not clear what relationship the three terms bear to each other.[70] We may perhaps assume that justice *(iustitia)* refers to the fair character of that law; "equity" *(aequitas)* to its constant and impartial application;[71] and "faith" *(fides)* to the general respect to which it is entitled and which it receives. At all events, *aequitas* and

---

[61] Cic. *de leg.* 1. 14. 40 ff.; 1. 15. 43; *de fin.* 2. 18. 59 (*de rep.* 3. 26).

[62] Cic. *de leg.* 1. 10. 28.

[63] This is an inference from the argument against justice given by Philus in *de rep.* 3. 11.

[64] Cic. *de rep.* 3. 5, *passim.*

[65] Cic. *de rep.* 3. 7; 8; *de leg.* 1. 18. 48.

[66] Cic. *de leg. loc. cit.*; *de fin.* 3. 21. 70.

[67] Cic. *de leg.* 1. 15. 42.

[68] See the quotation from Cicero in Placentinus: *summa institutionum,* 1. 1, cited by Carlyle: *Mediaeval Political Theory,* 2 (1909), p. 10.

[69] Cic. *de rep.* 3. 11; *de fin.* 5. 23. 67; *de n. d.* 3. 15. 38.

[70] Cic. *de fin.* 1. 16. 52; 2. 18. 59. *Iustitia* and *aequitas* are joined in at least two passages: *de off.* 1. 19. 64; *de am.* 22. 82; *ius* and *aequitas* in *parad.* 4. 1. 28. *Iustitia, aequitas,* and *fides* are combined in at least three places: *de fin.* 1. 16. 52; 2. 18. 59; *de rep.* 1. 2.

[71] Cic. *top.* 4. 23; Carlyle: *Mediaeval Political Theory,* 2 (1909), pp. 7 ff.

fides, like *iustitia,* originate in nature;[72] and reason urges men to pattern their conduct upon these principles.[73]

We have said that the existence of a universal law, eternal in duration and divine in character, is a presupposition of Cicero's theory of the state.[74] It follows that the whole world is the home of its subjects.[75] As Philus declares in the *Commonwealth,* a mån can call a structure of four walls his home only in a very narrow sense, since the entire universe is the true domicile which is shared by all rational beings, human and divine.[76] But the world is more than a home: it is the true state, of which God and man are fellow-citizens,[77] and within which exist the isolated phenomena which we describe as states. An inevitable consequence of this theory, but one which we have not found specifically expressed in Cicero, is the fact of dual citizenship.[78] If a man, as an individual, is bound by ties of affection and duty to the city and country in which he lives, he is no less bound, as a human being, by the obligations which he owes to the universal state.

It has been well said by Carlyle that nothing better illustrates the change in political theory between Aristotle and Cicero than the view held by the latter that human beings are naturally equal.[79] This belief is indeed implicit in Cicero's conception of reason as a natural and universal attribute of man.[80] In all men, moreover, the senses are affected in like ways by like causes.[81] Belief in goodness, approval of well-doing, and, on the contrary, detestation of savagery and baseness are instinctive with mankind.[82] Were not these natural

[72] Cic. *de fin.* 2. 18. 59; cf. *acad. post.* 1. 6. 23.
[73] Cic. *de fin.* 1. 16. 52.
[74] See Introduction, p. 48, above.
[75] Cic. *de rep.* 1. 13; 3. 22; *de fin.* 4. 2. 4; 5. 23. 67; *de leg.* 1. 5. 16; 1. 10. 28; 1. 15. 42; *de off.* 1. 7. 20; 1. 7. 23; 1. 16. 50 ff.; 3. 5. 21 ff.; 3. 6. 28; 3. 6. 31; 3. 17. 69; *de am.* 5. 19 ff.
[76] Cic. *de rep.* 1. 13.
[77] Cic. *de leg.* 1. 7. 23; 1. 23. 61; *de fin.* 3. 19. 64; *acad. post.* 1. 5. 21.
[78] This view is closely approximated in *de fin.* 4. 3. 7; see Marcus Aurelius: *Reflections,* 6. 44; 10. 15; 12. 36; Seneca: *de ot.* 4[31]. 1 ff.; *de tran. an.* 4. 4; Epictetus: *Discourses,* 1. 9. 1 ff.
[79] Carlyle: *Mediaeval Political Theory,* 1 (1903), p. 9.
[80] See Introduction, p. 48, above.
[81] Cic. *de leg.* 1. 10. 30.
[82] Cic. *de leg.* 1. 11. 32.

endowments debased by the "corruption of custom and the emptiness of opinion," men would be as equal in fact as they are in theory.[83]

THE ORIGIN OF THE COMMONWEALTH

We may now consider the origin of the commonwealth. Cicero finds in nature the source of all human goods and virtues, including that social impulse which marks man from his very birth as the future member of political associations.[84] Prompted by this social instinct and not by a sense of physical helplessness, men gather together for the sake of those mutual advantages and pleasures which are inherent in social groups.[85] Such a body of men becomes a commonwealth, however, only when certain further conditions are satisfied. There must, for example, be an adequate number of individuals in the group, since otherwise there cannot be a sufficient exchange of mutual and common advantages. A further prerequisite, before a commonwealth may properly be said to exist, is the evolution of unity of feeling and of an interest in the "people's affair."[86] Indeed, this interest is so important in Cicero's eyes that he regards the "people's affair" as a correct and succinct definition of a commonwealth. But a final step in the development of the group is necessary: the various members composing it must come to an agreement about the law which is to govern their conduct and relations toward one another.

def. of commonwealth

Nothing essential is added to this definition of the commonwealth by Cicero's analysis of the state *(civitas)*, since the *civitas* also is a natural institution and implies the existence of legal rules which express the sense of right of the group.[87] If we are to find any differentiation between the *res publica* and the *civitas*, it will perhaps be seen in the fact that in the former emphasis is laid on the common interest felt by citi-

---

[83] Cic. *de leg.* 1. 10. 28 ff.
[84] Cic. *de rep.* 1. 25; 26; *de leg.* 1. 8. 25 ff.; 1. 24. 62; *de off.* 1. 44. 157 ff.
[85] Cf. Cic. *de off.* 2. 21. 73, where it is said that helplessness has led men to found cities.
[86] We are indebted to Carlyle for this translation of the words *populi res.*
[87] Cic. *de fin.* 3. 19. 63; *de rep.* 1. 32; *de leg.* 2. 5. 12; *parad.* 4. 1. 27 ff.

zens in their society, while in the latter the institutions are stressed by which the people seek to make this interest effective.[88] It is at least to be noted that the state *(civitas)* is "an arrangement of the people," including social classes. There must also be instruments for determining what acts are in accordance with law, and what are not. In the *civitas*, moreover, there must be repositories of public authority, that is, magistrates; and there must be deliberative bodies who cooperate with the magistrates in giving direction, form, and sanction to the popular will. It is assumed by Cicero that political usages will become established in the state, and that public activities will be influenced, if not guided, by the traditions built up by "the fathers."[89]

GENERAL CHARACTERISTICS OF POLITICAL SOCIETY

Such is the nature of political society. At the risk of some repetition we feel it wise to describe certain general qualities by which it must be animated. We shall deal first with the legal nature of the state. For Cicero this is probably the most significant aspect of government, since he holds that nothing matches the law of a state in importance.[90] A human imitation of the divine and eternal law, it is the bond which holds political society together.[91] Without law the state cannot exist,[92] since by definition the state is a group of men united by law.[93] Cicero is very explicit as to the reason why law is an indispensable element of political society. It is necessary to have some common factor in the state which affects all men in the same way. We cannot presume or insure that character and ability will be equally distributed among all citizens. Neither can we wisely constrain each individual to have the

---

[88] Cic. *de rep.* 1. 26; see also Dunning: *History of Political Theories Ancient and Mediaeval* (1902), p. 120, n. 2.

[89] Cicero holds that it is important for the leading men of the state to maintain the soundest teachings of experience, since the character of the state is wholly dependent upon the character of the ruling class; see *de leg.* 3. 13. 30 ff.; *de sen.* 19. 67.

[90] Cic. *de leg.* 1. 4. 14.

[91] Cic. *de rep.* 1. 32.

[92] Cic. *de leg.* 2. 5. 12.

[93] Cic. *de rep.* 1. 25; 1. 32.

INTRODUCTION

same wealth.[94] Thus, according to Cicero, only law may be
shared by all citizens on equal terms. Indeed, the essential
quality of law, apart from the requirement that it be just,[95] is
that it applies equally to all and grants neither special exemp-
tions nor dispensations.[96]

The importance of law, to which we have just referred, is
closely approximated by that of justice. This also originates
in nature[97]; and we must there seek the pattern for justice
among men.[98] If the institutions of government set up by men
are to function at all, their activities must be marked by a
high degree of justice. This view, however, as Cicero recognizes, was not always held; and in the third book of the *Commonwealth* he puts into the mouth of Philus the arguments
which Carneades[99] had employed to show the conventional nature of human justice and the antagonism of true justice to
prudence. To establish the former of these points, Philus denies the existence of true justice, since experience and observation teach that there is no agreement about what is just
either in religious customs or in legal practices.[100] Some men,
for example, believe that it is right to deify animals; others
think it right to sacrifice human beings; while others even hold
that it is not right to represent the gods by statues. Some
peoples consider piracy an honorable calling; others view agriculture as an ignoble occupation; and others deem it proper
to increase the value of their own produce by forbidding their
subject states to raise the same produce. In the sphere of private life, women are sometimes legally subject to unjust dis-
crimination as compared with men, and one group of women is
privileged beyond other groups.[101] There is, moreover, no
uniformity of legal practice among men, and in any city the
same rules are never long observed.

It is also true, according to Philus, that even if justice and

[94] Cic. *de rep. ibid.*; *de off.* 2. 21. 73.
[95] Cic. *de leg.* 2. 5. 11; 2. 5. 13.
[96] Cic. *de rep.* 1. 32; *de leg.* 3. 19. 44.
[97] Cic. *de rep.* 3. 22; *de leg.* 1. 14. 40 ff.; *de fin.* 2. 18. 59.
[98] Cic. *de leg.* 1. 16. 44; 2. 5. 13; 2. 24. 61.
[99] See Introduction, pp. 26 f.
[100] Cic. *de rep.* 3. 9.
[101] Cic. *de rep.* 3. 10 ff.

the just man really exist, justice is often diametrically opposed
to the elementary dictates of prudence and the just man often
acts like a fool.[102]   What is true of individuals holds also for
states; and no state, least of all the Roman, could have ever
attained greatness if it had always pursued the course of justice.[103] Justice, as the term is used by men, is thus a convention
founded upon experience. It springs not from nature or from
inborn inclination but from weakness.[104]

We have given at this length the argument of Philus because
it apparently serves to introduce the famous definition of the
true law by Laelius, and also because of the importance of
justice in Cicero's theory of the state.   After Philus ends his
case, Laelius attempts to show that justice is a part of the
order of nature.[105] Most of his argument has been lost, but we
may suppose that he seeks to prove that justice is implicit in
the true, eternal, and universal law, and hence that justice
itself is true, eternal, and universal.[106] Apparent instances of
injustice—for example, the subjection of human beings to
other human beings—are in fact only apparent, since it is
truly just for the inferior to be subject to the superior.[107] The
answer of Laelius failed to satisfy some of the ancients, and
Lactantius, to whom we are indebted for our knowledge of the
argument, says that Laelius did not successfully refute Philus,
but that he confused natural justice, which Philus had called
folly, with civil justice, which Philus had called prudence.[108]
The real question of the existence and efficacy of natural justice Laelius, according to Lactantius, passed by as if it were a
trap.

The relationship between justice and harmony Cicero does
not clearly define; but it is natural to assume that harmony
is the effect of justice. It exerts its benign influence even prior

---

[102] Cic. *de rep.* 3. 12; 17; 19 ff.

[103] Cic. *de rep.* 3. 9; 12; 15; 18.

[104] Cic. *de rep.* 3. 13: *iustitiae non natura nec voluntas sed inbecillitas
mater est.*

[105] Cic. *de rep.* 3. 20.

[106] Cic. *de rep.* 3. 22.

[107] Cic. *de rep.* 3. 24. It is hardly necessary to point out that this
argument is inconsistent with Cicero's belief in natural equality; see
Introduction, p. 50, above.

[108] Cic. *de rep.* 3. 20.

to the evolution of a commonwealth by inducing wandering tribes to conform to the demands of social and political life.[109] In a long and well-known passage Cicero compares harmony in music with harmony in the state, and describes the latter quality as "the closest and best bond of security that can be found in any commonwealth."[110]

Among these general attributes of the state we may appropriately include Cicero's conception of political liberty. Freedom, in his view, is one of the major elements of any sound social order, since "nothing is sweeter than freedom, even to wild beasts."[111] It is apparently Cicero's idea that liberty is the end for which law is established, since men are slaves of the laws in order that they may be free.[112] Thus freedom is the absence of arbitrary control, for the control exercised by law, as being rational in essence and in origin, is not arbitrary. Moreover, since law should apply equally to all, liberty must be shared equally, if it is to have any real existence.[113] When we pass to the life of an individual, we find that Cicero's definition of freedom "as the power of living as you like" is so qualified that freedom means voluntary subjection to the laws and to moral principles. "What, indeed, is freedom? It is the power of living as we wish. Who then lives as he wishes, except the man who follows the path of rectitude, who rejoices in the performance of his duty, and whose way of life is circumspect and deliberate? He obeys the laws not, of course, because of fear; he complies with them and respects them because he judges that such a course is extremely advantageous. He says nothing, does nothing, thinks of nothing except in a free and voluntary manner. All of his plans and all of his acts proceed from himself, and he himself is also the judge of them. There is nothing which has greater influence with him than his own will and judgment."[114] This

---

[109] Cic. *de rep.* 1. 25.
[110] Cic. *de rep.* 2. 42.
[111] Cic. *de rep.* 1. 35. That this statement, which is put into the mouth of the advocates of democracy, represents Cicero's own view, may be inferred from *de rep.* 1. 31.
[112] Cic. *pro Cluent.* 53. 146.
[113] Cic. *de rep.* 1. 31.
[114] Cic. *parad.* 5. 1. 34; *de off.* 1. 20. 70.

definition of freedom, while applicable in a strict sense only to a philosopher,[115] seems to show that for Cicero freedom, in a political sense, is the absence of all external and arbitrary control except that which is inherent in law and morality.[116] Concretely, liberty means the positive right of citizens to participate in deliberative and executive functions.[117]

Cicero of course realizes that political liberty is often understood as a complete exemption from any form of social control, and that it is wrongly identified with license.[118] This latter condition results from an excess of freedom, since everything has a tendency to become extreme and in its extreme form passes into its opposite. This is true, for example, in the case of health and climate and fertility of soil. Hence, whether we are dealing with individuals or with states, the extreme of freedom becomes the extreme of slavery.

THE FORMS OF STATE AND THEIR CYCLE

Such, in brief, are the forces which bring the state into being and mark its life. Between all political associations formed in this way there is the tie of a common humanity. But all states are not alike. They tend rather to fall into certain general classes. Cicero holds that all existing governments, except the Roman, the Spartan, and the Carthaginian, fit into one of three categories. Each of these in turn includes a true and a perverted form of state.[119] A government is therefore either a monarchy or, when debased, a tyranny; an aristocracy or, if perverted, an oligarchy; or finally a democracy, or when degraded, a turbulent mob. Each of the three good types of state—and we must suppose that Cicero's statement

---

[115] It savors too strongly of the impossible, and absurd, ideal of the Stoic sage; see Arnold: *Roman Stoicism* (1911), pp. 102; 111; 299.

[116] Cic. *de rep.* 1. 27; 2. 23: *libertas quae non in eo est ut iusto utamur domino sed ut nullo*; see Justinian: *inst.* 1. 3. 1.

[117] Cic. *de rep.* 1. 27; Carlyle: *Mediaeval Political Theory*, 1 (1903), pp. 15 ff.

[118] Cic. *de rep.* 1. 44; 3. 13.

[119] Cic. *de rep.* 1. 26; 28. While in most of the references which Cicero makes to *tria genera rerum publicarum* he seems to mean only the good forms, it is clear that he includes the perverted types in his theory of constitutional cycles, as Polybius and others had done before him. Cf. Polybius: 6. 5 ff.

applies also to the debased types—derives its character from
the nature of the ruling element,[120] and its name from the or-
gan which wields deliberative authority. Such authority is of
course essential if the state is to enjoy long life—and this is
one end of government[121]—and must always be relative to the
particular history of the particular state.[122] If supreme power
is lodged in the hands of an individual, we call such a person
a king, and the form of government a monarchy. If it is
given to specially chosen members of the commonwealth, we
have an aristocracy. If, finally, all power is vested in the
people, the state is a democracy.

These forms of state, together with the perverted types that
accompany them, are not fixed and unchanging phenomena,
without historical origin or predictable future. On the contrary there is a natural cycle or course through which every
commonwealth moves, beginning with the political chaos which
characterizes the primal associations of men, and ending
probably with a similar condition of political disruption.[123]
Orderly government is first attained under a king, who in

---

[120] Cic. *de rep.* 1. 31.
[121] Cic. *de rep.* 3. 23.
[122] Cic. *de rep.* 1. 26. How we are to understand this somewhat cryptic
remark is not certain. It may refer, in the first place, to Cicero's view
that the state originates in a sound social instinct, and that this instinct,
if uncorrupted, necessarily gives birth to a sound form of state. The
circumstances that surround the beginning of each state will determine
where the chief power is lodged and what, accordingly, the form of government is to be. The perversion will arise only when the sound instinct
is corrupted. In the second place, the passage may be explained as in-
directly referring to Cicero's attempt to reconcile the constitutional
theories of Polybius with his own conception of Roman history.
[123] Cic. *de div.* 2. 2. 6., where he says that he first learned the *conver-
siones rerum publicarum* from Plato (see *Republic*, 545 c ff.). For
Cicero's theory of constitutional cycles see Schmekel: *Phil. d. mittleren
Stoa* (1892), pp. 74 ff.; Hinze: *Quos scriptores Graecos Cicero in libris
de re publica componendis adhibuerit* (1900), pp. 39 ff.; Cauer: *Ciceros
politisches Denken* (1903), pp. 67 ff. Cicero's chief source is of course
Polybius (see Introduction, pp. 33 f., above), although he seriously modifies and confuses Polybius' theory. According to the simple and logical
view held by the latter, each of the three simple forms of state has its
own peculiar and inherent defect, which causes it to decline in a definite
direction. This conception Cicero certainly understands (*de rep.* 1. 28)
and apparently intends to reproduce, though he does not follow the
principle in the two accounts which he gives of the successions of constitutions (*de rep.* 1. 29; 1. 42).

his turn is followed by a tyrant.[124]   A tyrant, however, may be expelled either by the aristocrats or by the people themselves.   After tyranny we may therefore have either aristocracy or democracy.   The democracy in this case would, according to Cicero, at first be moderate.   Since, however, he goes on to describe Plato's extreme democracy,[125] we should infer that democracy is succeeded by mob rule or ochlocracy.[126] The origin of ochlocracy, however, is confused by the further suggestion that it may arise directly from monarchy or aristocracy[127]—a view which contradicts the theory that constitutions degenerate into their opposites through an inherent weakness of a specified kind.[128]

But if we neglect the difficulties caused by this last confusing statement, we can perceive that Cicero has in mind a double or branching series of constitutions instead of the linear series of Polybius.   We may represent this relationship as follows:

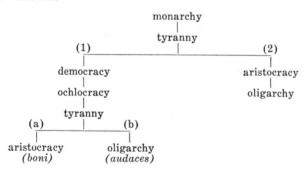

The second branch, which evidently agrees with Polybius,[129] would presumably complete itself in democracy and ochlocracy, though Cicero nowhere says so in the extant portions of the *Commonwealth*. In the first branch, the second tyranny, which follows ochlocracy, may be suppressed either by aristo-

---

[124] Cic. *de rep.* 1. 42; 44 ff.
[125] Cicero closely paraphrases *Republic*, 562 c ff.
[126] Cic. *de rep.* 1. 43.
[127] Cic. *de rep.* 1. 42.
[128] Cic. *de rep.* 1. 28.
[129] Polybius: 6. 7. 8 ff.

crats *(boni)* or by adventurers *(audaces)*.[130] Thus tyranny
would be followed by aristocracy or oligarchy—a development
which completely neglects the assumption that constitutions
degenerate because of a perversion of their governing element, since oligarchy, itself a perverted form, springs directly
from tyranny, another perverted form. What Cicero has done
is to take Polybius' straightforward series and to break it
in two at the point where tyranny passes into aristocracy, and
then to offer an alternative line of evolution.

Such a modification of Polybius' theory completely dis-
arranges the constitutional cycle, and in fact leads to no definite and logical scheme at all. The figure of the ball,[131] which
is tossed about from tyrants to aristocrats or democrats, and
from them to oligarchs or tyrants, is a true representation of
Cicero's constitutional cycle, but it wholly gives up the idea
that there is any logical succession.

The cause of Cicero's confusion lies clearly in his attempt
to modify Polybius' theory in the interest of what he believed
to be historical truth, and to make it accord with his own view
of the development of the Roman constitution. He proposes to
illustrate the cyclical development of constitutions by showing
how the Roman constitution naturally developed into the
mixed form of state.[132] Since, however, Polybius' theory applies only to the unmixed forms of government, while the merit
of the mixed type is, as we shall see,[133] that it is stable and
therefore does not fall within the constitutional cycle, the en-
deavor to combine the two ideas involves Cicero in a contradic-
tion at the start. Moreover, Cicero's conception of Roman history commits him to the view that the tyrant Tarquinius was
expelled, not by aristocrats as ought to have been the case according to the Polybian cycle, but by the whole people, that is,
by an insurgent democracy.[134] It is, in fact, this interpretation which suggests the alternative line of development,

---

[130] Cic. *de rep.* 1. 44.
[131] Cic. *de rep. loc. cit.*
[132] Cic. *de rep.* 2. 16; see also Polybius: 6. 4. 13.
[133] See Introduction, pp. 62 ff., below.
[134] Cic. *de rep.* 2. 30 ff., where it is implied that authority passed to the
people at the end of Tarquinius' rule.

wherein tyranny is followed by moderate democracy, and democracy in turn shows the normal tendency to become extreme.[135]

The chief cause of the degenerative tendency in the forms of state which constitute the cycle is their inherent and inevitable instability. To repeat Cicero's own phrase, the state is nothing but a ball passed about between contending factions or individuals.[136] Their instability, in turn, arises from the fact that in none of the simple good forms of government is there any restraint, natural or artificial, placed upon the normal tendency of the governing element to become perverted; while in the corrupt forms of government the indispensable condition of a true commonwealth, that it be founded upon an agreement about law and rights, is not realized at all.[137] The cause of this fluidity lies in the absence of internal cohesion and tension. Each individual is free to move and destroy the political balance by strengthening or weakening unduly some component of the government.[138] All such governments, accordingly, pass into the related perverted types or sometimes into wholly different types of state.

Naturally, therefore, Cicero rejects the three simple forms of state in his search for the best and perfect commonwealth. But he does not do so hastily. He considers their merits rather carefully before abandoning them and indeed admits that any one of them, if uncorrupted, will give a tolerable government.[139]. Monarchy he regards as the best of the simple types.[140] The position of the king in the state approximates that of God in the universe. The rule which reason exerts in the soul is royal in its nature and consequently like the rule of

---

[135] Cic. *de rep.* 1. 40. In his historical account of the evolution of the Roman state, Cicero shows how the power of the senate, together with the royal authority vested in the consuls, checks the ochlocratic tendency and gives rise to the mixed constitution; see Cic. *de rep.* 2. 32 ff. Various unsuccessful attempts to carry ochlocracy through to its logical culmination in a second tyranny (*de rep.* 2. 26) represent the power of the mixed constitution to resist change.

[136] Cic. *de rep.* 1. 42-44.

[137] Cic. *de rep.* 3. 31 ff.

[138] Cic. *de rep.* 1. 45.

[139] Cic. *de rep.* 1. 26.

[140] Cic. *de rep.* 1. 35-40; 45; 2. 23; 3. 35.

an individual. The authority wielded by the head of a family is by analogy a justification for monarchy. Finally, the soundness of the monarchical principle is attested by the fact that in emergencies the Romans revert to the dictatorship.[141] Nevertheless, monarchy is subject to fatal weaknesses. Even under a good king, such as Cyrus the Great, there is an excessive concentration of power in the hands of one person.[142] The people do not enjoy freedom[143]—and freedom is one of the necessary elements of a sound political life[144]—and the condition of the commons is not one which we should covet.[145] There is, moreover, no way by which we can guarantee that a king will not suffer a fatal change of character and degenerate into a pitiless tyrant like Phalaris of Agrigentum.[146]

Nor does aristocracy fare better at Cicero's hands. It is, he admits, an efficient and just form of government, and, according to its partizans, satisfies the natural principle that the best should be set over their inferiors,[147] and that positions of authority in the state should be given only to those who deserve them.[148] Moreover, aristocracy preserves a balance between the weakness of a single ruler and the rashness of many. And yet the defects inherent in aristocracy weigh more with Cicero than its alleged advantages. Popular liberty is so repressed, even under such an excellent aristocratic government as that at Massilia, that the resulting condition is a close approximation to slavery.[149] Nor is such a government stable, since it easily declines to an oligarchical conspiracy like that of the Thirty Tyrants at Athens.[150]

Cicero no less rejects democracy. Under this form of state he would probably admit that the people are free, at least in the usual sense of the term, since they control all the activities

---

[141] See Introduction, p. 81, below.
[142] Cic. *de rep.* 1. 27.
[143] Cic. *de rep.* 2. 23.
[144] See Introduction, p. 55, above.
[145] Cic. *de rep.* 1. 27.
[146] Cic. *de rep.* 1. 28; 32; 2. 23; 26; 28; 3. 30; 34.
[147] Cic. *de rep.* 1. 27; 34; 3. 24.
[148] Cic. *de rep.* 1. 34.
[149] Cic. *de rep.* 1. 27; 33.
[150] Cic. *de rep.* 1. 28; 3. 32.

of government both at home and abroad.[151] Moreover, if a democratic state views every issue solely with an eye to its own security and freedom, it has a fair degree of stability. Being a society founded upon equality of rights, it easily secures political harmony. None the less, Cicero refuses to approve democracy, because it does not recognize degrees of worth and readily lapses into a turbulent mob, as happened ultimately at Athens.[152] In Cicero's opinion democracy is the worst form of good state.[153]

THE COMPOSITE STATE AND ITS MERITS

For these reasons Cicero turns to the composite state as the ideal.[154] In his eyes this form of government, which includes the best elements of each of the unmixed types, possesses to a unique degree the virtue of stability.[155] There should be a royal element in the perfect state, just as certain activities ought to be carried on by the best men, and as in some fields the commons should be supreme. The blending of these three different elements checks the natural tendency to decay or change with which each of the simple forms is infected. It is only when the leaders of a composite state fall into exceptional degradation that its constitution will suffer modification. The inner

---

[151] Cic. *de rep.* 1. 31 ff.

[152] Cic. *de rep.* 1. 27; 28; 34.

[153] Cic. *de rep.* 3. 35.

[154] In *de rep.* 3. 13 Philus asserts that the *coniunctum civitatis genus* exists as the result of an agreement (*pactio*) made by the various discordant elements of the state in order to establish security and peace. Since Philus does not set forth Cicero's own views, we should not attribute to the latter this explanation of the origin of the mixed state, but should rather regard it as a form of proof of Philus' contention that justice exists only by convention. The immediate source of Cicero's own theory, which is developed in the following pages, is the historian Polybius. Polybius (6. 10; 6. 11. 11 ff.) describes the Roman constitution as it was after the battle of Cannae (216 B. C.), and aims to show that its peculiar excellence was due to its tripartite nature. The monarchical element is represented by the consuls or in emergencies by the dictator; the aristocratic by the senate; and the democratic by the people. As we shall have occasion to note (see Introduction, pp. 90 ff., below), Cicero does not follow this scheme closely.

[155] Cic. *de rep.* 1. 29; 45; 2. 23; 33; see also 2. 9; 17; and esp. 2. 22, where the so-called Servian constitution is described. See Cauer: *Ciceros politisches Denken* (1903), pp. 34 ff.

strength of such a government depends on the assignment of appropriate functions to each of the citizens, since "there is no cause for change when each individual is firmly set in his proper place, and when there is no inferior position into which he may rapidly decline."

Cicero feels, moreover, that the composite state is exemplified by the Roman commonwealth.[156] Accordingly, except for some minor deficiencies, Rome is the embodiment of the ideal.[157] It is Cicero's claim, put into the mouth of Laelius, that this is an original conception. While other writers on political theory, such as Plato, had described the ideal state in general, Cicero illustrates the nature of the perfect commonwealth by the description of a real state—a state, moreover, that had progressed by a natural course from its humble beginnings under the kings to its perfection in the years preceding the tribunate of Tiberius Gracchus.[158] The secret of Rome's excellence lies, according to Cicero, in the circumstance that Rome, unlike other states, owed its growth and final form to the labors of successive lawgivers and to the experience accumulated in the course of successive centuries.[159]

The doctrine of progress, to which we have just alluded, is one of the most interesting aspects of Cicero's political theory, though it must be confessed that it does not seem to have led him to sounder conclusions than those held by his predecessors. The Greek investigators, while acutely aware of the constant changes that occur in actual states, felt that, if the perfect state could be attained, it could be preserved unchanged through a wise and appropriate constitution. They placed an excessive and unjustifiable emphasis upon the form in which political life was to be cast and in this way sought to make static the fluctuating and passionate nature of man.

---

[156] Cic. *de rep.* 1. 46.

[157] Cic. *de rep.* 2. 30; 39; *de leg.* 2. 10. 23.

[158] Cic. *de rep.* 1. 46; 2. 11; 16. It is perhaps too much to say that Cicero thinks that the Roman state attained complete perfection in the years before Tiberius Gracchus, since in the *Laws* Cicero introduces some provisions which, so far as we know, had never been embodied in the Roman state.

[159] Cic. *de rep.* 2. 1; 21; Carlyle: *Mediaeval Political Theory*, 1 (1903), p. 14.

Polybius, perhaps more than any other, believed that the external form of political society was in reality the state itself. It is clear that Cicero had a glimpse of the profounder truth that states are always changing and that experience stored up in the course of successive generations is of greater value than the judgment of any individual, however wise. But he did not realize the consequences of this conception of progress. Indeed, if we understand him rightly, he would have the ideal state adopt the form of constitution that the Roman state had possessed in the middle of the second century B.C.[160] Apparently, he believes that a proper arrangement of the various elements of the state will insure a permanent and unchangeable form of political life. In spite of his knowledge of political development, Cicero would impose rigidity upon flux.

We have noted that the Roman state was Cicero's ideal. We should accordingly remember that in his two political treatises we have an intricate blend of reality with fiction. We find, for example, that his long account of Roman history, which purports to be factual, contains numerous generalities about an ideal state. We find several provisions in the third book of the *Laws* which diverge from Roman practice and which are designed to bring the Roman constitution into conformity with the requirements of a perfect commonwealth.

LOCATION OF THE PERFECT STATE

We may suppose, then, that a statesman addressing himself to the task of founding a perfect state would establish a composite commonwealth in which each of the three simple forms is equally represented. He would then naturally choose a location for the state. This must be selected always with an eye to permanence and security,[161] since governments should be so created that they may endure forever.[162] Such a location will not lie directly upon the seaboard. Not only is a maritime site exposed to the unexpected attacks of enemies, but it is also

---

[160] Cic. *de rep.* 3. 29; 2. 22.
[161] Cic. *de rep.* 2. 3 ff.; Cauer: *Ciceros politisches Denken* (1903), pp. 54 ff.
[162] Cic. *de rep.* 3. 23.

subject to moral contamination; and the citizens who live there are tempted to abandon the hardships of camp and tillage for the stirring and more lucrative careers of piracy and trade. This picture, which is drawn from the experience of Greece and Carthage, has of course a reverse. For a city located on the coast has great economic advantages: it can import and export at pleasure and thus share in the commercial intercourse of the world. It is naturally Cicero's desire that the ideal commonwealth should possess the advantages but not the disadvantages of a maritime location. He turns to Rome for his model, and places his city not far from the sea on the banks of a river open to commerce throughout the entire year.[163] The site, moreover, should be adapted in other ways for the development of urban life.[164] It must be healthful; it must be abundantly supplied with water; and the hills on which it is built must afford shade to its inhabitants and be visited by cooling breezes.

FAMILY LIFE IN THE PERFECT STATE

If a state is to have continuous life, its members must increase and multiply. Plato had proposed communism in wives and children as the method by which the guardians of his state should insure the propagation of sound and intelligent offspring.[165] Cicero rejects this notion emphatically,[166] and holds that the only proper relationship designed for the procreation of children is the institution of monogamous marriage. This, in turn, is closely connected with the social unit of the family, in which the oldest male rules over his wife, his children, and his grandchildren.[167] An element of great stability when subject to "paternal authority" *(patria potestas)*,[168] the family is the chief source in private life of that permanence which the ideal state establishes, embodies, and perpetuates.

---

[163] Cic. *de rep.* 2. 5.
[164] Cic. *de rep.* 2. 6.
[165] Plato: *Republic*, 457 b ff.
[166] Cic. *de rep.* 4. 5; 5. 5.
[167] Cic. *de rep.* 4. 6; *de off.* 1. 17. 54; see also *de rep.* 1. 43, a passage paraphrased from Plato, where nevertheless the idea of family control is stressed.
[168] For *patria potestas* see Gaius: *inst.* 1. 55; Justinian: *inst.* 1. 9.

EDUCATION IN THE PERFECT STATE

The children must, in their turn, be educated, if they are to give themselves intelligently to the service of the state. Because of the exceedingly fragmentary condition of the fourth book of the *Commonwealth* we cannot present a consecutive account of education in the ideal commonwealth. It is probable, indeed, that Cicero does not propose a state-controlled educational system, but that he would have the young taught within the family circle.[169] But it is at least clear that Cicero's conception of education provided both for physical and intellectual training; and that it stressed the necessity of inculcating moral principles. Training of the body is to precede that of the mind. In the extant fragments Cicero alludes to some plan of physical discipline unlike the Spartan.[170] He would not, for example, have young men exercise naked, nor would he have them, during military training, live in intimate association with their fellows and thus be exposed to the risk of moral impairment. More important, naturally, is intellectual instruction, since in Cicero's view mind and reason are the noblest endowments of man.[171] Education in ethical problems is more fully represented in the fragments of Book IV than any other aspect of the subject. The young are to be taught their duties toward the dead.[172] They are bidden to revere the departed and to respect their tombs. Similarly, Cicero inculcates the obligations which men are to observe toward their fellows. The young are taught that it is wrong to steal.[173] The principles of a simple and upright life are emphasized.[174] A severe prohibition is laid upon homosexual indulgence.[175]

Cicero naturally excludes from the system of education any

---

[169] A glance at Cicero's fourth book will show that this is a mere hypothesis, justified, in our opinion, by the fact that in the Roman practice, which Cicero usually follows, children were educated in the family; and by the emphasis laid upon family life; see Cic. *de rep.* 4. 3, below, and note; 5. 5.

[170] Cic. *de rep.* 4. 4.

[171] Cic. *de rep.* 4. 1.

[172] Cic. *de rep.* 4. 8; see also *de leg.* 2. 9. 22.

[173] Cic. *de rep.* 4. 3.

[174] Cic. *de rep.* 4. 7.

[175] Cic. *de rep.* 4. 3; 4.

form of instruction which might in any way lead the young
to emotional excess. It is accordingly probable that the young
are not taught lyric poetry.[176] Comedy, on the other hand,
Cicero appreciated, and it is likely, but by no means certain,
that he admits it into the curriculum.[177] The range of its activity, however, is narrowly restricted, since, in accordance with
the principle sanctified by the Twelve Tables, personal attacks upon the living are not allowed on the stage.[178] What
Cicero conceives to be the function of epic and tragic poetry in
education we do not know, but we may be reasonably sure
that his attitude was censorious. We are almost equally in the
dark as to the place held by music in the training of the
young.[179] That Cicero fully appreciates the significance of
music is quite apparent, since he twice quotes, without express
dissent, Plato's dictum that a change in the forms of music
used in education is equivalent to a change in the form of constitution.[180] We shall perhaps not go too far if we tentatively
conclude that Cicero restricts musical education to a knowledge only of those modes which have a tranquillizing effect on
the emotions or which fortify the soul against fear.

We are without means for knowing how far Cicero would
include instruction in political theory in the training of the
young. If we may trust the fragmentary excerpts made from
the *Commonwealth* by Nonius, it is probable that Cicero rec-
ommends the teaching of the elements of law.[181] Moreover, he
clearly inculcates the belief that Plato's communistic theory is
wholly wrong, and that property should be privately owned.[182]

---

[176] Cic. *de rep.* 4. 9.
[177] Cic. *de rep.* 4. 11.
[178] Cic. *de rep.* 4. 10.
[179] We are at a loss to explain the implicit criticism of Cicero contained in the twelfth chapter of Book 4, pp. 241 f., below. It is there suggested, though not specifically asserted, that one of the interlocutors in
the *Commonwealth* assumed the only function of music to be the excitement of pleasurable feelings. Since this is clearly at variance with
Cicero's attested views, we feel bound to regard the testimonium in
Aristides Quintilianus as essentially inaccurate, in so far as it would
imply that Cicero himself held the view criticized.
[180] Cic. *de leg.* 2. 15. 39; 3. 14. 32; cf. Plato: *Republic*, 424 b ff.
[181] Cic. *de rep.* 4. 8.
[182] Cic. *de rep.* 4. 5; cf. *de off.* 1. 7. 21, where it is stated that private
ownership of property is not a natural institution.

CHAPTER IV

THE INSTITUTIONS OF THE IDEAL COMMONWEALTH

RELIGIOUS INSTITUTIONS OF THE IDEAL COMMONWEALTH

Such are the conditions which surround the origin and life of the perfect commonwealth. These requirements, however, are of a general nature, and do not in a narrow sense affect the political structure of the state. To the outward form of the state, to the detailed regulations by which the state enforces its will and which determine the repositories of political authority, Cicero devotes two books of the *Laws*. Since, as we have shown,[1] Cicero regards social organization as closely related to the divine, it is natural that he should consider first the means by which the state endeavors to win the favor of the gods,[2] and second the ways by which the state, under divine favor, lives and functions. In the one case the state acts through religious ceremonial and priestly orders; in the other, through magistrates and groupings of the chief men and people.

The code of religious law is introduced by a preamble, suggestive in its form of Plato,[3] in which Cicero urges all citizens of the ideal commonwealth to believe implicitly in the supremacy of the deathless gods.[4] For the gods not only govern the universe, but they also perceive and record the acts and feel-

---

[1] See Introduction, p. 48, above.
[2] Cic. *de leg.* 1. 15. 43; see also Greenidge: *Roman Public Life* (1911), p. 162. We should perhaps state here the plan which we have followed in citing evidence in this and the following sections of the Introduction. We supply the passage from Cicero on which the statement in the text is based, and then give other evidence to show whether or not the view set forth by Cicero is in accord with the religious or political practices of the Roman state.
[3] Cic. *de leg.* 2. 6. 14.
[4] Cic. *de leg.* 2. 7. 15 ff.

ings of each individual. Accordingly, if reverence does not of itself inspire adoration, prudence will at least suggest the expedience of worshiping beings who will be both witnesses against us and judges of our conduct. The religious provisions themselves, which Cicero intentionally drew up in quaint and legalistic phraseology reminiscent of the Twelve Tables, open with a description of the proper attitude of worship.[5] The gods must be approached reverently, in purity of heart, and without costly ceremonial; and they will visit with punishment those who disregard these provisions. For reverence is dear to the gods, and the manner in which men worship them should conform to their wishes. If the law stresses purity of heart, it does not thereby imply that no importance is to be attached to purity of body. On the contrary, Cicero assumes that the body of a worshiper will be ceremonially clean. Since, however, mind is superior to body, and since the gods are entitled to the best that man may give, purity of mind must accompany purity of body in the worship of the gods. By forbidding costly ceremony the law opens the rites of religion to all, a provision which the gods approve, since they are displeased by any artificial restriction upon the number of those who seek to know and worship them.

The divinities who are to be thus approached do not all possess identical significance. Cicero mentions first, and hence perhaps esteems most important, the deities who have always been regarded as the gods of heaven (*di caelestes*).[6] The second place he assigns to deified mortals, like Hercules and Aesculapius, whose good deeds on earth have elevated them to the gods.[7] He places next such personified abstractions as Intelligence (*Mens*), Excellence (*Virtus*), and Faith (*Fides*). After these Cicero puts the dead, who are to be considered as gods and whose worship must be maintained.[8] Into this pan-

---

[5] Cic. *de leg.* 2. 8. 19; 2. 10. 24 ff.; *de rep.* 2. 14.
[6] Cic. *de leg.* 2. 8. 19. It should be noted that this division of the gods does not agree with that given in the old formula which Livy (8. 9. 6) preserves, in which the gods are described as either *di indigetes* or *di novensiles*; see Wissowa: *Religion und Kultus der Römer* (1912), pp. 18 ff.
[7] Cic. *de leg. loc. cit.*; 2. 11. 27.
[8] Cic. *de leg.* 2. 9. 22; 2. 22. 55 ff.

theon no new or imported gods will be admitted, unless they have been officially adopted by the state.[9] Furthermore, citizens will not be allowed to worship the personification of any evil abstraction, such as Insult *(Contumelia)*, Fever *(Febris)*, or Ill Fortune *(Mala Fortuna)*.[10]

An interesting survival of a view essentially proper to a city-state is the division of the field of religious observance into an urban and a rural sphere,[11] in each of which Cicero would have the best elements of traditional Roman ritual carefully preserved.[12] Certain practices, moreover, are at all times forbidden. Women, for example, must not participate in nocturnal sacrifices, except when duly performed in behalf of the people; and they must not be initiated into the mysteries, except the Greek rites of Ceres.[13] No wicked person *(impius)* may offer gifts to the gods in the hope of softening their anger towards him.[14] No one except the attendants of the Great Mother of the Gods may collect money for religious purposes; and even they may do so only on the proper days, so strongly does Cicero feel that the custom consumes property and disseminates superstition.[15] No one may dedicate land, which is the sacred possession of all the gods, to any special purpose. And in all offerings of gold, silver, or ivory, moderation must be preserved.[16]

In addition to these injunctions of a negative character

---

[9] Cic. *de leg.* 2. 8. 19; 2. 10. 25-26.

[10] Cic. *de leg.* 2. 8. 19; 2. 11. 28. This portion of the religious code represents Cicero's objection to the custom followed by the Romans. There was, for example, a goddess Fever in the Roman pantheon (see Wissowa: *Religion und Kultus der Römer*, 1912, pp. 245 ff.); a goddess Fortuna Mala (see Cic. *de n. d.* 3. 25. 63; Wissowa: *op. cit.* p. 262); and a god Robigo, to whom men offered sacrifices in order that rust might be averted from the grain (see Wissowa: *op. cit.* pp. 195 ff.).

[11] Cic. *de leg.* 2. 8. 19.

[12] Cic. *de leg.* 2. 9. 22; 2. 16. 40.

[13] Cic. *de leg.* 2. 9. 21; 2. 14. 35 ff. The objection which Cicero feels towards the mysteries in general is due to their licentious character, and his exemption of the rites of Ceres from this ban is due to their spiritual nature; see in general Schoemann: *Gr. Alt.* 2 (1902), pp. 385 ff.

[14] Cic. *de leg.* 2. 9. 22; 2. 16. 41.

[15] Cic. *de leg.* 2. 9. 22; 2. 16. 40. This provision is apparently derived from Roman custom: see Wissowa: *Religion und Kultus der Römer* (1912), p. 320.

[16] Cic. *de leg.* 2. 9. 22; 2. 18. 45.

there are in Cicero's code some general and unrelated provisions of a positive nature.[17]   For example, vows are to be strictly observed.   Violations of the religious law will be punished.   From those who are guilty of perjury two penalties are exacted.   Since, on the one hand, perjury is an offense against the gods, the punishment is death; and since, on the other hand, perjury intimately affects human life and interests, death is accompanied by disgrace.   Finally, anyone who takes or steals any offering or any private property deposited in a shrine for safe keeping is treated as a parricide.

These are the provisions which concern the general practices of religion.   In rural districts, where groves *(luci)* are the religious centers and where the shrines of the Lares are maintained, Cicero would have the simple pieties of ancestral and family worship carefully preserved.[18]   How strongly he realized the potency of the religion of the countryside may be seen from the regulations with which Cicero surrounds holidays.   These are to be days of relaxation, falling at such seasons of the year as naturally coincide with the end of the farmer's labor, when he, his family, and his slaves can make suitable offering of the season's fruits to the appropriate divinities.   In cities, on the other hand, the gods are worshiped in temples, where statues bring them vividly before the eyes and thoughts of men.[19]   Another form of ceremonial which accompanies urban development is public games *(ludi)*, consisting of musical and athletic contests.[20]   If Cicero is preoccupied more with the musical aspect of games, it is because, as we have seen, he appreciates the force of Plato's view that a change in the forms of music involves also a change in the form of government.

In each of these spheres of worship, all ritual is subject to the guidance of certain individuals.   According to Cicero's account, which is not clear, there are two main groups of religious functionaries.   The first of these contains the various

---

[17] Cic. *de leg.* 2. 9. 22; 2. 16. 41.
[18] Cic. *de leg.* 2. 8. 19 ff.; 2. 12. 29.
[19] Cic. *de leg.* 2. 8. 19; 2. 10. 26 ff.
[20] Cic. *de leg.* 2. 9. 22; 2. 15. 38.

priesthoods *(sacerdotia)*,[21] known collectively as the public priests *(sacerdotes publici)*. The priesthoods, in turn, fall into separate groupings. The pontiffs, who are first mentioned by Cicero, control the worship of all the gods. They preside over all public and private ceremonial, and supply information as to the proper forms of all ritual. Within their competence also falls the duty of punishing with death any Vestal who fails to keep her vow of chastity.[22] There are, moreover, certain priests assigned to the worship of a particular divinity.[23] These are the flamens *(flamines)*, whose duties are not specified by Cicero.[24] The third of these priesthoods is the group of women called Vestals *(virgines Vestales)*, who direct the worship of Vesta.[25] Probably six in number, these priestesses guard the sacred fire symbolical of the city's domestic life, and may never allow it to become extinguished. During incumbency, which probably lasts for thirty years, the Vestals are bound to preserve chastity; and any breach of faith on their part is punished with death.[26]

The second class of religious officials is composed of the augurs.[27] They expound the will of Jupiter by the interpretation of signs and auspices. They are to be masters of their art, for Cicero in the *Laws* holds that there is an art in divi-

---

[21] Cic. *de leg.* 2. 8. 20. The account which Cicero gives agrees essentially with the practices of Roman religion, though it should perhaps be noted that he does not mention the *rex sacrorum*; see in general Wissowa: *Religion und Kultus der Römer* (1912), pp. 479 ff.; 501 ff.

[22] Cic. *de leg.* 2. 9. 22; 2. 12. 29.

[23] Cic. *de leg.* 2. 8. 20; 2. 12. 29. Cicero has very little to say about the flamens. It is likely that there were fifteen of them, twelve minor flamens and a *flamen Dialis*, a *flamen Martialis*, and a *flamen Quirinalis*, each serving the god indicated by the proper adjective; see Wissowa: *op. cit.* pp. 504; 521.

[24] That is, unless we assume that the words *alterum ... adsciverit* in *de leg.* 2. 8. 20 refer to certain duties which the flamens perform at the express bidding of the senate and people. In this case, the flamens are to explain the obscure utterances of prophets and soothsayers whenever the senate and people command.

[25] Cic. *de leg.* 2. 8. 20; 2. 12. 29. This is a Roman institution; see Wissowa: *op. cit.* p. 504.

[26] Cic. *de leg.* 2. 9. 22; 2. 12. 29.

[27] Cic. *de leg.* 2. 8. 20 ff.; 2. 12. 31. This is an institution transferred from Roman practice; see Wissowa: *op. cit.* p. 523 ff.

nation.[28]   They are to determine, by appropriate ritual, whether the gods favor the state, its crops, and its priests. Their pronouncements, duly delivered after formal observation, are law to commanders in the field and to magistrates within the city.   Whatever they pronounce to be defective because it fails to meet the obligations of ritual is null and void. Their mandate is enforced on penalty of death.

It will readily be seen that the importance of the augurs in the sphere of religion is overshadowed by their importance in the sphere of politics.   This is what Cicero desired.   "The chief and pre-eminent power in the commonwealth is that associated with the authority of the augurs.   I do not in fact hold this view because I myself am an augur, but because it is inevitable that I should think so. What, indeed, is greater— if we raise the question of authority—than the power of disbanding assemblies and gatherings of the people presided over by the highest military and civil magistrates, of blocking their resolutions, or of nullifying such resolutions as they have passed? What is of deeper import than that a proposal already initiated should be quashed, if one augur says: 'Postpone'? What is more illustrious than to possess the power of compelling by a decree the consuls to resign their offices?   What is more holy than to have the power of giving or refusing to give magistrates the right to approach the people *(populus)* and the commons *(plebes),* or even of abrogating a statute which was illegally passed?"[29]

If events of an unusual character *(prodigia portenta)* occur under circumstances which suggest that they may reveal the divine will, the matter is reported to the Etruscan soothsayers on the order of the senate.[30]   In these cases, as well as in the case of objects struck by lightning or of eclipses, the Etruscans are to determine what expiatory offerings shall be made and what deities shall be placated.

---

[28] Cic. *de leg.* 2. 13. 32 ff.; cf. *de div.* 2. 72. 148, where Cicero sharply attacks divination. On this question see Cic. *de div.* (ed. Pease), Introduction, pp. 10 ff.

[29] Cic. *de leg.* 2. 12. 31.

[30] Cic. *de leg.* 2. 9. 21; 2. 14. 34. This is a custom drawn from the practice at Rome; see Wissowa: *op. cit.* pp. 543 ff.

The religious aspects of declaring war, concluding peace, or striking a treaty are dealt with by the Fetial College *(fetiales)*.[31] Their sanction is necessary if these diplomatic and international relationships are to possess legal validity.

By these provisions, short and incomplete though they be, Cicero feels that the ideal commonwealth will secure and preserve the favor of the gods. In its essentials, his code is a summary of Roman usage, not far different, as Atticus remarks, "from the laws of Numa and our customs."[32] Its place in an account of Cicero's political views is justified by the fact that in Roman belief political power, considered abstractly, flowed from the gods, and that human agents could properly exert political authority only when that authority was divinely sanctioned.

POLITICAL INSTITUTIONS OF THE IDEAL COMMONWEALTH

Cicero describes the political structure of the ideal state in Book III of the *Laws*. In that treatment, which consists of a number of more or less specific injunctions, he aims to supply the governmental agencies and processes which are necessary if the mixed and balanced type of state is to exist and function.[33] It has been claimed that the form in which Cicero presents these rules apparently approaches "more closely to the modern idea of a written constitution" than the work of "any other ancient statesman or political theorist."[34] We do not agree with this view. There does not appear to be any appreciable difference in its essential characteristics between this code and the various codes established by the Greek lawgivers, especially such statesmen as Solon, Lycurgus, Zaleucus, and Charondas.[35] In its form, its language, and the precision of certain of its provisions, Cicero's code bears some resemblance

---

[31] Cic. *de leg.* 2. 9. 21; 2. 14. 34; *de rep.* 2. 17; 3. 23. This institution is adopted from Roman practice; see Wissowa: *op. cit.* pp. 550 ff.

[32] Cic. *de leg.* 2. 10. 23.

[33] Cic. *de leg.* 3. 2. 4; 3. 5. 12.

[34] C. W. Keyes: "Original Elements in Cicero's Ideal Constitution," *Amer. Jour. of Phil.* vol. 42 (1921), pp. 309 ff., esp. p. 312.

[35] For Solon see Busolt: *Gr. Staatskunde*, 2 (1926), pp. 828 ff.; for Lycurgus, *ibid.* pp. 648 ff.; for Zaleucus, *op. cit.* 1 (1920), pp. 375 ff.; for Charondas, *ibid.* p. 377.

to the latter books of Plato's *Laws*.[36]   It is hardly true, moreover, to say that Cicero's draft contains "a complete constitution."[37]   We need take only two examples to illustrate the
incompleteness of the code: there is no adequate treatment
either of the powers and functions of the people or of the
judicial system.   There is, finally, nothing in Cicero's own
words—though, as has been suggested,[38] he may well have
been familiar with the idea—to suggest that he intended his
code to possess rigidity—nothing, for example, comparable
to the famous provision in the laws of Zaleucus.[39]   That there
are original elements in Cicero's code will be readily admitted
by all, but these suggested innovations concern the individual
provisions of his constitution.

His code, considered abstractly, deliberately places great
emphasis upon authority in the state.[40]   Implicit in nature and
exemplified by the relationship of God to the world and by
the traditional position of kings, the principle of authority is
essential to the existence of a household, a family, or a state;
and without it the human race and the entire universe would
wholly cease to be.   Within the sphere of political life we have
already seen that Cicero conceives the true and impersonal
source of authority to be law.[41]   But law, if it is to be effective
in the realm of human action, must be embodied in a human
agent.   This person is the magistrate or college of magistrates.[42]   "It can be truly affirmed that the magistrate is law
made vocal, while law is a voiceless magistrate."[43]   The
magistrate accordingly occupies an exalted station.   If he is
inferior to the laws of his state, he is nevertheless above the
people, and by virtue of his authority lays down provisions
that are right, useful, and in accordance with the law.[44]   But

---

[36] Cf. Plato: *Laws*, 751 a; 768 d.
[37] Keyes: *op. cit.* p 312; see Introduction, p. 86, below.
[38] Keyes: *op. cit.* p. 310 ff.
[39] Busolt: *Gr. Staatskunde*, 1 (1920), p. 377.   The provision referred
to, that a sponsor of a new law should make his proposal with a rope
around his neck, is also attributed to Charondas.
[40] Cic. *de leg.* 3. 1. 3 ff.
[41] See Introduction, p. 52, above.
[42] Cic. *de leg.* 3. 2. 5.
[43] Cic. *de leg.* 3. 1. 2.
[44] Cic. *de leg. loc. cit.*; 3. 3. 6.

he is not permitted to lose all contact with the people and thus to wield his powers perpetually. Cicero holds the eminently sound view, derived from Greek theory and particularly from Athenian practice,[45] that a good magistrate is one who has been an obedient citizen, that every good citizen ought to look forward to the time when he will be in authority, and that every magistrate should remember that in a short time he will again occupy merely private station.[46]

The magistrates play a rôle so important that Cicero regards the state as held together by magistrates, and considers its type as determined by the system in which its magistrates are arranged.[47] It is accordingly necessary for a candidate to have satisfied certain requirements before he is elected to an office in the ideal commonwealth. A candidate must, for example, have attained the minimum age required for the particular office concerned.[48] Furthermore, he may not hold the same office a second time until an interval of ten years has passed.[49] It is also probable that the magistracies can be held only in a certain order.[50] Corruption, of course, disqualifies a candidate and brings upon him a penalty commensurate with the offense.[51]

If we pass from candidates to magistrates, we find that in Cicero's constitution the latter all possess certain rights and conversely are bound by certain duties. Every magistrate may fine, scourge, or imprison a rebellious or dangerous citizen, provided that no magistrate of equal or superior authority (*par maiorve potestas*) intervenes, and provided that no

---

[45] Aristotle: *Politics*, 1283 b 42 ff.; Ferguson: *Greek Imperialism* (1913), pp. 55 ff.

[46] Cic. *de leg.* 3. 2. 5.

[47] Cic. *de leg.* 2. 27. 69; 3. 2. 5; 3. 5. 12.

[48] Cic. *de leg.* 3. 3. 9; see note on *de rep.* 1. 12, below. This provision is taken from Roman practice; see Greenidge: *Roman Public Life* (1911), p. 186.

[49] Cic. *de leg.* 3. 3. 8. In this requirement Cicero has retained a provision passed by Sulla in 81 B.C.; see Greenidge: *loc. cit.*

[50] Cic. *de leg.* 3. 3. 7; 3. 3. 9; see Keyes: "Original Elements in Cicero's Ideal Constitution," *Amer. Jour. of Phil.*, vol. 42 (1921), p. 315; Greenidge: *loc. cit.* This is apparently the Sullan rule.

[51] Cic. *de leg.* 3. 4. 11; 3. 20. 46. This is simply the Roman custom; see Greenidge: *op. cit.* p. 185; Keyes: *op. cit.* pp. 318 ff.

appeal is made to the people.[52]   Every magistrate, also, may preside over a court and may consult the auspices.[53]   But the most important general right of the magistrates is that of entering the senate after their term of office expires.[54]

Conversely, there are certain obligations which rest uniformly upon all magistrates. They must, as we have implied, recognize the principle of *par maiorve potestas,* and must allow defendants to appeal to the popular courts.[55]   When dispatched by senate or people on military or diplomatic service, they may engage only in wars that are legally sanctioned. They must keep their forces under control; they must spare allied states; they must enhance their country's honor and return home, not loaded with spoils, but crowned with glory.[56]

The great majority of the magistrates treated in Cicero's code function regularly and are constantly in being. We shall consider them one after the other, following the normal course taken by a person who enters upon a political career. At the foot of the list come the minor officials *(minores magistratus),* whose powers, though slight, probably entitle them to be counted among the magistrates.[57]   The members of this group

---

[52] Cic. *de leg.* 3. 3. 6; 3. 12. 27; *de rep.* 2. 31. This is probably a partial revival of the early powers of the Roman magistrate; see Keyes: *op. cit.* p. 319; Greenidge: *op. cit.* pp. 167 ff. According to the principle of *par maiorve potestas,* any magistrate could veto the acts of any magistrate of equal or inferior rank; see Greenidge: *op. cit.* p. 176.

[53] Cic. *de leg.* 3. 3. 10; 3. 12. 27. This is essentially the Roman usage, though there is some doubt as to whether the aediles (see Introduction, p. 78, below) had the right to preside over a *iudicium;* see Greenidge: *op. cit.* pp. 158 ff.; pp. 162 ff.

[54] Cic. *de leg.* 3. 3. 10; 3. 12. 27. It is not clear exactly what Cicero's provision, "*exque iis* [that is, *omnibus magistratibus*] *senatus esto,*" means. We hold, with Keyes (*op. cit.* pp. 313 ff.), that Cicero would have the senate constituted by the censors from all who have held any magistracy, and that no one except an ex-magistrate could be a member of the senate. If this interpretation be correct, we have (in Keyes's words) a "compromise between the older principle of free choice by the censors and the Sullan law attaching entrance to the Senate to the holding of a particular magistracy."

[55] Cic. *de leg.* 3. 3. 6; 3. 12. 27.

[56] Cic. *de leg.* 3. 3. 9; 3. 8. 18. On the intrusion of moral advice into a constitutional scheme, see Keyes: *op. cit.* p. 319.

[57] Cic. *de leg.* 3. 3. 6; Keyes: *op. cit.* pp. 313 ff. To all appearance, these magistrates correspond to those known as *vigintisexviri,* with the exception that the quaestors and the *tribuni militum* are included in the group; see Greenidge: *Roman Public Life* (1911), pp. 234 ff.

are divided into smaller units, each possessing distinct and differentiated powers. Some of them, named tribunes of the soldiers *(tribuni militum)*, serve in their appropriate capacity as the commanders of such troops as are put under their control. Others coin and guard the public moneys. Another group is set the task of preventing the escape of accused persons while their cases are pending, and of inflicting capital punishment on those convicted on a capital charge. Others, finally, hear and decide certain law-suits, perhaps those in which the freedom of a slave is at stake.

From the *magistratus minores* Cicero naturally proceeds to the aedileship which he makes a prerequisite for holding higher office.[58] The aediles form a college the membership of which is not stated; neither is it specified where they are elected, though it is probable that election took place in the tribal assembly of the people.[59] Upon their shoulders rests the obligation to maintain good order in the city, to provide for its grain supply, and to give the regular games which not only satisfy the popular desire for amusement but are also a form of religious ceremonial.[60]

With the censorship, which is next described by Cicero, we reach one of the chief magistracies of the state.[61] The college of censors, comprising two individuals and presumably elected in the assembly of the centuries, holds office continuously for five years and at no time during their incumbency is their power in abeyance.[62] By virtue of their authority in the do-

---

[58] Cic. *de leg.* 3. 3. 7. It is probable, as Keyes (*op. cit.* p. 315) suggests, that Cicero makes the *cursus honorum* rigid and requires that the offices be held in a certain order.

[59] This is entirely an inference from the Roman practice; see Greenidge: *op. cit.* p. 208. It will be noted that Cicero has quite neglected to specify the particular form of popular assembly in which any of his magistrates is elected. Cicero makes no distinction between curule and plebeian aediles.

[60] Cic. *de leg.* 3. 3. 7.

[61] Cic. *de leg. loc. cit.*

[62] In his treatment of the censorship Cicero has introduced a striking innovation. The Roman censors, while elected for five years, functioned actively for only eighteen months, so extensive and so potentially oppressive were their powers; see Greenidge: *op. cit.* pp. 216 ff., esp. p. 218; Keyes: *op. cit.* pp. 316 ff. The change which Cicero proposes greatly increases their authority. It is in part made necessary by some new powers conferred upon them; see below.

main of finance, the censors build and maintain public works, such as shrines, roads, and aqueducts, out of funds accruing to the treasury from public revenues. Similarly they keep the citizen-lists of the state which contain the name and financial status of every citizen. To secure a proper distribution of the electorate among the centuries, they institute classes based on wealth and age and allocate citizens to them; and they assign citizens to the appropriate tribes. In another sphere of censorial competence—that of moral supervision of the state—they possess authority to compel citizens to marry, and to regulate their lives in accordance with morality. Their control also extends over the field of public life. They exclude from the senate all senators or ex-magistrates who have been guilty of improper conduct. A more striking aspect of their authority is their power to demand from each retiring magistrate an account of his official conduct, and to prosecute all who cannot show that they have been honest and efficient.[63] A natural outgrowth of this function is the duty of maintaining the integrity of the laws, to keep them from being altered, and to insure that they are obeyed.[64]

In every state a clash of legal rights and interests is inevitable. If this disagreement is to be adjusted in an orderly and peaceable way—and this is the only decent procedure for civilized beings[65]—a legal system of some sort is necessary. In the form in which the Third Book of the *Laws* has been preserved there is no account of what we term criminal law, and the description of civil procedure is very vague.[66] Civil

---

[63] Cic. *de leg.* 3. 4. 11; 3. 20. 47. This is an attempt to develop an institution in Cicero's constitution similar to the *euthuna* in Athenian politics (Busolt: *Gr. Staatskunde*, 2, 1926, pp. 1076 ff.). There was nothing like it in Roman practice; see Keyes: *op. cit.* p. 317.

[64] Cic. *de leg. loc. cit.* It has been well pointed out by Keyes (*op. cit.* p. 316) that this new and interesting, if not very carefully described, function is probably taken from the duty of the *nomophylakes* introduced into the Athenian constitution by Demetrius of Phalerum (Busolt: *op. cit.* p. 925; Ferguson: *Hellenistic Athens*, 1911, pp. 44 ff.). This conception of Demetrius' may well have been derived, through his master Theophrastus and through Aristotle, from the function of the *nomophylakes* in Plato's *Laws* (752 ff.).

[65] Cic. *de off.* 1. 11. 34; see also *de leg.* 3. 18. 42.

[66] It is probable, as we have noted, that this aspect of political life was treated at length in the later books of the *Laws*; see *de leg.* 3. 20. 48.

law, because of the close relationship which it bears to the
Roman praetor, was perhaps regarded as the particular province of a magistrate. In Cicero's state the guardian of the
civil law is the praetor, who is assisted by such colleagues as
the senate and the people may deem necessary to provide.[67]
Elected probably in the assembly of the centuries, the praetors
may approach the people and the senate, seeking from the
former action of a legislative, judicial, or elective character,
and from the latter the passage of advisory decrees *(senatus
consulta)*.[68] While Cicero does not specify the military powers
of the praetors, it is clear from his discussion of the extraordinary office of *magister equitum,* that the praetor also commands certain units of the army.[69]

But the crown of the regular magistrates is the college of
two consuls.[70] In them the Roman kingship is in a fashion
perpetuated. Chosen in the assembly of the centuries, they
bear three names, each of which emphasizes one aspect of
their tripartite authority. They are called by the archaic title
of *praetores* because they lead the army; *iudices* because they
possess a limited judicial competence; and *consules* because, in
their capacity as executive officials, they seek the opinion of
their advisory body, the senate. Within the domestic sphere
of action *(domi),* they exercise their minor judicial powers
and their far greater authority of summoning and presiding
over the people when convened for legislative, judicial, or
elective purposes, and of submitting proposals to their judgment. They are also empowered to lay business before the
senate and to elicit its will expressed in the form of decrees
(senatus consulta).[71] While the consuls are limited within the
city by the principle of *par maiorve potestas* and by the threat
of tribunician intervention,[72] in the foreign sphere *(militiae)*
they wield supreme and incontestable authority. The sole

[67] Cic. *de leg.* 3. 3. 8. Cicero follows the Roman custom.
[68] Cic. *de leg.* 3. 4. 10; 3. 18. 40.
[69] Cic. *de leg.* 3. 3. 9; see Introduction, p. 81, below.
[70] Cic. *de leg.* 3. 3. 8; 3. 7. 15 ff.; *de rep.* 2. 31; 32. The account of the
consulate is, with perhaps one exception (see below), derived from Roman
practice.
[71] Cic. *de leg.* 3. 4. 10; 3. 18. 40.
[72] See Introduction, pp. 82 f., below.

objective by which their action is then guided is military advantage and the welfare of the state. "In their eyes the safety of the people shall be the highest law."[73]

These are the regular magistrates which exist in Cicero's state. It is not enough, however, that a constitution should provide only for the conditions of normal political life. It must possess, in addition, a certain elasticity, and must be able to set in motion a machinery capable of meeting the inevitable emergencies which put strain on any governmental system. Such an occasion is war or civil strife.[74] When either of these conditions arises, Cicero's constitution provides for the appointment of a dictator or "master of the people."[75] Chosen by the senate with the sanction of the gods, the dictator holds power for not over six months. During that period he wields the same authority as the two consuls collectively possess in normal times. The dictatorship, which in its historical form originated, according to tradition, in the early years of the Roman commonwealth,[76] is a temporary revival of monarchy.

Closely associated with the dictator in a subordinate capacity is the master of horse *(magister equitum)*.[77] This magistrate, as his name implies, is primarily military in character. He commands the cavalry contingents of the army, while the dictator leads the infantry. In the political sphere, the master of horse exercises the power wielded by the praetor in normal times.

---

[73] Cic. *de leg.* 3. 3. 8. The meaning which Cicero intends to give to the words just translated (*ollis salus populi suprema lex esto*) is not wholly clear. The phrase follows a statement of the powers of the consuls in the extra-urban sphere. We do not think that Cicero refers here to the powers of the consuls in domestic emergencies, since there is nothing that here connects them with the senate. We do not agree with Keyes (*op. cit.* pp. 317 ff.) that "Cicero here intends to give the consul extraordinary powers in cases of emergency, without the necessity of action by the Senate," since, as Keyes concedes, this provision would be glaringly inconsistent with the first sentence in his code (*de leg.* 3. 3. 6): "Let all forms of public authority be subject to law." It is our view that the phrase *ollis . . . esto* refers exclusively to the authority of the consuls when in the field on military or diplomatic missions; see du Mesnil's commentary (p. 207) on the words *ollis salus.*
[74] Cic. *de leg.* 3. 3. 9. Cicero copies Roman practice.
[75] Cic. *de rep.* 1. 40; cf. Polybius: 6. 18. 9.
[76] Cic. *de rep.* 2. 32.
[77] Cic. *de leg.* 3. 3. 9. This is essentially the Roman custom; see Greenidge: *Roman Public Life* (1911), pp. 195 ff.

Another public emergency may be said to exist when there are no higher magistrates.[78] This condition may result from losses in war, and theoretically may be brought about by a delay in holding the elections of the magistrates for any subsequent year. If such a situation arises from any cause whatever, the right to take the auspices—a function attaching to all magistrates[79]—reverts to the senate. Immediately this body appoints one of its own members as temporary ruler or *interrex*, who in turn presides over the senate and holds consular elections.[80] This step, Cicero implies, signifies the return of normal political life.

There are, finally, emergencies which arise when some part of the public business is of so difficult a nature that it cannot be intrusted to any of the ordinary magistrates.[81] This is likely to occur in connection with war or provincial administration.[82] When it is necessary to do so, the people appoint a special functionary *(legatus)*, who must in no way derive profit from his mission,[83] and empower him to accomplish his particular task.

Unable to emancipate himself from the preconceptions natural to a Roman, Cicero embodies in his constitution the anomalous and unwieldly plebeian organization which was so much a part of the Roman state. Accordingly, he places another system of regular officials, chosen exclusively by the plebs, at the side of the hierarchy of magistrates elected by the entire people.[84] The tribunes *(tribuni)*, whose historical prototypes were, according to tradition, created to thwart the consuls and the senate,[85] are the instruments used by the plebs

---

[78] Cic. *de leg. loc. cit.*
[79] See Introduction, p. 77, above.
[80] Cic. *de leg.* 3. 3. 9.
[81] Cic. *de leg.* 3. 4. 10.
[82] Cic. *de leg.* 3. 3. 9.
[83] Cic. *de leg. loc. cit.;* 3. 8. 18.
[84] It is, as Greenidge (*Roman Public Life*, 1911, p. 233) points out, hardly proper to call the tribune a magistrate, since he lacked two of the essential marks of the magistracy, insignia and the right to take the auspices. It seems probable that, in Cicero's plan of government, the plebian officials retain the same technical inferiority. On the plebeian assembly see Introduction, p. 86, below.
[85] Cic. *de rep.* 2. 34, below, and note; *de leg.* 3. 7. 16.

to protect themselves against invasion of their rights.[86] Ten in number, the tribunes have the right to issue binding and unlimited prohibitions which make legally void all acts of which they disapprove. The ambit of their authority is the city. Whatever measures they carry through the assembly of the plebs (if we may assume that such a body exists) possess the same authoritative character as is accorded the laws passed in the assemblies of the *populus*. While the tribunes may not approach the people *(populus)*, they may preside over the senate and elicit its will.[87] By virtue of their duty to protect the people—a task that they are never permitted to abandon—sacrosanctity invests their persons.

In the second part of Book III of the *Laws*, where many of the provisions of the code are analyzed in detail, Quintus Cicero pronounces an unfavorable judgment upon the tribunate and, while retaining it in the constitution, would greatly restrict its powers and would allow the tribunes solely the right of aiding the oppressed.[88] The tribunate, in Quintus' opinion, is the offspring of dissension, and its natural tendency is to keep dissension alive. In reply to Quintus, Marcus explains what he conceives to be the true function of the tribunes.[89] Strangely enough, the tribunate is intended to play a repressive rôle, curbing the otherwise uncontrollable impulses of the commons. The plebeians, when their passions are enkindled, are not themselves amenable to reason. Their leaders, on the contrary, will realize the necessity of maintaining public order and will accordingly hold their followers in check. Since, moreover, the tribunate is exclusively reserved to plebeians, it will satisfy the political vanity of the commons. It will create the illusion in the minds of the poor that they are the equals of the rich.

While it is true that Cicero places the emphasis on the magistrates, he does not wholly neglect the consideration of other governmental agencies. We shall devote our attention first to the senate, since it is into this body that all ex-magis-

[86] Cic. *de leg.* 3. 3. 9.
[87] Cic. *de leg.* 3. 4. 10; 3. 18. 40.
[88] Cic. *de leg.* 3. 8. 19 ff.
[89] Cic. *de leg.* 3. 10. 23 ff.

trates automatically pass.[90] In this way the experience and competence of its members are assured, while high standards of personal conduct are guaranteed by the supervision of the censors.[91] It is, in fact, Cicero's desire that the senate, exemplifying the perfection and maturity of political wisdom, should be the model by which public life is guided and adjudged.

The senate is thus a council. If its latent powers are to be utilized, it must be so organized that its will can be elicited and applied. This task Cicero imposes upon those persons who may preside over its meetings. With particular care he enumerates the magistrates who are so empowered: the consuls, the praetors, and the tribunes; and in emergencies the dictator, the master of horse, and the *interrex*.[92] It it clear, furthermore, that the order in which the magistrates are mentioned is also the order of precedence, except that in the case of the interrex such a question cannot arise.

The senate must conduct its business in an orderly and dignified manner.[93] Since its judgment has value only in so far as it represents the opinions of its members, it is the duty of every senator to be present. If he fails to attend sessions, he is obliged to give an adequate explanation, and if he fails to do so, he is censured.[94] In all debates senators speak only when they have been called upon by the presiding officer to express their views.[95] Since, moreover, the senate is a large body, with a membership of approximately three hundred, all discussion must be brief and germane to the issue. Debate, finally, if it is to be fruitful of wise decisions, must be based upon a reasonable amount of sound information. Each senator, accordingly, should be thoroughly familiar with the condtion of the state, its military strength, its fiscal resources, the nature and extent of its diplomatic relationships, the forms of senatorial pro-

---

[90] Cic. *de leg.* 3. 3. 10; 3. 12. 27; see Introduction, p. 77, above. Cicero keeps pretty close to the Roman practice.
[91] Cic. *de leg.* 3. 3. 7; 3. 3. 10; 3. 12. 28 ff.
[92] Cic. *de leg.* 3. 4. 10.
[93] Cic. *de leg. loc. cit.*
[94] Cic. *de leg.* 3. 4. 11.
[95] Cic. *de leg. loc. cit.*; 3. 18. 40.

cedure, and—an unusual provision for a new state—the precedents of statecraft which the men of old established.

The constitutional function of the senate is to pass decrees *(senatus consulta)* in response to magisterial appeals for advice. If this action is unopposed by a magistrate equal or superior to him who submits the question, the decree possesses legal force and must be obeyed by the magistrates.[96] If, on the other hand, it is vetoed by a competent magistrate, the decree, perhaps called under these circumstances an *auctoritas,* is preserved in writing, not as an instrument of legal validity, but simply as a record of the action taken.[97]

There is no limit, apparently, to the questions upon which the senate may be approached. On the contrary, Cicero seems to assume that no magistrate will act, at least in any important matter, without previously ascertaining the senate's will, although there is no provision in the code which compels him to do so. The major province affected by senatorial decrees is legislation. In this way a form and sanction are given to proposals which the magistrates, in their turn, must submit to the final decision of the people. Certain, perhaps typical, examples of the senate's powers are specifically mentioned.[98] It cooperates with the people, probably in the way just suggested, in declaring war and concluding peace, and in the lesser matter of determining the number of praetors. It decides, independently it would appear, when the appointment of a dictator is necessary, and even appoints him. Whenever there are no magistrates, the senate automatically becomes the repository of the auspices, and chooses, in some manner not defined by Cicero, the *interrex,* who initiates the return to normal political life by presiding over consular elections in the assembly of the centuries. In the domain of religion the senate orders

---

[96] It is very important to note that by this provision Cicero seeks to put an end to the technically *de facto* authority of the Roman *senatus consultum,* and to give it a legal character; see Introduction, p. 89, below; cf., however, Keyes (*op. cit.* pp. 312 ff.), who thinks that the provision equates *senatus consulta* to *leges.*

[97] Cic. *de leg.* 3. 3. 10; 3. 12. 28; cf. *ad fam.* 8. 8, where a *senatus consultum* and *auctoritas* are given.

[98] Cic. *de leg.* 3. 3. 8 ff.

prodigies to be referred to the Etruscan soothsayers for interpretation.[99]

Cicero's treatment of the position and authority of the people, like his treatment of the senate, is very summary. Moreover, it is confusing; for, while clearly providing some form
of organization for the commons as well as for the whole *populus,* he does not adequately describe either of them or differ-
entiate their powers and functions. The *populus* acts through
two assemblies. In the *comitia centuriata,* which possesses the
greater deliberative faculty,[100] the citizens are divided into
classes based on their wealth, age, and military duties.[101] These
classes are composed of centuries, units essentially military in
character, through which the people vote. The *comitia centuriata* is thus not only an organization of the people based on
the army, but it is also one in which political power is based on
the possession of wealth. The intention in this arrangement
was that those persons whose property interests were most
deeply involved in the well-being of the state should have the
greatest influence in determining its policy, while, on the other
hand, the poor should not be wholly excluded from participat-
ing in the public life of their country. The other assembly of
the *populus* is the *comitia tributa.*[102] Here the citizens are
grouped and vote by tribes which are based upon geographical
distribution. It seems probable, furthermore, that Cicero includes among popular organs of government some distinct assembly in which the plebeians meet and function, but he has
failed to describe its composition or to note the respects in
which it differs from the two groupings of the *populus.*[103]

---

[99] Cic. *de leg.* 2. 9. 21.

[100] Cic. *de leg.* 3. 19. 44.

[101] Cic. *de rep.* 2. 22. We assume that, since Cicero expressly states in
connection with his treatment of the magistrates that he is closely following the Roman practices, he keeps fairly close to Roman practice in
other respects; see *de leg.* 3. 5. 12. Hence we suppose that the description of the so-called Servian constitution is at least in the main a picture
of the arrangements which should be realized in the ideal state.

[102] Cic. *de leg.* 3. 3. 7; also 3. 19. 44.

[103] Whether there was such a plebeian assembly in ancient Rome is a
matter of considerable doubt; see the extended discussion in Botsford:
Roman Assemblies (1909), pp. 119 ff. It is nevertheless clear that, unless
Cicero was guilty of striking inaccuracy or pointlessness, he implies the
existence in his ideal state of a separate plebeian organization; see *de*

Popular assemblies so complicated and extensive as these afford an easy field for the political agitator. This weakness Cicero recognizes and accordingly insists that all meetings of the people preserve order and decorum.[104] Whenever violence attends a gathering of the people, the magistrate who presides at the meeting is held responsible, whether he instigates, permits, or merely fails to prevent the disorder;[105] and conversely any person who causes civil uprising to subside shall be acclaimed as a beneficent citizen *(salutaris civis)*.[106]

Proposals laid before the people, whether of an elective, judicial, or legislative character, are subject to restrictions which seriously affect their freedom of action. Cicero, it is true, considers these limitations as applying primarily to the magistrates who approach the people; but this is in part a superficial analysis, since the constitutional result is a reduction of the people's authority. Magistrates who lay proposals before the people must yield to the report of unfavorable auspices.[107] While the ostensible object of this provision is to prevent the passage of unwise legislation,[108] the actual consequence is to decrease the power of the popular assemblies, since there is no way by which the augurs can be compelled to confine their objections to purely constitutional grounds, and since the augurs and the magistrates form really one single class.[109].

Furthermore, the necessity of observing the principle of *par maiorve potestas* carries with it a narrowing of the

leg. 3. 3. 9 and 3. 4. 10: "The right of approaching the people (i. e. *populus*) and the senate (i. e. *patres*) shall belong to the consul, the praetor, the master of the people, the master of the horse, and to him whom the senate selects for the purpose of electing the consuls (i. e. the *interrex*); and the tribunes whom the commons (i. e. *plebes*) shall elect to protect their own interests, shall have the right of approaching the senate, and shall bring any necessary proposal before the commons (i. e. *plebes*)."

[104] Cic. *de leg.* 3. 4. 10 ff.; 3. 18. 42.

[105] Cic. *de leg.* 3. 4. 11.

[106] Cic. *de leg. loc. cit.*; 3. 19. 42 f. The provision by which Cicero attaches responsibility to the presiding official was a departure from Roman custom; see Keyes: *op. cit.* p. 315.

[107] Cic. *de leg.* 3. 4. 11; 2. 8. 21; 2. 12. 31; 3. 19. 43.

[108] Cic. *de leg.* 3. 12. 27.

[109] Cic. *de leg.* 2. 12. 31; also Introduction, p. 73, above.

people's authority.[110] Under this rule whether the people may vote on any measure whatever depends, in the last analysis, on magisterial judgment or caprice, since any magistrate, with the exception of the dictator and *interrex,* can be prevented by any other magistrate of equal or greater competence from laying any proposal before the people.

Even when the people are allowed to vote, their various assemblies are exposed to influences which, however well intended, cannot fail to be sinister and subversive of freedom of action. Cicero expressly rejects the secret ballot, and in its place institutes a form of open voting carried out under the scrutiny and exhortation of the chief citizens *(optumates).*[111] Such a procedure, by giving a specious impression of freedom, removes the ground for strife between the commons and the *optumates,* while in reality it confirms the latter class in their exercise of authority.[112] Their judgment, accordingly, is the decisive element in all matters nominally submitted to popular suffrage.

But the chief barrier to an effective assertion of power by the people rests on a provision the existence of which Cicero tacitly assumes. The rule of Roman public law that the people, as such, do not possess any inherent right of assembling and discussing pending questions, much less of making proposals about them, underlies Cicero's view of popular authority.[113] The people meet only at the bidding of a magistrate, and only to consider such proposals as he chooses to submit. They may not take the initiative, and their action is thus effectively subordinated to the judgment of the ruling class.

Nevertheless, there are some provisions in Cicero's constitution which facilitate efficiency in legislation and in the performance of other popular functions. Legislators, electors, or jurors, at least if they are to act intelligently, must have access to information about the topics laid before them. This

---

[110] Cic. *de leg.* 3. 4. 11; see Introduction, pp. 76 f., above.
[111] Cic. *de leg.* 3. 3. 10; 3. 15. 33 ff. This suggestion is original, and seems to be an attempt to combine the merits of the secret ballot with the old procedure of *viva voce* voting; see Keyes: *op. cit.* pp. 314 f.
[112] Cic. *de leg.* 3. 17. 39.
[113] Greenidge: *Roman Public Life* (1911), pp. 159 f.

is particularly necessary in the case of a primary assembly, the members of which are ill informed and less experienced in the issues of politics.[114] This problem Cicero recognizes, and accordingly requires magistrates who submit proposals or recommend candidates to the people to acquaint them with the pending questions and to supplement their own views with opinions of other magistrates and even of private citizens.[115]

Within these bounds and under these conditions the people exercise their powers. They elect their regular magistrates, those of the *populus* being chosen in the assembly of the centuries or of the tribes, and those of the *plebs* in some form of plebeian organization.[116] The *populus*, but not the *plebs*, selects special functionaries *(legati)*, and defines and confers their powers.[117] Furthermore, the *populus*, meeting in the *comitia centuriata*, hears and decides all criminal cases in which the crimes were committed within the city, and in which the penalty involves death or corporal punishment.[118]

Legislation, however, is the field in which the people's authority is most minutely defined. Theoretically, they may legislate on any question whatever, although it is probable that Cicero conceives of legislation as a cooperative act in which the action of the senate habitually, and perhaps necessarily, precedes and thus controls or modifies that of the people.[119] But the rulings of the people, whether passed by *populus* or *plebs*, are the chief source of law, and, as such, must

---

[114] It may be naturally objected that such was not the case in the Athenian government, in which the *ekklesia* exerted an exceedingly wide authority. At Athens competence in politics was insured by a number of factors, chief among which was election by lot and rotation of office. See Headlam: *Election By Lot at Athens* (1891), pp. 88 ff.; 161 ff.

[115] Cic. *de leg.* 3. 4. 11. This is an institution adopted from Roman custom.

[116] Cic. *de leg.* 3. 3. 9 ff.; see Introduction, p. 86, above.

[117] Cic. *de leg.* 3. 4. 10.

[118] Cic. *de leg.* 3. 3. 6; 3. 3. 10; 3. 4. 11; 3. 19. 44. This is a provision which, according to Cicero, existed in some form in the time of the Roman monarchy and which was given a definite legal status by the law of the Twelve Tables; see *de leg.* 3. 19. 44; *de rep.* 2. 31.

[119] Such, at any rate, is the procedure followed in declarations of war and the resumption of diplomatic relations (*de leg.* 3. 3. 9), and in enlarging the praetorian college (*de leg.* 3. 3. 8); see also *de rep.* 2. 32. It is not clear how far Cicero would have the senate guide the people's legislative acts, since the phrase (*de leg.* 3. 3. 10), "The decrees of the

conform to the requirements of law and possess a truly legal character. The statutes drawn up by man should seek to reproduce the qualities of the divine law discovered by God.[120] In the moral sphere legislation should aim to protect the good and to correct the bad,[121] and in this way to make possible a happy and peaceful life.[122] Furthermore, it should deal with only one topic at a time, since in this way simplicity and utility are best secured.[123] A law, finally, must be of universal application, for the very essence of a rule for political society consists in the fact that it recognizes no privileged individuals but exerts its pressure evenly upon all citizens alike.[124]

CICERO'S INSTITUTIONS AS PARTS OF THE COMPOSITE STATE

It is Cicero's design to construct a form of state which can be adopted by future generations, and which because of its inner cohesion cannot readily fall into decay.[125] He seeks to attain this end by creating a composite state in which a balance would be preserved between a popular element, an aristocratic element, and a royal element. We may now appropriately ask what institutions in the constitution laid down in the *Laws* correspond to each of these factors.

There can be no doubt that the various assemblies in Cicero's constitution represent the democratic element in the ideal state.[126] This is the function ascribed to the people by Polybius, Cicero's chief source, in the famous analysis of the Roman constitution which he incorporated in the sixth book of

---

senate shall possess legal force" (*eius decreta rata sunto*), is ambiguous. See Introduction, p. 85, above, where we suggested that the words mean that the senate's decision possesses binding force only for the magistrate who consults it. This principle would result in senatorial control over legislation, if the only proposals set before the people were drawn up by the senate.

[120] Cic. *de leg.* 2. 5. 13; see Introduction, p. 52, above.
[121] Cic. *de leg.* 1. 22. 58.
[122] Cic. *de leg.* 2. 5. 11.
[123] Cic. *de leg.* 3. 4. 11; 3. 19. 43. This rule is taken from the Roman provisions against *leges saturae*. Such a prohibition existed as early as the *Lex Acilia de repetundis* (122 B. C.) and was re-enacted by the *Lex Caecilia Didia* of 98 B. C.
[124] Cic. *de leg.* 3. 4. 11; 3. 19. 44.
[125] Cic. *de rep.* 1. 45; *de leg.* 3. 2. 4; 3. 13. 29.
[126] Cic. *de rep.* 1. 45; 2. 33.

his history.[127] Nothing else in the governmental scheme set forth by Cicero can in any way be regarded as democratic in its nature.

While it is certainly less easy to fix the element which represents aristocracy,[128] it seems very probable that Cicero has assigned this rôle to the unit formed by the senate and the magistrates with the exception of the consuls. This is a conclusion to which Cicero was naturally led,[129] since in his state, as in the Roman commonwealth on which his theory was based, magistrates automatically become senators, and senators are inevitably close in sympathy and interest to the class of which they have once been members and into which they temporarily return whenever they hold another office.[130] This class Cicero calls the *boni*,[131] the *optumates*,[132] or the *principes*.[133] To its collective authority contribute the principle of *par maiorve potestas*[134] and the great powers of the augurs over public acts.[135] Its interests are further confirmed by the scheme of open voting which Cicero introduces into the popular assemblies, since thus the people are "privileged to comply honorably with the wishes of the good."[136]

If, then, we conclude that the *optumates* are the aristocratic constituent of the perfect state, we may inquire what is the representative of monarchy. To the present writers it seems perfectly clear that no satisfactory answer can be given to this question, due possibly to the development and change in Cicero's ideas in the interval between the composition of his

---

[127] Polybius: 6. 11. 11 ff.; 6. 14.
[128] In Polybius aristocracy is represented by the senate; see Polybius: 6. 11. 11 ff.; 6. 13.
[129] The particular circumstance which, more than any other, tended to this end, was the history of the *nobiles* in the late Roman Republic; see Mommsen: *Röm. Gesch.* 1, pp. 783 ff. (Eng. trans. 2, pp. 295 ff.); Greenidge: *Roman Public Life* (1911), pp. 128 ff.
[130] Cic. *de leg.* 3. 3. 10; see Greenidge: *Roman Public Life* (1911), pp. 263 ff.
[131] Cic. *de leg.* 3. 17. 38; 39; see *de rep.* 1. 44.
[132] Cic. *de rep.* 1. 34; 2. 23; perhaps 6. 2; *de leg.* 3. 3. 10; 3. 17. 38 ff.; 2. 12. 30; 3. 7. 17; 3. 15. 34.
[133] Cic. *de rep.* 1. 45; 2. 32; *de leg.* 3. 9. 19; 3. 13. 30.
[134] Cic. *de leg.* 3. 4. 11; see Introduction, pp. 87 f., above.
[135] Cic. *de leg.* 2. 12. 31; see Introduction, p. 87, above.
[136] Cic. *de leg.* 3. 17. 39; see Introduction, p. 88, above.

two political works, and due certainly to the fragmentary form in which these works are preserved. It is at least indisputable that Cicero himself is confusing, since in different places he equates different elements with the monarchical factor. In one passage he describes the collective body of magistrates in such a way as leads us to believe that here we have the equivalent of kingship.[137] In another, the dictatorship is represented as a very close approximation to monarchy.[138] And yet neither of these institutions seems truly royal in nature. A temporary and extraordinary office, like the dictator's, cannot be the repository of continuous and normal functions, like the king's. Nor is there sufficient evidence to justify us in applying to the entire body of regular magistrates the royal attribute which is categorically applied to only one of them.

Accordingly, it is our belief that Cicero intended the college of consuls to be the representative of monarchy. It is royal in character.[139] It is probable, moreover, that Cicero followed Polybius, who embodied in the consuls the authority of the king.[140] What makes Cicero's view difficult to accept is that, except in connection with war, the consuls do not occupy a position sufficiently differentiated from the other magistrates or sufficiently imposing in itself to be justly considered as the counterpart of the king. Within the range of political functions, the tribunes certainly wield as great authority; and the censors, especially in the form given to the office by Cicero, are at least their equals and probably their superiors. The reason for this confusion is not far to seek. Although Cicero has based his account on Polybius, he has introduced discordant modifications. Such, for example, is his proposal to extend the active incumbency of the censors to five years. He

---

[137] Cic. de rep. 2. 33.
[138] Cic. de rep. 2. 32.
[139] Cic. de leg. 3. 3. 8; 3. 7. 15 ff.; de rep. 2. 31; 32.
[140] Polybius: 6. 11. 11; 12; 6. 12. His account is logically developed, and the Roman government is neatly divided into a monarchical element, the consuls; an aristocratic element, the senate; and a democratic element, the people. His arrangement possesses schematic excellence rather than historical accuracy, and is possible only because he wholly disregards the tribunes, a seriously disturbing element.

has failed to reflect that this change, which destroys or at least greatly reduces the pre-eminence of the consuls, leaves the system without any genuine equivalent of monarchy. Nevertheless, although it seems hardly logical to found the importance of the consulate on functions neither essentially political nor constantly exercised, we may tentatively conclude that it is in the military powers of the consuls and perhaps the external splendor of their position that Cicero sees their equivalence to the king.

Unsatisfactory as this conclusion is, it is rendered still more unsatisfactory by the presence in Cicero's theory of a *rector* or *moderator* or *princeps rei publicae*. We cannot determine with any precision what rôle this "philosophical director" plays, since the treatment of the subject in the fifth and sixth books of the *Commonwealth* is most fragmentary, and since there is no mention of him in the present text of the *Laws*. To all appearances, however, it was Cicero's intention, at the time when he composed the *Commonwealth,* to include in his ideal state an ideal statesman—one individual whose authority should be comprehensive and far-reaching.[141] That his position in the constitutional system is one of great eminence cannot be denied. He is to be nurtured on glory.[142] It is his task to make the lot of his people happy and prosperous.[143] He considers not merely their practical advantages but also their dignity. His province it is to know the cycles of political change and to be able to pilot the state through the storms that

---

[141] The character of the *rector* has been the subject of considerable discussion. The present writers take the view that the word *rector* refers to one person of distinct position and authority, and not to a member of an aristocratic class. They are led to this conclusion because the several philosophical and historical antecedents of the *rector* suggest only one person, and because the citation made by Peter of Poitiers (Cic. *de rep.* 5. 7, below) can refer, in their opinion, only to one separate individual. For different treatments of this view see Reitzenstein: "Die Idee des Principats bei Cicero und Augustus," *Nachrichten der Gött. Ges. d. Wiss.* (1917), pp. 399 ff.; 436 ff.; "Zu Cicero de re publica," *Hermes* (1924), pp. 356 ff.; E. Meyer: *Caesars Monarchie und das Principat des Pompejus* (1922), pp. 180 ff. For the opposite view, namely, that the *rector* is one of a class, see Richard Heinze: "Ciceros 'Staat' als politische Tendenzschrift," *Hermes* (1924), pp. 73 ff.

[142] Cic. *de rep.* 5. 6; 7; 2. 29.

[143] Cic. *de rep.* 5. 3.

threaten it.[144]   As a driver guides an elephant, so the *rector* is to guide his people.[145]   In time of civil strife he considers the merits of the contending factions, and does not content himself with merely counting the numbers on either side.[146] Trained thoroughly in law and in the Greek literature from which the speculative basis of law is to be learned, the ideal statesman is "wise, just, self-controlled, and eloquent."[147]   He possesses at once the active courage of Marcellus and the wise hesitancy of Maximus.[148]   Nothing must distract him from his chief objective, which is to be the bailiff and steward of the commonwealth; and to that end all his studies in law or in agriculture must contribute.[149]   The philosophical statesman never ceases to improve himself.[150]   At all times he aims to be the model which his subjects may imitate, and the mirror in which they may behold the image of a perfect life and character.

This is indeed an august conception. It is an abiding expression of Cicero's belief in the potency of moral and political virtue. If we feel that the *rector's* authority is too vague and ill-defined to be an element in a true political system, we must in part ascribe this to the very defective condition of that portion of the *Commonwealth* in which the subject was treated. In part also the vagueness is due to the philosophical sources from which Cicero derived the *rector*.

The ideal statesman whom Cicero describes bears a strong likeness to the "kingly man" whom Plato delineates in the *Statesman*.[151]   In this work, which is "a logical exercise in the art of definition by way of differentiation rather than a political treatise," the "kingly man" is described as one whose rule is over voluntary subjects, is directed to the management of

---

[144] Cic. *de rep.* 1. 29; 6. 1.
[145] Cic. *de rep.* 2. 40.
[146] Cic. *de rep.* 6. 1.
[147] Cic. *de rep.* 5. 3; 6. 1.
[148] Cic. *de rep.* 5. 8.
[149] Cic. *de rep.* 5. 3.
[150] Cic. *de rep.* 2. 42.
[151] Plato: *Statesman*, 259 ff.; 276 e; 292 b ff.; Ernest Barker: *Greek Political Theory: Plato and his Predecessors* (1918), pp. 271 ff., who cites the above passage from the *Statesman*; E. Meyer: *Caesars Monarchie und das Principat des Pompejus* (1922), p. 184.

society, and is based on the knowledge of political science. These preconceptions also underlie Aristotle's idea of the statesman,[152] whose function as "a moral and spiritual force" is the elevation of the "character and intellect" of the state.

But our inquiries into the philosophical antecedents of the *rector* must not be confined to these two great thinkers. One of the chief sources of the ideal statesman is found in the political commonplaces that are reproduced in the Neo-Pythagorean fragments.[153] These set forth the superior merits of kingship. The king, created by God in his own image,[154] bears the same relation to his state that God bears to the universe.[155] As it is the duty of the king ever to pattern his conduct upon that of God,[156] so it is implied that his subjects should imitate the qualities of a virtuous king.[157] The vicegerent of God on earth and the sole medium by which men partake of the divine element in the universe,[158] the king becomes in fact a living embodiment of law.[159] His authority is in one passage limited to the duties inherent in leading armies, dispensing justice, and worshiping the gods,[160] but the general tenor of the fragments belies such a restriction. For it is surely implied that the power of the king on earth, like that of God in the universe, will be without substantial let or hindrance.[161]

Such ideas as these seem to have passed into the body of political commonplaces during the Hellenistic period. They reflect the spirit that led to the deification of Alexander.

---

[152] Newman: *Politics of Aristotle*, 1 (1887), pp. 561 ff.

[153] These fragments are chiefly found in Stobaeus' *florilegium*. They are undated and their authorship is unknown, though they are attributed to members of the older Pythagorean school. For the reasons which lead to the belief that these fragments represent the political commonplaces of the Hellenistic age, especially as regards kingship, see the forthcoming article, "The Political Theory of the Hellenistic Kingship," by Professor E. R. Goodenough, in the first volume of the Yale Classical Studies.

[154] Stobaeus: *florileg.* 47. 22.

[155] Stobaeus: *op. cit.* 48. 61-62.

[156] Stobaeus: *op. cit.* 47. 63.

[157] Stobaeus: *op. cit.* 47. 62. It is interesting to note that the idea that the *rector* should be a model for the conduct of his fellow-citizens is present in Cic. *de rep.* 2. 42.

[158] Stobaeus: *op. cit.* 47. 22.

[159] Stobaeus: *op. cit.* 48. 61-62.

[160] Stobaeus: *loc. cit.*

[161] Stobaeus: *op. cit.* 47. 63.

Wherever the Neo-Pythagoreans spread and flourished, these notions passed as current change. It is quite possible that these views became known to Cicero through the Neo-Pythagorean group that centered around his friend Nigidius Figulus.

In the philosophical sources the legal aspect of the *rector* is at best imperfectly conceived. He stands as a powerful force operating on the state from without rather than from within. On the other hand, it has been suggested that the *rector* had Roman antecedents as well, and that these would have supplied Cicero with a legal form and definite function for his *rector*. The idea, for instance, may have been derived from the traditional interpretation of the rôle played by the mythical king Numa.[162] The *rector* finds a more historical prototype in the constitutional place which the Elder Africanus desired to hold after the end of the Second Punic War.[163] Perhaps the hope of filling such a position was in the mind of Scipio Aemilianus; and possibly this was the future destined for him by enlightened members of the Roman aristocracy.[164]

But, according to the view of those who hold that the *rector* had also a Roman source, we do not need to carry our inquiries back of Cicero's own time. It is certainly true that the conditions in Rome suggested the advantages of some form of dictatorship. It is no less true that, when Cicero wrote the *Commonwealth*, he had a high opinion of Pompey's ability and character, and referred to him as *princeps rei publicae*.[165]

---

[162] Cic. *de rep.* 5. 2.
[163] E. Meyer: *op. cit.* p. 185; Heitland: *Roman Republic* (1909), sect. 492.
[164] Cic. *de rep.* 6. 12; *de am.* 25. 96; Heitland: *op. cit.* sect. 714.
[165] For a more detailed account of the conditions prevailing in Rome at the time when Cicero was at work upon the *Commonwealth*, see Introduction, pp. 44 f., above. The chief passages in Cicero that refer to Pompey's career at the time in question are as follows: *ad fam.* 5. 7. 3. (dated 62 B. C.); *post. red.* 2. 4 (57 B. C.); *de domo*, 25. 66 (*ibid.*); *pro Sestio*, 39. 84 (56 B. C.); *pro Plancio*, 39. 93 (54 B. C.); *ad fam.* 1. 9. 11 (*ibid.*); *ad Att.* 8. 11. 1 (49 B. C.), where Pompey is considered in retrospect. For the general theory that Cicero took Pompey as the model of the *rector*, see E. Meyer: *op. cit.* pp. 189 ff. The present writers do not feel that the extant evidence permits as confident a conclusion as Meyer draws; and they do not believe that Cicero seriously expected "ihm (i. e. Pompey) gegenüber eine viel selbständigere, führende Stellung einnehmen zu können, als die des Laelius neben Africanus."

Cicero may possibly have thought that he discerned in Pompey certain of the qualities that marked the "kingly man" in Greek philosophy. It is further possible that Cicero, in an amateurish way, may have sought to create in his ideal constitution a position that Pompey might properly fill. But in our opinion the view that Cicero aimed to supply Pompey with a theory and an office cannot be proved from Cicero's own words, and is at the most only a plausible reconstruction.

At all events, even if we assume that Cicero was led, consciously or unconsciously, to unite with the idea of the "kingly man" the narrower idea of a Roman extraordinary magistrate, it is clear that in the extant fragments of the *Commonwealth* he regarded the *rector* much as Plato had regarded the "kingly man" or the Neo-Pythagoreans the king.. What function he performed in the composite state we do not know, so scanty is the evidence. Cicero may have intended him to be the unofficial head of the state, and to occupy with respect to the whole government a position analogous to that held by a *iuris consultus*—Scaevola, for example—with respect to young men entering upon a legal career. Such unofficial authority was the basis of the prestige attaching to the leading member of the Roman senate who was called *princeps senatus*;[166] and such was the position which Cicero arrogated to himself as the leader of the faction which opposed and was crushed by Antonius.[167]

We are now able to see one of the reasons why the *rector* is a puzzling element in Cicero's scheme of government. At the time when he wrote the *Commonwealth*, he was under the influence of Greek philosophy and introduced the *rector* as the counterpart of Plato's "kingly man." With the passage of time, Cicero's views changed. It is at least highly probable that Pompey's subsequent career and the activities of Julius Caesar destroyed any attachment on Cicero's part to the extra-legal principle behind the *rector*. Accordingly, when he came to write the *Laws*, he did not include the *rector* among the elements of the constitution.

---

[166] Gellius: *noct. Att.* 14. 7. 9.
[167] Cic. *ad fam.* 12. 24. 2.

If we may regard the *rector* as a part only of that system set forth in the *Commonwealth,* we are entitled to conclude that in the perfect state as delineated in Cicero's later and more mature work, the *Laws,* the three elements are the consuls, the group of *optumates* comprehending all other magistrates and the senate, and the commons. What Cicero has actually done, however, is to create a government in which there are only two separate factors, the people on the one side and the great and powerful class of *optumates* on the other. For, as we have suggested, there is no marked distinction between the consuls and the other magistrates; and the inevitable tendency of the principle of *par maiorve potestas* and of the augural procedure is to weld into one the interests of all the magistrates. With the senate the connection of the magistrates is equally close, since every senator is an ex-magistrate and almost every magistrate has been a senator and will be so again. And it is furthermore clear that in the government that Cicero would establish political initiative and control are vested, not in the people, but in the *optumates.*

If Cicero has in truth failed to create a form of state in which monarchy, aristocracy, and democracy are equally represented, he has borne witness to the truth of Tacitus' ironical dictum that the composite state can be more easily praised than realized.[168] And yet this failure does not in any serious way detract from the importance of his work. The significance of the *Commonwealth* and the *Laws* lies elsewhere.[169] It lies

---

[168] Tacitus: *Ann.* 4. 33. 1.

[169] While it is not the purpose of this Introduction to trace the influence of Cicero's *Commonwealth* on subsequent thinkers and statesmen, we feel that we should register a complete dissent from the view set forth by Eduard Meyer (*op. cit.* p. 189), that "darin liegt die grosse geschichtliche Bedeutung der Schrift Ciceros: sie enthält nicht nur die theoretische Formulierung der Stellung, die Pompejus für sich erstrebt, sondern zugleich auch die Grundzüge der Staatsordnung, die Augustus im Principat zu verwirklichen gesucht und in der Tat durch einen mit unvergleichlichem staatsmännischem Geschick abgewogenen Kompromiss zwischen Theorie und Praxis dauernd begründet hat. Wie es dem Scipio sein Ahn im Traume verkündet, ist denn auch Augustus wirklich im Tode als *Divus* zu den Göttern aufgestiegen." There is, so far as we can see, no evidence for this conclusion; and it is, moreover, inherently improbable, since, at least in the present text of Cicero, there is no reference, even of the vaguest kind, to the two great bases of Augustus'

in their noble insistence that it is the duty of all men to serve their country, in their inculcation of the principles of justice and fair-dealing, in their recognition of the universal society, founded upon reason and including all rational beings within its ambit. This denotes an advance in political thinking. To us it is an astounding paradox that Aristotle, who, if he did not breed "great Alexander to subdue the world," was at least aware of his achievement, should have devoted his comprehensive treatment of politics solely to a study of the city-state, while the Tigris and Euphrates resounded with the clash of his pupil's arms. Cicero, it is true, has not wholly progressed beyond this narrow view of political life. If he believes in the existence of the great society which is as broad as humanity itself, he supplies us with no governmental institutions by which that society can express itself. If we meet in him, as in Polybius, a broader outlook than we find in Thucydides, Plato, or Aristotle, we must remember that his advance is only in the general theory of political relations. Nevertheless, it is an advance; and we may fairly claim that Cicero's conception of the state marks the intermediate stage between the city-state of which Aristotle made so profound an analysis and the world-state of which the Edict of Caracalla is the symbol and expression.

---

power, his tribunician authority and his military *imperium*. To attribute to Cicero, on the ground of hardly fifty lines of text, at once fragmentary and ambiguous, the theoretical source of perhaps the most important governmental institution of Western Europe is a procedure which, in our opinion, cannot be justified.

BIBLIOGRAPHY

I

EDITIONS OF CICERO

a. *De re publica:*

Mai, Angelo: *M. Tullii Ciceronis de re publica quae supersunt*, Rome, 1822, *editio princeps*, text and commentary.

Moser, G. H.: *Ciceronis de re publica libri*, Frankfort on Main, 1826, text and commentary.

Ziegler, K.: *M. Tulli Ciceronis de re publica librorum sex quae manserunt*, Leipzig, 1915, text only. This text is the basis of the present translation, and all deviations from it are indicated in the notes.

Keyes, C. W.: Cicero: *de re publica, de legibus*, London and New York, 1928, text and translation.

b. *De legibus:*

Turnèbe, A.: *M. T. Ciceronis de leg. lib. III*, Paris, 1552, text and commentary.

Moser and Creuzer: *M. Tullii Ciceronis de legibus libri tres*, Frankfort on Main, 1824, text and commentary.

Bake, J.: *M. Tulli Ciceronis de legibus libri tres*, Leyden, 1842, text and commentary.

du Mesnil, A.: *M. Tullii Ciceronis de legibus libri tres*, Leipzig, 1879, text and commentary.

Vahlen, J.: *M. Tullii Ciceronis de legibus libri*, Berlin, 1883, text only. This text is the basis of all references made to the work.

c. *Academica:*

Reid, J. S.: *M. Tulli Ciceronis academica*, London, 1885, text and full commentary. This text is the basis of all references made to the work.

d. *De finibus:*

Madvig, N.: *M. Tullii Ciceronis de finibus bonorum et malorum libri quinque*, Copenhagen, 1876, text and commentary.

Schiche, Th.: *M. Tulli Ciceronis de finibus bonorum et malorum libri quinque*, Leipzig, 1915, text only. This text is the basis of all references made to the work.

Reid, J. S.: *M. Tulli Ciceronis de finibus bonorum et malorum libri I, II*, Cambridge, 1925, text and full commentary.

e. *De officiis:*

Holden, H. A.: *M. Tulli Ciceronis de officiis libri tres*, Cambridge, 1899, text and commentary.

Atzert C.: *M. Tulli Ciceronis de officiis libri tres*, Leipzig, 1923, text only. This text is the basis of all references made to the work.

f. *De divinatione:*

Pease, A. S.: *M. Tulli Ciceronis de divinatione liber primus*, Urbana, 1920; *liber secundus*, Urbana, 1923, text and full commentary. This text is the basis of all references made to the work.

1 0 0

INTRODUCTION

g. *Tusculanae disputationes:*
   Dougan, T. W.: *M. Tulli Ciceronis Tusculanarum disputationum libri quinque*, Cambridge, vol. 1, 1905, text and commentary.
   Pohlenz, M.: *M. Tulli Ciceronis Tusculanarum disputationum libri quinque*, Leipzig, 1918, text only. This text is the basis of all references made to the work.

h. *De natura deorum:*
   Mayor, J. B.: *M. Tullii Ciceronis de natura deorum*, Cambridge, vol. 1, 1891; vol. 2, 1883; vol. 3, 1885, text and full commentary.
   Plasberg, O.: *M. Tulli Ciceronis de natura deorum libri tres*, Leipzig, 1917, text only. This text is the basis of all references made to the work.

i. *Paradoxa:*
   Klotz, R.: *M. Tullii Ciceronis paradoxa ad M. Brutum*, Leipzig, 1876, text only.

j. *Topica:*
   Klotz, R.: *M. Tullii Ciceronis ad C. Trebatium topica*, Leipzig, 1876, text only.

k. *De amicitia:*
   Reid, J. S.:*M. Tulli Ciceronis Laelius de amicitia*, Cambridge, 1902, text and commentary.

l. *De senectute:*
   Reid, J. S.: *M. Tulli Ciceronis Cato maior de senectute*, Cambridge, 1879, text and commentary.

II

WORKS ON LITERARY HISTORY

Christ-Schmid: *Geschichte der griechischen Literatur*, Munich, 1912-1920.

Duff, J. W.: *A Literary History of Rome*, London, 1914.

Petersson, T.: *Cicero, A Biography*, Berkeley, 1920.

Schanz, M.: *Geschichte der römischen Literatur*, Munich, erster Teil, erste Hälfte, 1907; zweite Hälfte, 1909.

Sihler, E. J.: *Cicero of Arpinum*, New Haven, 1914.

III

WORKS ON PHILOSOPHY

Adam, J.: *The Republic of Plato*, Cambridge, vol. 1, 1905; vol. 2, 1907, text and commentary.

Arnold, E. V.: *Roman Stoicism*, Cambridge, 1911.

Barker, E.: *Greek Political Theory: Plato and his Predecessors*, London, 1918.

Burnet, J.: *Greek Philosophy, Part I, Thales to Plato*, London, 1914.

Carlyle, R. W. and A. J.: *History of Mediaeval Political Theory in the West*, New York, vol. 1, 1903; vol. 2, 1909; vol. 3, Edinburgh and London, 1915.

1 0 1

ON THE COMMONWEALTH

Cauer, F.: *Ciceros politisches Denken*, Berlin, 1903.
England, E. B.: *The Laws of Plato*, Manchester, 1921, text and commentary.
Hicks, R. D.: *Stoic and Epicurean*, New York, 1910.
Hinze, C.: *Quos scriptores Graecos Cicero in libris de re publica componendis adhibuerit*, Halle, 1900.
Keyes, C. W.: "Original Elements in Cicero's Ideal Constitution," *Amer. Jour. of Phil.* vol. 42 (1921), pp. 309 ff.
Newman, W. L.: *The Politics of Aristotle*, Oxford, vols. 1 and 2, 1887; vols. 3 and 4, 1902.
Schmekel, A.: *Phil. d. mittleren Stoa*, Berlin, 1892.
Usener, H.: *Epicurea*, Berlin, 1887.
von Arnim, J.: *Stoicorum veterum fragmenta*, vol. 1, Leipzig, 1921; vol. 2, Leipzig and Berlin, 1923; vol. 3, Leipzig and Berlin, 1923; vol 4, Leipzig, 1924.
Welldon, J. E. C.: *S. Aurelii Augustini episcopi Hipponensis de civitate Dei contra paganos libri XXII*, London, 1924.
Zeller, E.: *Die Philosophie der Griechen in ihrer geschichtlichen Entwicklung*, Leipzig, vol. 1.1, 1923; vol. 1.2, 1920; vol. 2.1, 1922; vol. 2.2, 1921; vol. 3.1, 1923; vol. 3.2, 1923.

IV

HISTORICAL WORKS

Beloch, K. J.: *Griechische Geschichte*, vol. 1.1, Berlin and Leipzig, 1924; vol. 1.2, Strassburg, 1913; vol. 2.1, Strassburg, 1914; vol. 2.2, Strassburg, 1916; vol. 3.1, Berlin and Leipzig, 1922; vol. 3.2, Berlin and Leipzig, 1923; vol. 4.1, Berlin and Leipzig, 1925.
Bouché-Leclercq, A.: *Manuel des institutions romaines*, Paris, 1886.
Busolt, G.: *Griechische Staatskunde*, Munich, vol. 1, 1920; vol. 2, 1926.
Buettner-Wobst, Th.: *Polybii historiae*, Leipzig, vol. 1, 1922; vol. 2, 1924; vol. 3, 1883; vol. 4, 1904.
Ferguson, W. S.: *Hellenistic Athens*, London, 1911.
Girard, F.: *Manuel élémentaire de droit romain*, Paris, 1924.
Greenidge, A. H. J.: *Roman Public Life*, London, 1911.
History of Rome, London, vol. 1, 1904.
Grote, G.: *History of Greece*, London, 1869-1870.
Heitland, W. E.: *The Roman Republic*, Cambridge, 1909.
Meyer, E.: *Geschichte des Altertums*, Stuttgart and Berlin, vol. 3, 1915; vol. 4, 1915; vol. 5, 1902.
Caesars Monarchie und das Principat des Pompejus, Stuttgart and Berlin, 1922.
Mommsen, Th.: *Römische Geschichte*, Berlin, reprinted, vol. 1, 1912; vol. 2. 1908; vol. 3, 1909. (English translation by W. P. Dickson in Everyman's Library).
Römische Staatsrecht, Leipzig, 1887-1888.
Pauly-Wissowa: *Realencyclopädie*, Stuttgart, 1894-, *passim*.
Schoemann, G. F.: *Griechische Staatsalterthümer*, Berlin, vol. 1, 1897; vol. 2, 1902.

PART II

ON THE COMMONWEALTH

TRANSLATION

NOTE ON TYPOGRAPHY

The typographical form in which the translation is presented perhaps requires a word of explanation. (1) We have used Roman type in all passages which are in the Vatican palimpsest or which are presented in other sources as Cicero's own words. (2) We have printed in italics all passages, whether derived from other works of Cicero or from later writers, which reproduce the sense but not the actual words of Cicero's *Commonwealth*. (3) We have employed square brackets to enclose words which we have supplied either in order to complete the apparent meaning before or after a lacuna, or to expand for the sake of greater clarity the meaning of words or phrases which, if closely rendered, would have required commentary. This privilege we have utilized but seldom.

CICERO

ON THE COMMONWEALTH

BOOK I

I. [Without a sense of public duty, Manius Curius, Gaius Fabricius, and Tiberius Coruncanius] would not have freed [Italy] from the attack [of Pyrrhus.[1]] Without this feeling Gaius Duelius, Aulus Atilius, and Lucius Metellus would not have banished the fear of Carthage.[2] Without it, the two Scipios would not have quenched with their own blood the rising fire of the Second Punic War; nor, when fresh fuel had been added to the flames, would Quintus Maximus have stayed its violence, nor Marcus Marcellus have stamped it out. Without it, Publius Scipio Africanus would not have snatched the brand of war from before the city's gates, and hurled it within the enemy's walls.

Now take the case of Marcus Cato,[3] who serves as the model of an active and virtuous life for all of us whose interests, like his, are political. Unknown and without an inherited tradition of public service, he might surely have enjoyed himself in quiet repose at Tusculum, a healthful and convenient place. But he was a fool, as your philosophical friends believe,[4] because he chose to ride the storms and tempests of public life until advanced age, rather than to live a life of ease amid the calm and restfulness of Tusculum.

---

[1] Seventeen leaves (thirty-four pages) of the palimpsest are lost at the beginning. Our reconstruction of the first sentence, which we adopt from Mai, is based on *Tusc.* 1. 37. 89 ff. and *parad.* 1. 2. 12.

[2] These were generals in the First Punic War.

[3] Marcus Porcius Cato the Censor (234-149 B. C.), the famous model of ancient Roman austerity and the persistent foe of Greek learning and manners, was for some thirty-five years the most influential man in Rome. He also composed the earliest history of Rome in Latin, the *Origines,* cited by Cicero (*de rep.* 2. 1, below).

[4] *Ut isti putant.* Cicero's introduction was probably addressed to his brother Quintus. The reference is clearly to the philosophy of Epicurus, according to whom, "The wise man will play no part in politics" (Diog. L. 10. 119; cf. Cic. *ad fam.* 7. 12. 2; *de rep.* 1. 6, below; *de leg.* 1. 13. 39).

I pass by countless men who have individually contributed their share to the safety of the state; and others, whose lives are too nearly[5] contemporaneous, I do not mention for fear that someone may complain that he or one of his family has been slighted. I content myself with this one assertion: The need and love for noble actions, which nature has given to men that they may defend the common weal, are so compelling that they have overcome all the enticements of pleasure and of ease.

II.   But merely to possess virtue as you would an art is not enough, unless you apply it. For an art, even if unused, can still be retained in the form of theoretical knowledge, but virtue depends entirely upon its use. And its highest use is the government of a state and the actual performance, not the mere discussion, of those deeds which your philosophers rehearse in their secluded retreats. For, even when philosophers express just and sincere sentiments about these matters, they merely state in words what has been actually realized and put into effect by those statesmen who have given states their laws. From whom, we may ask, comes our sense of moral obligation and our reverence toward the gods? From whom do we derive that law which is common to all peoples, or that to which we apply the term civil?[6] From whom comes our feeling for justice, for honor, for fair dealing? Whence our sense of shame, our self-control, our avoidance of what is base, our craving for a name and reputation? From whom is derived our courage in the face of toil and danger? Assuredly, from those statesmen who have developed these qualities by education and have embedded some of them in custom and have enforced others by the provisions of their laws. Xenocrates,[7] one of the most distinguished of philosophers, was once asked, so the story goes, what his pupils gained from his instruction. He replied that of their own free will they would perform the duties they would be forced to do by the laws.

---

[5] With Mai, we read *haut* before *procul*. The text is corrupt.

[6] On the meaning of *ius gentium* and *ius civile* see Gaius: *inst.*, ed. Poste (1904), 1. 1, and commentary.

[7] Xenocrates of Chalcedon was the head of the Academy second after Plato, i. e., from 339 to 314 B. C.

A statesman, therefore, who by his authority and by the punishments which his laws impose obliges all men to adopt that course which only a mere handful can be persuaded to adopt by the arguments of philosophers, should be held in even greater esteem than the teachers who make these virtues the subject of their discussions. For what argument of your philosophers is so carefully wrought out that it should be preferred to a state firmly established under public law and custom? Cities "mighty and imperial," to quote Ennius,[8] ought, in my opinion, to be considered superior to hamlets and outposts. Similarly, those who by their advice and influence rule such cities must, I feel, be assigned a far higher place in respect to wisdom itself than those who take no part in any public duty. Since, therefore, we are powerfully moved to increase the resources of the human race, since we desire through our planning and toiling to render life safer and richer, and since we are spurred on to this agreeable task by nature herself, let us persevere in that course which has ever been chosen by the best of men, and let us not heed the trumpets which sound retreat and would recall even the soldiers who have already advanced.

III. Against these conclusions, clear and indisputable though they be, those who take the opposite view urge, first, the toil which must be borne if the commonwealth is to be defended. But in truth this is a light burden for an alert and active man, and one which he must scorn to consider, not only when engaged in affairs of such pith and moment, but even when engaged in unimportant interests or duties or mere matters of business. Moreover, these objectors cite the grave risks involved in a political career. They hold up the base fear of death before the eyes of brave men, although brave men usually find it more pitiable to be worn out by the natural infirmities of age than to have the opportunity of surrendering for their country, as they prefer, the life which in any case they must surrender to nature.

---

[8] For Ennius (239-169 B. C.), the first important figure in Latin literature and the friend of Cato the Censor and Scipio Africanus the Elder, see Schanz: *Gesch. d. röm. Lit.* 1. 1 (1907), pp. 109 ff.

And yet it is upon this point that our critics think themselves resourceful and adroit, for they string together the misfortunes of distinguished men and the injuries that have been heaped upon them by ungrateful states. Of these they enumerate the well-known instances to be found in Greek history: the victorious Miltiades,[9] conqueror of the Persians, with the wounds not yet healed which he received facing the enemy in a glorious victory, yielding up in an Athenian prison the life which he had saved from the weapons of the enemy; and Themistocles,[10] banished from the country which he had set free, fleeing in terror, not to the harbors of Greece which he had saved, but to the harbors of Persia which he had humbled!

Nor is it only among the Athenians that we find instances of fickleness and inhumanity towards distinguished citizens;[11] but, though these traits of character had their origin at Athens and were frequently manifested there, they have infected, so the critics say, our own stable commonwealth. They cite, for example, the exile of Camillus,[12] or the downfall of Ahala,[13] or the unpopularity of Nasica,[14] or the banishment of Laenas,[15] or the conviction of Opimius,[16] or the exile of

---

[9] For Miltiades, commander of the Greek forces at Marathon, see Kirchner: *Prosopographia Attica* (1903), no. 10212.

[10] For Themistocles, the most brilliant and versatile politician of the first quarter of the fifth century B. C., see references in Kirchner: *Prosopographia Attica* (1901), no. 6669.

[11] Such examples as the ostracism of Aristides, and the execution of the generals after Arginusae in 406 B. C. (Cic. *de rep.* 4. 8, below), of Socrates in 399 B. C., and of Phocion in 318 B. C. (Ferguson: *Hellenistic Athens*, 1911, pp. 32 ff.) give weight to the judgment which Polybius (6. 44. 3) pronounced upon Athens: "The Athenian *demos* at all times resembles a ship without a pilot."

[12] According to tradition, he conquered Veii, suffered exile, and was recalled to defend Rome against the Gauls.

[13] Gaius Servilius Ahala was exiled for his summary execution of Spurius Maelius. See Cic. *pro domo*, 32. 86; *in Cat.* 1. 1. 3.

[14] For Publius Cornelius Scipio Nasica, leader of the senatorial mob that killed Tiberius Gracchus, see Greenidge: *History of Rome*, 1 (1904), pp. 141 ff.

[15] Publius Popilius Laenas, consul in 132 B. C., member of the special commission to try the followers of Tiberius Gracchus, was exiled as the result of a law passed in 123; see Greenidge: *op. cit.* pp. 146; 199 ff.

[16] Lucius Opimius, consul in 121 B. C., crushed the movement led by Gaius Gracchus. Twelve years later he was condemned by the Mamilian

Metellus,[17] or the disaster of Gaius Marius and the murder of
the chief men of the state,[18] or the ruin of many of them which
followed shortly after.[19] Already, indeed, they add my name
to the list; and, I suppose, it is because they think that my
foresight and the dangers I incurred have kept for them their
life of ease, that they bewail my misfortunes more deeply and
more affectionately. And yet, when those very men cross the
sea for purposes of education and travel, I can hardly say why
[they are surprised that I brave the greatest perils for my
country's sake . . . .]

(The last leaf of the third quaternion is missing)

IV. . . . . . since, at the close of my consulate, I had taken
an oath before the people that [the state] was safe [because of
my efforts]—and the Roman people put the same value upon
my services—[20] I might easily have set off [the pride of this
achievement] against the anxiety and suffering which all my
injuries entailed. And yet my misfortunes carried more of
honor than of hardship, less of humiliation than of fame. For
the happiness which I reaped because good men regretted my
exile was greater than my sorrow because bad men rejoiced
at it. But even if the result had been different from what I
have said, how could I have complained? In view of my great
deeds, nothing indeed had happened to me which I had not
foreseen, nothing worse than I had anticipated. I was free, to

Commission, ostensibly for his part in the Jugurthine War; see Greenidge: *op. cit.* pp. 248 ff.; 378.

[17] For Quintus Caecilius Metellus Numidicus, a general who fought
Jugurtha, exiled because he refused to support the agrarian law of
Saturninus, see Greenidge: *op. cit.* ch. 7; Heitland: *Roman Republic*
(1909), sect. 813.

[18] We read *et* before *principum*. For Marius see Heitland: *op. cit.*,
Book 6, *passim*, esp. ch. 40 and sect. 858 ff.

[19] This apparently refers to the proscriptions of Sulla on his return
from Asia in 83-82 B. C.; see Heitland: *op. cit.* ch. 7.

[20] Cicero refers to the speech which he attempted to deliver when he
retired from the consulate. It was the custom for the retiring consuls
to take public oath that they had not violated the laws. When Cicero
tried to comply with the custom, he was prevented by the tribune
Metellus Nepos, who asserted that Cicero had acted illegally in inflicting
summary punishment upon the Catilinarian conspirators. Accordingly,
Cicero modified the customary oath as indicated in the text, and declared
that by his action in connection with the conspiracy of Catiline (63 B. C.)
the state was saved. See Cic. *in Pis.* 3. 6 ff.; *ad fam.* 5. 2. 7 ff.; Heitland:
op. cit. sect. 1044.

a greater extent than other men, to derive enjoyment from a quiet life because of the delightful variety of the studies which I had followed from boyhood; and if some unusual disaster were to visit all men, I should have suffered no exceptional fate beyond that which came to all. Nevertheless, that I might save my fellow citizens, I was not the man to shrink from facing the wildest storms—nay, even the thunderbolts themselves—or to hesitate in securing at my own peril a peace which all might share. For the conditions upon which our country bore and reared us were not that she should expect no maintenance at our hands, or that she should merely serve our convenience and supply us with a safe retreat for our idleness and an undisturbed place for our repose. Her terms were rather that she herself should claim for her own advantage the greater share of our most important powers of mind, ability, and wisdom; and that, in return, she should give us for our private needs only so much as she might find superfluous.

V. To the evasions by which men would fain excuse themselves from public duties, in order to enjoy retirement the more comfortably, we must by no means give ear. It is asserted, for example, that political life attracts in general only utterly worthless men, to be compared with whom is disgusting, and to contend with whom, especially when the mob is aroused, is deplorable and dangerous. Therefore, it is said, a wise men does not grasp the reins of government, since he cannot restrain the mad lunges of the untamed rabble, nor does a free man strive against vile and savage opponents, or submit to the lash of insult, or suffer injuries that a wise man should not bear. As if a good and brave and high-minded man could find a more honorable reason for entering public life than the desire to avoid the rule of scoundrels or to prevent them from rending the commonwealth, while he himself, though eager to aid, looks impotently on![21]

VI. And who, moreover, can approve of the exception that they make when they say that the wise man will not assume a rôle in political life except under the compulsion of circum-

---

[21] Cf. Plato: *Republic*, 347 b ff.

stances? As if a greater compulsion could come to any man than came to me! And yet what could I have done in that emergency had I not then been consul? And how could I have been consul if I had not from early youth persisted in that course of life by which, though born in the equestrian order, I finally attained the highest position in the state?[22] You cannot aid the state at a moment's notice or when you wish, although she is faced with great danger, unless you are in a position to do so. It has always seemed especially strange to me in the discourses of the learned, that men who admit that they cannot pilot the ship when the sea is calm, because they have never learned how nor troubled about such knowledge, nevertheless declare that they will take the helm when the waves are highest.[23] Your philosophers, indeed, assert openly—and they even pride themselves not a little upon it—that they have not learned, nor do they teach, anything about the principles either of founding or preserving the state. According to them, such knowledge should be the province, not of scholars and philosophers, but of practical politicians. How, then, is it becoming for them to proffer their aid to the commonwealth only under the pressure of necessity, although they do not know how to perform the far easier task of ruling the state when no emergency confronts it? But even if we grant that the philosopher of his own accord does not generally condescend to deal with affairs of state, though he does not refuse the duty if circumstances make it necessary, nevertheless I should feel that the philosopher ought by no means to neglect the science of politics, since he should be forearmed with all the weapons which he may sometime be obliged to use.

VII. I have spoken thus at length because in the present work I have projected and undertaken a discussion of the commonwealth. That it might not be in vain, I had first to banish

---

[22] The higher offices in Rome were limited in practice, though not in theory, to the *nobiles*, that is, members of families whose ancestors had held such offices; see Mommsen: *Röm. Staatsrecht*, 3. 1 (1887), pp. 458 ff. Cicero was a *novus homo*, one of the exceptional men who attained high office without being born in the privileged class.

[23] Cf. Plato: *Republic*, 488 a ff.

the reluctance that is felt toward entering politics. But if there still are any who are influenced by the prestige of philosophers, I would have them give earnest attention for a moment to thinkers whose influence and renown have great weight with the learned. These thinkers, even though not actually holding public office, have investigated and treated many problems of the state; and I accordingly feel that they have performed some public function. I notice that nearly all of those whom the Greeks called the Seven Sages[24] passed their lives in the midst of public affairs. There is, indeed, nothing in which human excellence can more nearly approximate the divine than in the foundation of new states or in the preservation of states already founded.

VIII. Now it has been my good fortune not only to have performed some memorable service in the course of my public career, but also to have attained a degree of skill in the exposition of political theory.[25] Both as a result of experience, therefore, and also because of my zeal for learning and teaching, I became an authority on matters touching the state. The scholars of the past, on the other hand, had been either acute in argument but without any record of achievement, or they had been commendable for their conduct of public office but without skill in presenting their arguments.

In fact, however, I am not obliged to develop a theory of politics which is either new or of my own devising. On the contrary, I have only to reconstruct from memory a discussion

---

[24] The Seven Sages lived in the sixth century B.C. and, as the list is generally given, included Solon of Athens, Periander of Corinth, Chilon of Sparta, Pittacus of Mitylene, Bias of Priene, Thales of Miletus, and Cleobulus of Lindus. See Bury: *History of Greece* (1916), p. 321; Beloch: *Gr. Gesch.* 1. 1 (1924), p. 427; 1. 2 (1913), pp. 352 ff.

[25] The text of this paragraph is corrupt, an entire clause having been lost; the English is accordingly a paraphrase rather than a translation. Cicero clearly intends to present the combination of scholarly interests and political experience as his chief qualification as a writer on political philosophy; see Cic. *de leg.* 3. 6. 14. Since, so far as we know, he had not previously published any work on the subject, the "skill in the exposition of political theory," to which he refers, must have been gained from his studies and his duties as a jurisconsult, and displayed by the occasional insertion of political ideas into his speeches; see e. g., *pro Cluent.* 53. 146. Cicero (*de leg. loc. cit.*) mentions Demetrius of Phalerum as the only one beside himself who has combined the theoretical with the practical side of politics.

held by the wisest and most famous men of a certain period of our history, and repeated to us by Publius Rutilius Rufus,[26] while we were once spending several days together in Smyrna during your youth. In this discussion practically nothing, I believe, has been omitted which might concern in any important way the theory of politics.

IX. At the time of the Latin holidays in the year when Tuditanus and Aquilius were consuls,[27] Publius Africanus, the son of Paulus, had decided to remain on his country estate. His most intimate friends had promised that they would visit him frequently. Accordingly, on the morning of the first holiday, there came to him first of all his nephew, Quintus Tubero. After Scipio had hailed him cordially and had expressed his pleasure at seeing him, he asked: What, Tubero, you abroad so early? Surely this holiday afforded you a convenient opportunity for your literary work.

TUBERO: As far as I am concerned, one time is as good as another for my books; they are never busy. But it is a rare privilege to find you at leisure, especially in such a time of public commotion.[28]

SCIPIO: Nevertheless, at leisure you do find me, although it is my hands that are unoccupied, and not my mind.

---

[26] See the account of the persons of the dialogue in the Introduction, p. 6.

[27] The date is 129 B. C. The Latin holidays were a movable festival in honor of Jupiter Latiaris. It took place, during the republican period, shortly after the consuls' inauguration and before the departure of the retiring consuls to their provinces. The center of the cult was the god's shrine on Mons Albanus at Alba Longa; and the worship goes back to the time when the various peoples of Latium formed the Latin League *(nomen Latinum)*, and had not yet submitted to Rome. See Wissowa: *Religion und Kultus der Römer* (1912), pp. 40 ff.; 124 ff.; Fowler: *Religious Experience of the Roman People* (1911), pp. 40; 61; 172.

[28] After the death of Tiberius Gracchus in 133 B. C., the state was convulsed by the prosecution of his followers and by the agitations incident to his agrarian legislation. Scipio Aemilianus, the chief speaker in this dialogue, opposed the operation of the land-law, because he believed it to be a burden on the Italians. The concern which Cicero represents him as feeling was justified. "Ancient historians regarded the murder of Gracchus as epoch-making, as the turning point in the history of Rome, as the beginning of the period of civil war," Greenidge: *History of Rome*, 1 (1904), p. 143; see also *ibid.* pp. 110-158; Heitland: *Roman Republic* (1909), sects. 689-714; Mommsen: *Röm. Gesch.* 2 (1908), pp. 86-96 (Eng. Trans. 3, pp. 84 ff.).

TUBERO: You ought to relax your mind also. Many of us, indeed, are ready, as we decided, to spend this leisure with you, if it suits your convenience.

SCIPIO: It is quite agreeable to me, provided we may ultimately receive some fresh light on matters worthy of serious consideration.

X. TUBERO: Since you suggest it, if I may say so, and make me hopeful of hearing your answer, let us first consider this question before the others arrive: What truth is there in what was reported in the senate about the second sun?[29] There are, indeed, many men—and of sound judgment, too—who affirm that they have seen two suns. We cannot therefore refuse credence to the report, but must rather seek its explanation.

SCIPIO: How I wish that we had our friend Panaetius[30] here with us! He is always investigating problems of astronomy, as well as other problems, with the greatest enthusiasm. But for my part, Tubero—with you I may speak my mind plainly— I do not altogether agree with our friend in matters of this sort. Why, he talks about those things whose nature we can scarcely conjecture with such assurance that he appears to see them with his eyes or actually to touch them with his hands. Therefore, I always feel that Socrates was even wiser, since he resigned all interests of this character, and declared that problems of natural philosophy either transcended human reason or in no way concerned human life.[31]

TUBERO: I cannot understand, Africanus, why the tradition was established that Socrates rejected all such discussions and investigated only the problems of human life and conduct. Indeed, what more trustworthy authority can we cite than Plato? And Plato, in many passages of his works, even where he represents Socrates as discoursing about ethics and politics, makes

---

[29] The parhelia or sun-dogs is the name for this phenomenon; see *Enc. Brit.* (ed. 11th), s. v. Halo. Their appearance in the year 129 B. C. is mentioned elsewhere by Cicero; see *de n. d.* 2. 5. 14. Many ancient references to them may be found in Pease's note on Cic. *de div.* 1. 43. 97.

[30] On Panaetius see Introduction, p. 28.

[31] The character of Socrates' teaching has been the subject of much dispute. The ancient authorities are cited by Zeller (*Phil. d. Greich.* 2. 1, 1922, pp. 132 ff.), who takes the view mentioned by Cicero. For the opposite view see Burnet: *Greek Philosophy*, 1 (1914), ch. 8, esp. pp. 145 ff.

him eager to introduce arithmetic, geometry, and harmony, after the manner of Pythagoras.[32]

SCIPIO: What you say is true, but I presume you have heard, Tubero, that after the death of Socrates Plato went first to Egypt to carry on his studies, and later to Italy and Sicily, that he might thoroughly master the discoveries of Pythagoras.[33] He was very intimate with Archytas[34] of Tarentum and Timaeus[35] of Locri, and acquired the papers of Philolaus.[36] Since at that time the name of Pythagoras was greatly honored in those places, Plato devoted himself to the Pythagoreans and their researches. Thus, as he had been devotedly attached to Socrates and had wished to attribute everything to him, he interwove the charm and argumentative skill of Socrates with the mysticism of Pythagoras and the well-known profundity of his varied lore.

XI. When Scipio had finished these remarks, he caught sight of Lucius Furius Philus arriving unannounced; and after greeting him in a most affectionate manner, he took him by the hand and made a place for him on his own couch. At the same time Publius Rutilius, the source of our information

---

[32] Pythagoras was the founder of the school which bore his name. It was at first partly a religious society and partly a school which devoted itself especially to the study of arithmetic and musical harmony, but the character of Pythagoras was so overlaid with myth by later writers that it is impossible to be certain what he taught. See Zeller: *Phil. d. Griech.* 1. 1 (1923), pp. 380 ff.; Eng. trans., *Pre-Socratics*, 1 (1881), pp. 324 ff.; Burnet: *Greek Philosophy*, 1 (1914), ch. 2.
[33] The ancient evidence relative to Plato's travels is cited by Zeller: *Phil. d. Griech.* 2. 1 (1922), pp. 402 ff.; see also Wilamowitz-Moellendorff: *Platon*, 1 (1920), pp. 241 ff.
[34] Archytas of Tarentum was a Pythagorean philosopher contemporary with Plato. He was reputed to have been equally distinguished as a statesman, a general, and a mathematician and philosopher. On Plato's third journey to Sicily and after his quarrel with Dionysius, it was the intercession of Archytas which secured his release. The fragments are collected in Diels: *Vorsokratiker*, 1 (1912), pp. 322 ff.
[35] Timaeus of Locri was a Pythagorean philosopher of whom practically nothing is known; see Plato: *Timaeus*, 19 e ff.
[36] Philolaus, either of Croton or Tarentum, was the first of the Pythagoreans who committed the theories of the school to writing. He was a contemporary of Socrates. The fragments are collected by Diels: *Vorsokratiker*, 1 (1912), pp. 301 ff. See Burnet: *Early Greek Philosophy* (1908), pp. 320 ff. According to tradition, the book of Philolaus became the source of Plato's *Timaeus;* see Zeller: *Phil. d. Griech.*, 2. 1 (1922), p. 410, n. 2.

115

about this discussion, had arrived. Scipio greeted him also and bade him take a seat by Tubero.

PHILUS: What are you doing? Our arrival did not, I hope, interrupt any discussion of yours?

SCIPIO: Not at all. You, indeed, are constantly and earnestly investigating such problems as Tubero had just begun to examine. Our friend Rutilius, even when encamped under the very walls of Numantia,[37] would sometimes investigate questions of this sort with me.

PHILUS: What topic, I repeat, had come up for discussion?

SCIPIO: Those two suns; and I desire to hear from you, Philus, what you think about them.

XII. He had just said this, when a slave announced that Laelius had already left his house and was on his way. Then Scipio, putting on his sandals and his outer garments, left the apartment. After strolling up and down a little while in the portico, he greeted Laelius upon his arrival, and also several others who had come with him, Spurius Mummius, an especial friend, and Gaius Fannius and Quintus Scaevola, sons-in-law of Laelius and young men of scholarly interests who were then of an age to be eligible for the office of quaestor.[38] After Scipio had welcomed them all, he took a turn up and down the portico, making Laelius the center of the group. For between these two friends there was a kind of rule that when they were in camp Laelius should worship Scipio like a god because of his extraordinary renown in war, while in private life Scipio should revere Laelius as a father, because he was the older. After they had walked up and down once or twice and had

---

[37] The campaign against Numantia in Spain lasted from 143 to 133 B. C. Until 134 B. C. the war was wholly a failure from the Roman point of view, since the Roman army was ill-trained, lazy, disobedient, and dissolute, and its commanders were incompetent and scheming. In 134 B. C. Scipio Aemilianus took command. He imposed severe standards of discipline, and with the reformed army invested Numantia and forced it to surrender in 133 B. C. See Livy: *epit.* 59; Appian: *res Hisp.* 98; Eutropius: 4. 17; Heitland: *Roman Republic* (1909), sects. 604-609; Mommsen: *Röm. Gesch.* 2, pp. 13-17 (Eng. trans. 3, pp. 13-17).

[38] The minimal ages for the magistracies were determined by the Lex Villia Annalis (180 B. C.). That for the quaestorship was twenty-eight; see Heitland: *Roman Republic* (1909), sects. 615-616; Mommsen: *Röm. Staatsrecht*, 1 (1887), pp. 505-507; 529 ff.

exchanged a few words, and after Scipio had expressed his very great pleasure at their arrival, he decided that they should sit down together in the sunniest spot in the meadow, since it was the winter season. The suggestion met with their approval. At this point there arrived a man distinguished for his wisdom and a dear friend of the whole group, Manius Manilius. He was welcomed most cordially by Scipio and the others and seated himself next to Laelius.

XIII. PHILUS: It does not seem to me that the arrival of our friends makes it necessary for us to change the subject of discussion. We must deal with the matter more carefully, however, and our discourse must be worthy of their attention.

LAELIUS: What, I ask, were you doing, or what was the discussion which we interrupted?

PHILUS: Scipio had asked me what I thought about the fact that two suns have certainly been seen.

LAELIUS: Really now, Philus! Have we already settled the problems that may affect our private and public life, that we are investigating what goes on in the sky?

PHILUS: Why, do you not think that our private life is affected by the knowledge of what is done and what happens in our home? And our home is not a structure of four walls, but is this entire universe, which the gods have given us as a habitation and as a country, to be shared in common with them.[39] Surely, if we remain in ignorance of these cosmic problems, we must remain ignorant of many important matters. For my part, I take delight in the knowledge and study of natural phenomena, as indeed you do yourself, Laelius, in common with all men who love wisdom.

LAELIUS: I shall not stop you, especially since it is the

---

[39] This sentence is attributed by von Arnim to the Stoic Chrysippus; see *Stoicorum veterum fragmenta*, 3 (1923), fr. 338. It was a not uncommon way of expressing the fundamental Stoic principle that nature is ruled by reason and that reason is at once a divine and human attribute; see von Arnim: *op. cit.* 2, Chrysippus, fr. 1127-1131; 3, fr. 333-339; Cic. *de n. d.* 2. 31. 78; 2. 53. 133; *de fin.* 3. 19. 64; *de leg.* 1. 7. 22-23; 2. 10. 26. This doctrine was the metaphysical basis for the conclusion that all men form a single society or brotherhood, ruled by a single law, and that virtue consists in a life according to nature. See Hicks: *Stoic and Epicurean* (1910), pp. 41 ff.; 76.

holiday season. But are we to hear any further discussion or have we come too late?

PHILUS: There has been no discussion as yet. And since the question is untouched, I shall be glad, Laelius, to yield you the opportunity of treating the subject.

LAELIUS: By no means. Let us hear from you rather; that is, unless perhaps Manilius thinks that the two suns ought to be restrained from trespass by an injunction directing that each sun shall possess its own portion of the sky in accordance with the terms of its former possession.[40]

MANILIUS: Come, Laelius, are you going to make sport of that profession in which you yourself are an adept and without which, furthermore, no one can know what is his own and what is another's? But we can discuss that later. Let us now hear Philus, who, I perceive, has already been asked to give an opinion about more important matters than Publius Mucius or I.[41].

XIV. PHILUS: There is nothing new in what I shall report, nor anything which I myself have thought out or discovered. For I recall that once before, when this same phenomenon was said to have occurred, Gaius Sulpicius Gallus,[42] a very learned man, as you know, happened to be at the house of Marcus Marcellus, his colleague in the consulate. Gallus asked that the celestial globe be brought in which the grandfather of Marcellus had taken at the capture of Syracuse as his only share of all the booty carried off from that rich and splendid city.

---

[40] According to Cicero (de off. 1. 30. 108), Laelius' disposition was marked by *magna hilaritas*, of which the witticism contained in these lines is not perhaps a fair example. The interdict *uti possidetis* was an injunction issued by the praetor to confirm one of two litigants in the *ad interim* use of property until its ownership had been decided. See Gaius: *inst.*, ed Poste (1904), 4. 160; p. 599; Buckland: *Text-book of Roman Law* (1921), p. 734.

[41] For Publius Mucius Scaevola, a jurisconsult and author of a work on law, see Schanz: *Gesch. d. röm. Lit.* 1. 1 (1907), pp. 339 f. His part in the Gracchan troubles is referred to by Cicero: *de rep.* 1. 19, below.

[42] Gallus, praetor in 169 and consul in 166 B. C., was well known for his interest in literature and astronomy; see Cic. *Brut.* 20. 78; *de sen.* 14. 49. He is also mentioned in ch. 15, below, although in Livy's account of the same event (44. 37), he predicted the eclipse and thus prevented a panic in the Roman army.

Though I had often heard of this famous globe, because of the renown of Archimedes,[43] I was not much impressed by the appearance of the thing itself, because there was another globe, more beautiful and more generally known, also made by Archimedes, which this same ancestor of Marcellus had placed in the Temple of Virtue. But as soon as Gallus began to explain in a thoroughly scientific way the theory of the instrument, I came to the conclusion that the genius of Archimedes transcended human nature. For Gallus told us that the invention of the solid and compact globe in the Temple of Virtue was ancient, and that the first one had been fashioned by Thales[44] of Miletus. Subsequently, Eudoxus[45] of Cnidus, Plato's pupil, as Gallus said, marked on the globe the stars that are fixed in the sky. Many years after Eudoxus, Aratus[46] adopted from him the entire detailed arrangement of the globe and described it in verse, not displaying any knowledge of astronomy but showing considerable poetical skill.

But Gallus declared that the globe at Marcellus' house, which showed the motions of sun and moon and of those five wandering stars or planets, as they are called, could not be constructed in solid form. All the more remarkable, therefore, was Archimedes' discovery, since he had devised a method of construction whereby, extremely different though the movements of the planets are, the mere turning of the globe would keep them all in their unequal and different orbits. When Gallus rotated the globe, the moon really followed the sun on the bronze globe by the same number of revolutions as are the days it lags behind in the sky. Thus it happened that on the

---

[43] For Archimedes (c. 287-212 B. C.), the most original mathematician and physicist of the ancient world, see the brief account by Heiberg: *Science and Mathematics in Classical Antiquity* (1922), pp. 57 ff.

[44] For Thales (c. 624-c. 547 B. C.), see Burnet: *Greek Philosophy*, 1 (1914), pp. 17 ff. The statement below (ch. 16), that he discovered the cause of eclipses, is erroneous.

[45] Eudoxus (c. 408-355 B. C.), a pupil of Plato and Archytas (Diog. L. 8. 86), was a celebrated astronomer and mathematician. See Heath in *The Legacy of Greece* (1923), pp. 117 ff.; Heath: *Aristarchus of Samos* (1913), pp. 190 ff.

[46] Aratus of Soli in Cilicia (c. 310-c. 245 B. C.) was the author of the *Phaenomena*, a didactic poem written under the influence of the Stoics, in which he embodied the astronomical observations of Eudoxus; see Christ-Schmid: *Gesch. d. gr. Lit.* 2. 1 (1920), pp. 163 ff.

globe there occurred a solar eclipse just like the real eclipse; and also that the moon passed into that tract of space covered by the earth's shadow when the sun [and the moon were on opposite sides of the earth.]

(Of the six inside leaves of the sixth quaternion five are missing. Mai supposes the following to be the fifth leaf of the six, in which case four leaves are missing in this place)

XV. SCIPIO: . . . . . .was, both because I liked [Gallus] myself and because I knew that he had especially won the heart of my father Paulus and was dear to him. The event which I recall happened while I was a mere stripling. My father was consul in Macedonia, and we were in camp together. Our army was thrown into utter confusion through superstitious fear because on a cloudless night suddenly the full bright moon had gone into eclipse. Gallus, who was our legate about a year before his consulate, hastened on the next day to explain publicly in the camp that there was no supernatural element in the eclipse. The phenomenon which had just happened would, he added, always recur at those particular times when the position of the sun was such that its rays could not reach the moon.

TUBERO: What! Do you mean to say that he could give this explanation to men almost fresh from the farm, and that he presumed to discuss such matters before those uneducated soldiers?

SCIPIO: He did, indeed, and with great . . . .

(Probably one leaf is missing)

SCIPIO: . . . . . [Gallus] indulged neither in excessive display nor in a style of speech unsuited to the character of a dignified man. What he accomplished was indeed important, since he had lifted from the minds of those distracted men an unreasonable and superstitious fear.

XVI. A similar occurrence took place also in that tremendous struggle which the Athenians and the Lacedaemonians waged against each other with extreme intensity. There was an eclipse of the sun, and darkness suddenly fell. Since the hearts of the Athenians had been seized by great terror at the event, the famous Pericles, who was the chief man of the state by virtue of his influence, his oratory, and his wisdom, taught his fellow-citizens, according to the story, the explanation of the eclipse which he had learned from his master Anaxagoras.[47] The phenomenon, he said, happened of necessity at definite times when the moon completely covered the face of the sun. Accordingly, he added, although an eclipse did not occur at every new moon, it could occur only then. After he had discussed and thoroughly explained the event, the people's hearts were released from fear. At that time, you see, the explanation of the eclipse, that it occurs whenever the moon comes between the earth and the sun, was new and not generally known, although it is said that Thales of Miletus had first discovered its cause. Later, however, the cause of solar eclipses was understood even by our poet Ennius. For he writes that approximately in the three hundred and fiftieth year after Rome was founded,

> Upon the Nones of June the moon fronted the sun, and
> there was night.

And so great is the accuracy of astronomical knowledge that from this eclipse, noted as we see in Ennius and our pontifical records,[48] the earlier eclipses have been calculated even as far back as the famous one on the Nones of August in the reign of Romulus. In the darkness of that eclipse Romulus, according to tradition, was exalted to the gods because of his good works,[49] although in reality he met a natural end.

---

[47] Pericles (born c. 500 B.C.) was the leader of the Athenian democracy from 461 B.C. until his death in 429. The story which Cicero gives here is attested by Plutarch: *Pericles*, 35.2; Valerius Maximus: 8. 11. Anaxagoras of Clazomenae (c. 499-428 B.C.) lived at Athens for about thirty years under the patronage of Pericles, until the latter's political enemies brought about his banishment on a charge of impiety. See Burnet: *Greek Philosophy*, 1 (1914), pp. 76 ff.; the fragments are collected in Diels: *Vorsokratiker*, 1 (1912), pp. 375 ff.

[48] The pontifical records were documents, preserved by the chief pontiffs, in which they entered the outstanding events of their respective periods. It was a form of record which carries us back to the early period in Rome's history when every aspect of life, public and private, was overshadowed by religion. See Wissowa: *Religion und Kultus der Römer* (1912), p. 389.

[49] For Euhemerism, the belief expounded by Euhemerus of Messene (end of fourth century B.C.), see Pauly-Wissowa: *Realencyclopädie*, s. v. Euemeros.

XVII.   TUBERO: Do you see, Africanus, that what seemed otherwise a moment ago,..........?

(The second leaf of the seventh quaternion is missing)

SCIPIO: ....what others see. What, I ask, can a man think glorious in human life, who has contemplated these realms of the gods? What can he regard as enduring, who has learned the nature of eternity? What meaning can fame have for him who has seen how small is the earth, even the whole of it, and especially that portion inhabited by man, and how insignificant is that part of the habitable globe to which we are limited? For we are unknown to most races, even though we hope that our renown will fly and wander far and wide.

Lands, buildings, herds, and a countless store of gold and silver are generally accounted the goods of life. But how fortunate should we judge the man who rejects this view and refuses to call such objects good, because to him their enjoyment appears trifling, their use insignificant, and their ownership uncertain, and because he realizes that often the most debased of men have these possessions beyond all measure! Only such a man may truly claim all things as his own, not by a title derived from the law of the Quirites, but by virtue of the right which inheres in wisdom; not because of a formal contract under the civil law, but by virtue of that general law of nature which forbids that anything should belong to any one, except to a man who knows how to use and employ it wisely.[50] Such a man considers our military commands and civil magistracies among necessary, not among desirable things, to be undertaken only as a public duty, not to be sought for the sake of glory and reward. Such a man, finally, can make the same asser-

---

[50] The doctrine that only the wise man is rich was a favorite Stoic paradox; for many similar passages see von Arnim: *Stoicorum veterum fragmenta*, 3 (1923), pp. 154 ff. The principle that the right to property depends upon its wise use had considerable importance in ameliorating the legal status of slaves; see Gaius: *inst.*, ed. Poste (1904), 1. 53; Justinian: *inst.*, ed. Moyle (1912), note on 1. 3. 2. Ownership *ex iure Quiritium* was an ancient form of title; see Gaius: *inst.*, ed. Poste, pp. 151 ff. The formal contract, or *nexum*, mentioned by Cicero, was a form already long obsolete in his day; see Buckland: *Text-book of Roman Law* (1921), pp. 426 ff.

tion about himself that, according to Cato, my grandfather Africanus used to make, that he never accomplished more than when doing nothing, and that he was never less lonely than when he was alone.

Who can really believe that, when Dionysius[51] by employing every device wrested freedom from his subjects, he accomplished more than his fellow-citizen Archimedes, when the latter, though apparently idle, constructed the sphere you have just described? Who would not agree, moreover, that a man who does not meet in the crowds of the forum a single congenial acquaintance is more lonely than one who either communes alone with himself, or who is, in a sense, present in an assembly of the learned, because he delights himself with their discoveries and writings? Who can think anyone richer than the man who lacks nothing that nature truly requires; or mightier than the man who accomplishes all his aims; or happier than the man who has been freed from every disturbance of soul; or more firmly established in fortune's favor than the man whose possessions are such that he can, as the proverb says, bear them with him even from shipwreck? What military command, what magistracy, what kingly prerogative excels the power of him who looks down upon the world, who thinks that everything in it is human and inferior to wisdom, and who therefore reflects only upon eternal and divine truths?[52] Such a man is persuaded that, although others may be called human, only those are really so who have been refined by the truly humane arts.

I am accordingly inclined to feel that the story told by Plato,[53] or whoever else it was, is very much to the point. A storm at sea had cast him upon the deserted shores of an un-

[51] Dionysius was tyrant of Syracuse from 405 B.C. until his death in 367. Under him Syracuse became the dominant power in the Greek world. His authority was based on force, and in maintaining it he took away the freedom of his subjects. See Bury: *History of Greece* (1916), pp. 642 ff.

[52] The passage beginning "Who can think anyone richer" and running to "eternal and divine truths" is regarded by von Arnim as a paraphrase of the Stoic Chrysippus; see *Stoicorum veterum fragmenta*, 3 (1923), fr. 600.

[53] Vitruvius *(de arch.* 6. 1. 1) relates this story about Aristippus.

known land. While his companions were filled with terror because they were unacquainted with the place, Plato noticed on the sand some geometrical figures. Immediately he bade his comrades be of good cheer, saying that he discerned the traces of human beings. This conclusion he drew, you may be sure, not from the cultivation of the land which he saw before his eyes, but from the evidence of scientific interest. This is the reason, Tubero, why I have always delighted in learning, in cultivated men, and in those studies which you have made your own.

XVIII. LAELIUS: I do not have the courage to reply to what you have just said, Scipio, nor do I [think] that you or Philus or Manilius..........

(The seventh leaf of the seventh quaternion is missing)

LAELIUS:[54] ...... .in [Tubero's] family on his father's side belonged our friend, whom [Tubero] would do well to imitate,

A man exceeding wise, shrewd Aelius Sextus,[55]

who was "exceeding wise," and was so called by Ennius, not because he sought answers to insoluble questions, but because his advice would release those who consulted him from care and anxiety. When he argued against Gallus' studious interests, the famous words of Achilles in the "Iphigenia"[56] were ever on his lips:

Astronomers' constellations in the sky men seek and look for,
When Jove's she-goat or scorpion or some creature strangely
   named arises;
What is before his feet, none observes; all study heaven's
   tracts.

And yet sometimes he would take the opposite view—I can say this for I often used to hear him, and gladly, too—and

---

[54] This speech is incorrectly attributed by Ziegler to Scipio.

[55] Sextus Aelius Paetus Catus, consul in 198 B.C. and censor in 194, was a jurisconsult and the author of a work on the law of the Twelve Tables called *Tripertita*, apparently because he treated first each law, second the interpretation of it, and third the appropriate form of statutory process *(legis actio)*. The book was generally known as the *ius Aelianum*. See Schanz: *Gesch. d. röm. Lit.* 1. 1 (1907), pp. 337 ff.

[56] A play bearing this title is attributed both to Ennius and to Naevius (c. 270-199 B.C.). The translation of the quotation and of the preceding line follows Mai's text.

would declare that Zethus in Pacuvius'[57] play was too little a friend of learning. He was more pleased by the Neoptolemus of Ennius, who said [in the play of that name] that he would be a philosopher but only to a limited degree; to be a philosopher and nothing else did not at all suit him.

Although the studies pursued by the Greeks give you such pleasure, there are others, of a more liberal character and of a more extended application, which we can bring to bear either upon our private business or even upon the commonwealth itself. In truth, the value of these more speculative studies that you are interested in—if, indeed, they have any value at all—lies in the fact that they sharpen somewhat the minds of the young, and, as we may say, stimulate them to a greater facility in learning more important matters.

XIX. TUBERO: I agree with you, Laelius, but I ask you: What are the subjects that you deem more important?

LAELIUS: I shall express my views—rest assured of that—and perhaps I shall earn your contempt by doing so. For while you are asking Scipio questions about what happens in the heavens, I feel that these practical matters immediately before our eyes are a more worthy object of investigation. Why, indeed, does Tubero, the grandson of Lucius Paulus and the nephew of Africanus here, a member of Rome's most distinguished family and a citizen of so glorious a commonwealth —why, I repeat, does such a man inquire how two suns could have appeared in the sky, and does not rather ask why there are two senates in one commonwealth and now practically two peoples? For, as you see, the death of Tiberius Gracchus and, even before then, his entire conception of the tribunate divided one people into two factions.[58] The critics and slander-

---

[57] Pacuvius, called by Cicero (*de opt. gen. orat.* 1. 2) the greatest of the Roman tragic poets, was born at Brundisium in c. 220 B. C. and died probably at Tarentum in c. 130 B. C. See Duff: *A Literary History of Rome* (1914), pp. 224-227; Schanz: *Gesch. d. röm. Lit.* 1. 1 (1907), pp. 129 ff.

[58] For Gracchus' conception of the tribunate see Greenidge: *A History of Rome*, 1 (1904), pp. 132 ff. The persons mentioned in the following sentences, with the exception of Metellus, were attached to the party of Tiberius. Metellus was at odds with Scipio over some personal matter. Laelius gives the conservative interpretation of Gracchus' reform.

ous foes of Scipio continue the disturbance which Publius Crassus and Appius Claudius began; and now, even though these two are dead, they still control that second party in the senate which Metellus and Publius Mucius induce to desert Scipio and his followers. The allies and the Latin League have been aroused. Our treaties have been broken. Every day the agrarian commission is treacherously devising some new and revolutionary measure. Loyal citizens are harassed. And yet, the factious element does not allow our friend Scipio to relieve this dangerous condition of the state, although he is the only one who can do so. Therefore, my young friends, if you will take my advice, do not trouble yourselves about this second sun. For it is a matter of indifference whether its existence be impossible or whether we suppose that it really exists, as appears to be the case, so long as it does not cause us trouble. Either we can know nothing of such matters or, even if we fully understand them, we cannot thereby become either better or happier men. On the other hand, we can bring about the union of senate and people, and our condition is serious unless we do so. We know that such union does not exist now, and we see that, if it were realized, we should live both better and happier lives.

XX. MUCIUS: What studies do you think we should master, Laelius, in order to bring about the end that you desire?

LAELIUS: Assuredly, such subjects as would make us useful to the state. For service to the state I consider the most glorious function of the wise and the chief mark or duty of the good. Accordingly, in order that we may spend this holiday in discussions conducive to the highest interests of our country, let us request Scipio to explain what he regards as the best form of constitution for the state. After that we shall conduct other inquiries. When these are answered, I hope that we shall immediately arrive at the discussion of our present political situation, and explain the meaning of the perils that are now upon us.

XXI. When Philus and Manilius and Mummius had expressed their hearty approval.........

(The fourth leaf of the eighth quaternion is missing)

1 2 6

There is no pattern to which we prefer to compare the commonwealth.[59]

Therefore, if you please, bring down your conversation from the remote heavens to these nearer topics of earth.[60]

LAELIUS: ....I desired [you to discuss this question], not only because it was fitting that the state should be discussed preferably by its leading citizen, but also because I recalled that in your frequent discussions with Panaetius and Polybius[61]—the two Greeks most thoroughly versed in political science—you assembled much evidence for the view which you set forth, that by far the best form of constitution was the one bequeathed us by our ancestors. You are accordingly more at home in this subject than any one else; and so, if you will expound your views of the commonwealth—let me speak for my friends here as well as for myself—you will confer a favor upon all of us.

XXII. SCIPIO: I cannot indeed say that there is any subject to which I habitually devote more ardent or earnest thought than the very one which you, Laelius, propose. Now I observe that every workman, at least if he is a master workman, makes it the object of all his thoughts, deliberations, and efforts to improve his skill in his special craft. Since my sole duty, which I inherit from parents and ancestors, has been the watchful supervision and performance of public tasks, should I not confess that I was less energetic than a mere craftsman if I did not bestow on the greatest of professions as much effort as artizans devote to their petty tasks?[62] But I am not satisfied with the literature on this subject which the greatest and wisest men of Greece have left us, nor am I bold enough to prefer my own conclusions to theirs. I ask, therefore, that when you hear my arguments you will bear this in mind: that I am neither wholly ignorant of Greek researches nor minded to accord them preference over our own

---

[59] Diomedes: *gram. Lat.*, ed. Keil, 1, p. 365, 20.

[60] Nonius, p. 85. 18; p. 289. 8.

[61] On Panaetius and Polybius and their relation to the Scipionic Circle, see Introduction, pp. 27 ff.

[62] This passage should be compared with Aristotle: *Nic. Eth.* 1094 a 26 ff.; *Politics*, 1282 b 14 ff.; *Mag. mor.* 1182 a 32 ff.

authors, especially in the field of politics; that I am, rather, simply a typical Roman citizen who, because of a father's care, received a liberal education, who has been fired from boyhood with the love of learning, but who nevertheless has gained a far wider training from experience and a father's precepts than he has derived from the study of books.

XXIII. PHILUS: Assuredly, Scipio, I am convinced that no one has excelled you in native ability, while in the practical knowledge derived from the holding of high public office you are without an equal. The wide range of interests which has ever been yours we all know. If, then, as you say, you have applied your mind also to the science or art of politics, as we may call it, I am extremely indebted to Laelius. For I expect that your words will be much more fruitful than the whole body of Greek political speculation.

SCIPIO: Great, indeed, is the anticipation you arouse with reference to my discourse. And that is the heaviest burden which can be placed on anyone who is to discuss a serious subject.

PHILUS: However great our hopes may be, you will surpass them, as you always do. For there is no danger that, when you discuss the commonwealth, you will fail in effective presentation.

XXIV. SCIPIO: I shall do what you wish to the best of my ability and shall proceed immediately to the discussion. First, however, I must lay down one rule which, I believe, should guide all men in any discussion aimed to remove error: namely, that, if they agree to discuss a certain subject, that subject shall be first defined. Only if the definition meets with approval will it be proper for us to embark upon our discussion. For assuredly the nature of the subject can never be understood unless we first comprehend what it is. Since, therefore, the commonwealth forms the subject of our inquiry, let us first consider its precise definition.

After Laelius had expressed his approval, Scipio continued: In spite of what I have said, in the analysis of a thing so well-known and obvious as the state, I shall not go back to its primal constituents. I shall not, for example, follow the

usual custom of scholars in this field, and begin with the first
union of male and female, with the propagation of offspring,
and with the family relationships that ensue.[63] Nor shall I
define too frequently what each term means and in how many
ways it is used. Since I am speaking before experienced men
who, at home and abroad, have played an honorable part in
the greatest of states, I shall not commit the fault of making
the subject of my discourse obvious, while the discussion itself
is obscure. The task, indeed, which I have undertaken is not
to elaborate like a schoolmaster every detail of the topic; nor
do I bind myself to cover the entire field in my treatment and
leave no gaps at all.

LAELIUS: For my part, I am looking forward to the very
type of discussion which you promise.

XXV. SCIPIO: The commonwealth, then, is the people's
affair; and the people is not every group of men, associated
in any manner, but is the coming together of a considerable
number of men who are united by a common agreement about
law and rights and by the desire to participate in mutual advantages.[64] The original cause of this coming together is not
so much weakness as a kind of social instinct natural to man.
For the human kind is not solitary, nor do its members live
lives of isolated roving; but it is so constituted that, even if
it possessed the greatest plenty of material comforts, [it would
nevertheless be impelled by its nature to live in social groups
. . . .]

(The second leaf of the ninth quaternion is missing)

For what is the commonwealth except the people's affair?[65]
Hence, it is a common affair, that is, an affair belonging to a
state. And what is a state except a considerable number of

---

[63] This may refer to Aristotle: *Politics*, 1252 a 24 ff. (see Newman:
The Politics of Aristotle, 1, 1887, p. 34), or it may refer to some Stoic
work on the state; cf. Cic. *de off*. 1. 17. 53 ff. The Stoics explained
human conduct by an instinct of self-preservation, which included the
appetite which brings the sexes together and the love of offspring; see
Cic. *de off*. 1. 4. 11; *de fin*. 3. 19. 62; Polybius: 6. 6. 2. The complaint
of verbalism made below was very often directed against the Stoic
Chrysippus; see Cic. *de rep*. 3. 8, below.
[64] See Introduction, pp. 51 f.
[65] We have translated the context from Augustine, which Ziegler
prints in the apparatus criticus.

men brought together in a certain bond of harmony? The view that we meet in the Roman authors is as follows: In a short time a scattered and wandering aggregate of men became a state through harmony.

Augustine: epist. 138. 10; CSEL. 44, p. 135. 8.

Scholars have not attributed the founding of cities to a single first principle.[66] *For some hold that, when men first sprang up from the soil, they lived a roving life in the forests and plains, and were united by no bonds either of speech or of law, but made their beds in the leaves and grass and had caves and crevices in the rocks for houses, and were a prey to the more powerful wild beasts and animals. Later, they say, those men who had been torn by wild beasts or had seen their comrades torn, and had made their escape, were driven by consciousness of their danger to ally themselves with other men. From them they sought aid, at first making their wants known by signs and gestures. Afterwards they experimented with the beginnings of speech and, by giving names to things, gradually developed a system of language. These scholars believe, further, that, when men perceived that even in large numbers they needed to be protected against animals, they began to build towns, either with a view to making themselves safe at night, or for the purpose of warding off the attacks of animals, not by fighting them hand to hand, but by interposing barriers for their own protection . . . To other scholars, on the other hand, these views have appeared little better than madness, as in fact they were. These scholars held that the reason why men came together in groups is not to be found in the depredations of wild beasts, but rather in the social nature of mankind. Consequently, they said, men formed societies because it is their nature to shun solitude and to seek the relationships of social intercourse.*

Lactantius: inst. 6. 10. 13-15; 18.

XXVI. SCIPIO: .... [These gregarious impulses] are, so to speak, the seeds [of social virtues]; nor can any

---

[66] The first part of this section from Lactantius is clearly derived from Lucretius (5. 805-1116, *passim*). Mai supposed that Cicero discussed different views of the origin of the state, and Ziegler hesitatingly retains the passage. The contrast is between the Stoic and Epicurean theories.

other source be found for the remaining virtues or, indeed, for the commonwealth itself. Such groups, therefore, brought into being for the reason I have mentioned, first settled themselves in a fixed abode that they might have dwellings. And when they had fortified this abode, either by taking advantage of the natural features of the land or by building artificial works, they called such a group of buildings, with the places set aside for shrines and for common use, either a town or a city. Consequently, every people, which is a number of men united in the way I have explained, every state, which is an organization of the people, every commonwealth, which, as I have said, is the people's affair, needs to be ruled by some sort of deliberating authority in order that it may endure. This authority, in the first place, must always be relative to the peculiar grounds which have brought the particular state into being.[67] It must, in the second place, be delegated either to a single man, or to certain selected persons, or it must be retained by all the members of the group.

When, therefore, the supreme power is in the hands of one man, we call that man a king and that form of government a monarchy. When it is in the hands of certain selected persons, the state is said to be ruled by the will of an aristocracy. And a state is democratic—for that is the term used—when all authority is in the hands of the people themselves.[68] Any one of these three forms of government, while not, of course, perfect nor in my judgment the best, is nevertheless a passable form of government, if the bond holds which originally united its members in the social order of the commonwealth; and one may be better than another.[69] For either a just and wise king, or an aristocracy of leading citizens, or even the people themselves—though this last is the least desirable form of the

---

[67] This sentence suggests Aristotle's statement that even the founder of an ideal state is dependent upon the materials at his disposal, such as the location of his city, the number and character of his people, and the resources of the country; see *Politics*, 1325 b 40 ff.

[68] With this classification of states compare Herodotus: 3. 80. 3-6; Thucydides: 2. 37. 1; 6. 39. 1; Plato: *Republic*, 545 b ff.; *Statesman*, 291 d ff.; Aristotle: *Politics*, 1279 a 22 ff.; *Rhetoric*, 1365 b 31 ff.; Polybius: 6. 4. 2 ff.; Tacitus: *ann.* 4. 33.

[69] The Latin text of this last clause is corrupt.

three—appears capable of carrying on a stable government so long as injustice and greed have not crept into the state.

XXVII. Nevertheless, in a monarchy all except the king are too much excluded from the protection of the law and from participation in deliberative functions, though these rights belong to the whole people. In a government dominated by an aristocracy the mass of the people have hardly any share in freedom, since they have no part in common deliberative and executive powers. And when the state is governed by the people, even though they be just and self-disciplined, yet their very equality is inequitable in that it does not recognize degrees of merit.[70] Therefore, even if Cyrus[71] the Persian was a perfectly just and wise king, nevertheless the condition of the commons—that is, the commonwealth, as I have said above—does not seem to have been one which we should particularly covet, since it was subject to the caprice of a single man. Similarly, even if our clients, the Massilians,[72] are governed with the greatest justice by their oligarchy of nobles, still in a people so situated there exists something like slavery. And even if the Athenians at certain periods after the fall

---

[70] A reference to proportional as against absolute equality. The distinction depends on Plato's definition of justice as the performance of function (*Republic*, 433 b), and the principle is clearly stated in the *Laws*, 757 a ff. See also Isocrates (3. 14): "The essence of justice is . . . that unequals should not receive equal treatment, but that individuals should both act and be honored in accordance with their merits." The theory of proportional equality is developed by Aristotle especially. See *Nic. Eth.* 1131 a 10 ff.; *Politics*, 1280 a 7 ff.; 1301 b 29 ff.; 1318 a 10 ff. When developed as a legal conception, proportional justice becomes the Roman principle *ius suum cuique tribuere*.

[71] Cyrus the Great ruled from 558 to 529 B. C. The endearing personality which Cicero attributed to him perhaps originated in Xenophon's biographical romance, the *Cyropaedeia*, the unhistorical character of which is noted in *ad Q. fr.* 1. 1. 8. 23. Plato (*Laws*, 694 a) says that under the rule of Cyrus the Persians were free.

[72] See Strabo: 179 c and d, where we read: "The Massiliotes are governed by an aristocracy which is more orderly than any other. They have created a council of six hundred members who are called *timouchoi* (honor-holders) and who are invested with the honor of their office for life. The assembly is directed by fifteen men whose duty is the administration of current business; and the three who have most power preside over the fifteen. No *timouchos*, however, may become one of these three unless he has children and unless his ancestors have been citizens for three generations." See Gilbert: *Gr. Staatsalt.* 2 (1885), pp. 259 ff.; E. Meyer: *Gesch. des Alt.* 3 (1915), pp. 670 ff.; Busolt: *Gr. Staatskunde*, 1 (1920), pp. 357 ff.

of the Areopagus conducted all public business through enactments and decrees of the people, still their state did not preserve its glory, since it failed to regard differences of worth.[73]

XXVIII. I am speaking of the three types of government, not as they are when they have become disordered and deranged, but as they are when they maintain their true character. In this condition, each type is subject, first, to the defects which I have mentioned, and in addition has other faults likely to be fatal to its permanence. For each of these types of commonwealth has a tendency to slip headlong into that form of evil government which is most closely related to it.[74] Take, for example, a king at his best, a Cyrus, who was an endurable or, if you like, even a lovable ruler. Nevertheless, his character may change, for there lurks in him the utterly inhuman Phalaris into whose likeness arbitrary power in the hands of one man readily and easily degenerates.[75] Furthermore, the government of the Massilian state by a few chief men is closely approximated by the oligarchical conspiracy of the Thirty Tyrants which once ruled Athens.[76] And finally, at Athens the Athenians themselves—to seek no other [authority—admit] that the absolute power of the people degenerated into the irresponsible madness of a mob..........

(The seventh leaf of the ninth quaternion is missing)

---

[73] In 462-1 B. C. the democratic party, under the leadership of Ephialtes and Pericles, took from the Areopagus all its significant powers. The aristocratic tradition of Athenian history represents the epoch before the fall of the Areopagus as the golden age of Athens; see Isocrates: 7. 20 ff.; Plato: *Gorgias*, 515 e; Aristotle: *Const. of the Athenians*, 29. 3; Ferguson: *Hellenistic Athens* (1911), pp. 419 ff.

[74] See Polybius (6. 4. 8), where he mentions the natural tendency of monarchy to change to the related evil form of government, or tyranny; of aristocracy to lapse to oligarchy; and of democracy to decline into ochlocracy. On the cycle of constitutions see Cic. *de rep.* 1. 42, below, and note; also Introduction, pp. 57 ff.

[75] Phalaris, the tyrant of Agrigentum (sixth century B.C.), was noted in antiquity as the inventor of a hollow bronze bull into which his enemies were put and roasted to death. See Cic. *de div.* (ed. Pease), 1. 23. 46; *de rep.* 3. 30, below; Grote: *History of Greece* (ed. Murray, 1870), 4, pp. 305 ff.; Beloch: *Gr. Gesch.* 1. 1 (1924), p. 360.

[76] The régime of the Thirty Tyrants and of the Ten Commissioners who followed them occurred in 404-3 B.C., and was set up by Lysander. The arbitrary character of their rule, as indicated by Aristotle *(Const. of the Athenians*, 35. 4; 36. 2, ed. Sandys, 1912, where the notes give many other references), justifies Cicero's description of their rule as *consensus et factio*. See E. Meyer: *Gesch. des Alt.* 5 (1902), pp. 18 ff.

XXIX. SCIPIO: ....a veritable scoundrel [comes to the front;] and from this condition of the state there may arise an aristocracy or a tyrannical government by a party or a monarchy or, quite frequently, even a democracy.[77] And likewise it often happens that from this last type there grows up one of those forms of state which I have noted before. For there is a remarkable rotation and, if I may say so, cycle of changes in the life of states. It is the business of a philosopher to understand the order in which these changes occur; but to foresee impending modifications, and at the same time to pilot the state, to direct its course, and to keep it under control, is the part of a great statesman and a man of all but godlike powers.[78] There is, accordingly, a fourth kind of commonwealth which, in my opinion, should receive the highest approval, since it is formed by the combination, in due measure, of the three forms of state which I described as original.[79]

XXX. LAELIUS: I know, Africanus, that you prefer this composite type of state, for I have often heard you say so. But still, if there is no objection, I should like to know which of the three unmixed kinds of state you consider the best. For it will be of some use to know.........

(The first leaf of the tenth quaternion is missing)

XXXI. SCIPIO: ....and every state varies according to the character and inclination of its sovereign.[80] Consequently, no state except one in which the people have supreme power provides a habitation for liberty, than which surely

---

[77] The lacuna which precedes this sentence prevents us from understanding with certainty the relation which the sentence bears to Cicero's theory of constitutional cycles. It would appear that the "scoundrel" (taeterrimus) refers to the tyrant; and that the "tyrannical government by a party" refers to the Thirty Tyrants mentioned at the end of the preceding chapter.

[78] Cf. Aristotle: Politics, 1308 a 33 ff.; Polybius: 38. 21. 3.

[79] The locus classicus on the composite type of state is Polybius: 6. 3. 7 ff.; see also Aristotle: Politics, 1265 b 33 ff.; Newman: The Politics of Aristotle, 2 (1887), p. xiii; esp. Cambridge Ancient History, 6 (1927), pp. 532 ff.

[80] With this compare Aristotle's statement that a constitution is an arrangement of magistracies, especially the highest (Politics, 1278 b 9 ff.). Following the question put by Laelius at the end of the preceding chapter, Scipio states the arguments in favor of each of the unmixed kinds of state, beginning with democracy.

nothing can be sweeter. But if liberty is not equally enjoyed by all the citizens, it is not liberty at all.[81] And yet, how can all citizens have an equal share in liberty—I pass over the citizens in a monarchy, for there, of course, the subjection of the people is neither concealed nor questionable—but even in those states in which all men are nominally free? They do, of course, cast their votes; they elect the civil and military officials; their suffrages are solicited for purposes of election and legislation. Nevertheless, the powers which they bestow they would have to bestow, even against their will; and they do not possess the powers which others seek to obtain from them. For they have no share in military commands, or in advisory councils, or in special jury panels.[82] These offices are in fact reserved to men of ancient family or to men of wealth. But in a free people, as at Rhodes or at Athens, there is no citizen who [is not eligible to all the offices of state][83]........

(The third leaf of the tenth quaternion is missing)

XXXII. SCIPIO: [The advocates of democracy] affirm that, [when] one man or a few men become wealthier and more powerful than the other citizens, their pride and arrogance give rise [to special privileges], because the inactive and the weak give way and submit to the pretensions of the rich.[84] So long, however, as the people actually retain their power, these thinkers hold that no form of government is better, more liberal, or more prosperous, since the people have control over legislation, the administration of justice, the making of war and peace, the concluding of treaties, and over the civil status

---

[81] See Cic. *de rep.* 2. 23 (end), below, and note.

[82] Cicero apparently refers to the fact that at Rome the possession of *nobilitas* (see note 22 on ch. 6, above) was usually necessary if a man aspired to important political offices or to a military career.

[83] If our reconstruction of the meaning of the sentence be correct, Cicero's statement is accurate, generally speaking, for Athens, though there were some exceptions. On Rhodes cf. Cic. *de rep.* 3. 35, below, and for a general treatment of the Rhodian constitution see Gilbert: *Gr. Staatsalt.* 2 (1885), pp. 174 ff. Aristotle mentions the eligibility of all citizens to magistracies and to jury service as typical of democracy, and election by all or by lot as the democratic mode of filling offices: see *Politics*, 1300 a 31 ff.; 1301 a 11 ff.

[84] For Aristotle also the fundamental difference between democracy and oligarchy lies not in the number of rulers but in the contrary interests of the rich and poor; see *Politics*, 1279 b 11 ff.

and property of each individual citizen.[85] This, according to
their view, is the only form of government which can properly
be called a commonwealth, that is, the people's affair; and
therefore, while there are many instances where the people's
affair is freed from the yoke of kings and patricians, there is
none of a free people's demanding a king or an aristocratic
form of government. They assert, moreover, that it is not
right for democracy in general to be condemned because an
uncontrolled populace has defects; that, so long as a people is
harmonious and subordinates everything to its safety and freedom, there is no form of government less subject to revolution
or more stable; and that the kind of state in which harmony
is most easily attained is one in which the interests of all the
citizens are the same.[86] Dissension, as they hold, arises from
diversity of interests, whenever the well-being of some is contrary to the well-being of others. Consequently, when the
government was in the hands of aristocrats, the form of the
state has never remained stable. Still less has this been the
case with monarchies, for, in Ennius' words,

> In a kingdom there is no sacred fellowship or trust.

Since, then, law is the bond that holds political society together,[87] and since equality of rights is a part of law, by what
principle of right can an association of citizens be held together, when the status of these citizens is not equal? For,
if it is not thought desirable that property should be equally
distributed,[88] and if the natural capacities of all men cannot
possibly be equal, yet certainly all who are citizens of the
same commonwealth ought to enjoy equal rights in their mu-

---

[85] See Polybius: 6. 14. 3 ff., where the author, in enumerating the
democratic elements of the tripartite Roman constitution, mentions among
the powers of the people those here described as characteristic of democracy.

[86] Compare Plato: *Republic*, 461 e ff.

[87] See Aristotle's argument (*Politics*, 1286 a 7 ff.) that law should
be supreme in the state; also *op. cit.* 1292 a 32; 1295 a 14 ff.

[88] See Aristotle's criticism of various plans for equalizing property:
Politics, 1266 a 37 ff.; also Cic. *de off.* 2. 21. 73. For Aristotle also legislation implies the equality in birth and power of those who are to be
subject to the law; see *Politics*, 1284 a 11 ff.

tual relations. What, indeed, is a state, if it is not an association of citizens united by law?[89].........

(The sixth leaf of the tenth quaternion is missing)

XXXIII. SCIPIO: ....in fact, [the advocates of democracy] do not think that the other forms of government deserve even the names by which they would be called. Why, indeed, should I apply the word king—a name which belongs properly to Jupiter the Most High—to a human being who is greedy for lordship and exclusive dominion and who is the slave-driver of an oppressed people? Should I not rather call him a tyrant? For mercy is as possible in a tyrant as cruelty in a king.[90] Accordingly, the only concern of the people is whether they are the slaves of a kindly or of a harsh master, since under this form of government they are inevitably the slaves of someone. Moreover, how was it that, at the time when Spartan political institutions were supposedly at their best, this famous people contrived to have only good and just kings, although they had to take as king anyone who happened to be born of the royal family? And as for aristocrats, who can tolerate those who have assumed this title, not as the result of popular grant but as the result of their own election? What, I ask, is the criterion by which your aristocrat is judged? Is it learning, or culture, or scholarly tastes, as I hear? When.........

(The eighth leaf of the tenth, and the first leaf of
the eleventh quaternion are missing)

XXXIV. SCIPIO: ....if a state [chooses its rulers] at haphazard, it will be overthrown as quickly as a ship will founder if its pilot is chosen by lot from among the passengers.[91] But if a free people chooses those to whose guid-

---

[89] Since a lacuna immediately follows the word *civium*, it is impossible to tell whether the sentence ends with that word; and indeed *civium* may belong to the following sentence which has been lost. For the idea see Cic. *de rep.* 1. 2; 25, above; 6. 13, below; *parad.* 4. 1. 27 ff.

[90] We follow the manuscript and translate *rex*.

[91] In the lacuna Cicero passes to the arguments for aristocracy. The reference in the first sentence following the lacuna is to election by lot and to Socrates' criticism of it. This criticism, which is mentioned in Xenophon (*Mem.* 1. 2. 9), was probably one of the grounds for the prosecution of Socrates. Until the end of the fourth century B. C., all

ance it will submit itself, and if it chooses for this purpose all its best citizens—provided, of course, that the people wish to be secure—surely, then, the safety of the state has been founded upon the wisdom of its ablest members. This is particularly true since nature has contrived to make the men who are superior in courage and ability rule over the weak, and the weak willing to submit themselves to the best.[92] This perfect relationship between men has been overthrown, according to the partizans of aristocracy, by the false notions that prevail about human excellence. For, as few men possess excellence, so few are able to recognize and judge it. Thus, being ignorant of its nature, the masses suppose that men of wealth, influence, and important family connections are the best. When, as a result of this error on the part of the commons, the wealth rather than the excellence of a few men has come to control the state, these leaders cling stubbornly to the title of aristocrats, utterly lacking though they may be in the substance of excellence. For riches and reputation and power, if devoid of wisdom and of moderation in conduct and in the exercise of authority, are characterized by shamelessness and insufferable arrogance. There is, indeed, no uglier kind of state than one in which the richest men are thought to be the best.[93]

Athenian magistrates were chosen by this method, with the exception of military commanders, certain financial officials, and a few others. See Gilbert: *Gr. Staatsalt.* 1 (1893), p. 240; Schoemann: *Gr. Alt.* 1 (1897), p. 432; Busolt: *Gr. Staatskunde,* 2 (1926), p. 1064; Headlam: *Election by Lot in Athens* (1891), *passim.* In fact, election by lot was so universal in popular governments of the Greek world that it was often regarded as the criterion of democracy. See Herod. 3. 80; Pseud. Xen. *Ath. pol.* 1. 2; Plato: *Republic,* 557 a; Aristotle: *Rhetoric,* 1365 b 32; *Politics,* 1317 b 17 ff.; Busolt: *Gr. Staatskunde,* 1 (1920), p. 420.

[92] The natural superiority of the wise is the foundation of Plato's theory of government, and the principle is stated in the *Laws* (690 a ff.). For Aristotle also the rule of reason is natural; see *Politics,* 1252 a 30 ff.; 1254 b 2 ff., where this is made the basis of his famous defense of slavery; 1293 b 38 ff. The inferior, whether in nature or in art, exists always for the sake of the better; see *ibid.* 1333 a 21. A similar type of reasoning appears in Cic. *de rep.* 3. 24 and 25. below, where it apparently has Cicero's approval, in spite of the discrepancy with his own theory of natural equality.

[93] It is to be noted, however, that Cicero's solution of the practical problem of giving the best men a controlling power in the state is a property qualification for the suffrage; see his account and apparent approval of the Servian constitution in *de rep.* 2. 22, below. In this

On the other hand, when excellence governs the common-wealth, what can be more glorious? For then he who rules over others is not himself the slave of any base desire; the requirements which he lays upon his fellow-citizens he has fulfilled himself; he does not impose upon the people laws which he does not himself obey;[94] he holds up his own life before his fellow-citizens as the law by which they may guide their lives. If one such man were able to accomplish effective-ly all the business of the state, there would be no need for others; and if the body of citizens could always discover this perfect ruler and agree in regard to him, no one would demand specially chosen leaders. The difficulty of determining policy wisely has caused the transfer of authority from the king to several persons; and, conversely, the ignorance and reckless-ness of the commons have caused it to pass from the many to the few. Thus, between the weakness inherent in a single ruler and the recklessness inherent in the many, aristocracy has come to hold a middle place. Nothing, in fact, can be more perfectly balanced; and as long as an aristocracy guards the state, the people are necessarily in the happiest con-dition, since they are free from all care and anxiety. Their ease has been put into the safe-keeping of others, who must protect it and take care that nothing arises to make the people believe that their interests are being neglected by their leaders.

Now the equal rights of which democracies are so fond cannot be maintained. Indeed, no matter how free and un-trammeled popular governments may be, they are still excep-tionally prone to confer many favors on many men, and show decided preferences in the matter of individuals and in the matter of high rank. And what is called equality is, in reality,

---

respect he is at one with Aristotle, whose best practicable state is one ruled by the middle class; see *Politics*, 1295 b 1 ff.; also Plato's second-best state in the *Laws*, 744 b ff.; 756 b ff.

[94] The view that a ruler is bound to respect law passed into the *corpus iuris civilis*: "Our authority depends upon the authority of law. And in fact, to subject the imperial authority to law is a greater thing than empire" (*cod.* 1. 14. 4; cf. 6. 23. 3). As a qualification of the principle that the emperor is *legibus solutus*, the doctrine became an important element in the political theory of the Roman lawyers, and it exerted a profound influence upon mediaeval political theory. See Carlyle: *Medi-aeval Political Theory*, 3 (1915), pp. 38 ff.; 137 ff.

extremely unequal. For when the same importance is attached to the high and the low—and in every community these two classes necessarily exist—that very equality is most unequal. Such a condition cannot arise in states that are governed by aristocracies.

Arguments of much this character, Laelius, and others of the same kind, are usually put forward by those who praise most highly the aristocratic form of government.

XXXV. LAELIUS: But of the three simple forms of state, Scipio, which do you especially approve?

SCIPIO: You frame your question well when you ask, "Which of the three" I especially approve, because I do not approve any one of them considered separately and by itself. I prefer rather the mixed form, which is a combination of all three, to any one taken by itself. Still, if I had to express preference for one of the unmixed forms, I should choose monarchy [[95]and accord it first place. In this kind of state] we find that the king is described as if he were a father, planning for his subjects as if they were his children, and zealously protecting them [but never reducing them to subjection. Thus it is much better for the weak and ignorant] to be guarded by the care of one man, who is at once the strongest and the best man in the state. There are, to be sure, the aristocrats, who claim that they do this better than the king, and assert that there would be greater wisdom in a number of men than in one, and withal the same justice and good faith. Finally, the people themselves declare loudly that they do not wish to obey either one man or several. Nothing, they say, is sweeter than freedom, even to wild beasts; and no citizen possesses freedom when he is subject either to a king or to an aristocracy.

Thus I prefer monarchy for the love which the king bears to his subjects; aristocracy for its wisdom in counsel; and democracy for its freedom. When I compare them, I find it hard to decide which feature we desire the most.

LAELIUS: I suppose so, but the rest of the subject can hardly be developed if you leave this point unsettled.

---

[95] The Vatican manuscript is mutilated at this point; we base our translation on Mai's supplement.

XXXVI. Scipio: Then let us imitate Aratus, for when he addresses himself to treat an important subject, he thinks it necessary to begin with Jupiter.

Laelius: What has Jupiter to do with it, or what resemblance does this discussion bear to Aratus' poem?

Scipio: This resemblance: it is proper for us to begin our discourse with him who all men, learned and unlearned alike,[96] agree is the sole king of all gods and men.

Laelius: But why?

Scipio: Why do you suppose, except for the reason that is before your very eyes? It may be that the rulers of states, with an eye to the practical side of life, created this belief in order that it might be thought that there was one king in heaven, who, as Homer says, moved all Olympus with his nod and was considered both king and father of all creatures. In this case the belief finds powerful support and a cloud of witnesses, if we may so describe all the witnesses in the world, in the circumstance that all peoples in decrees—passed of course by their rulers—have expressed their agreement that nothing is superior to monarchy, since they believe that all the gods are ruled by a single divinity. Or, on the other hand, it may be that the belief rests, as we have been taught, upon the errors of ignorant men and is like the myths. Nevertheless, let us hear the views of those whom I may call the common teachers of educated men, who see with their eyes, as it were, those things which we scarcely know by hearsay.

Laelius: And who are the men you refer to?

Scipio: Those who by their investigations into natural philosophy have come to the conclusion that the whole world [is governed] by [a single] soul. . . . . . .[97]

(The eighth leaf of the eleventh, and the first leaf
of the twelfth quaternion are missing)

---

[96] We read, with Halm, *pariter* for *expoliri*.

[97] For the completion of the sentence see Cic. *de n. d.* 1. 14. 37. Scipio gives three theories of the belief in divine providence: (1) It may have been invented by statesmen for political purposes; see Polybius: 6. 56. 6 ff. (2) It may be a popular myth—the Epicurean view that all religious belief is superstition and that the gods do not concern themselves with human affairs; see Lucretius: 2. 646 ff.; 3. 978 ff.; Hicks: *Stoic and Epicurean* (1910), pp. 298 ff. (3) It may be a philosophical conclusion—the view of the Stoics, who hold that nature is governed by

*It is a long task to summarize the views about Almighty
God held by Thales or Pythagoras or Anaximenes[98] in ancient
times, or more recently by the Stoics, Cleanthes, Chrysippus,
and Zeno,[99] or among the Romans by Seneca,[100] who followed
the Stoics, and by Cicero himself. For all of these attempted
to define the nature of God, and also asserted that the world
was ruled by God alone. They said, moreover, that God himself was not subject to any natural law since all natural law
proceeded from him.*
Lactantius: epit. 4. 3

XXXVII. SCIPIO: .... but if you like, Laelius, I shall give
you witnesses that are neither too ancient nor at all uncivilized.

LAELIUS: That is the kind of witness I want.

SCIPIO: Do you note that our own city has been less than
four hundred years without kings?[101]

LAELIUS: That is a fact. It is less than four hundred years.

SCIPIO: And is four hundred years a very long time in the
life of a city or state?

LAELIUS: In fact, the state is hardly full grown in that
time.

SCIPIO: Then within these four hundred years there was a
king at Rome?

---

the world-soul. Cicero presents the Stoic view at length in the second
book of *de n. d.*; see also *de rep.* 1. 13, above, and note. This threefold
interpretation of religion is ascribed to Quintus Mucius Scaevola the
Pontifex by Augustine (*de civ.* 4. 27; 6. 5) on the authority of Varro.
Since Cicero studied law under Scaevola, he probably learned of the
theory from him; see Cic. *de am.* 1. 1. Scaevola in turn probably got it
from Panaetius; see Zeller: *Phil. d. Griech.* 3. 1 (1923), pp. 586 ff.

[98] Anaximenes of Miletus (second half of the sixth century B.C.)
followed Anaximander as head of the Ionian School. The fragments
are collected by Diels: *Vorsokratiker*, 1 (1912), pp. 22 ff.

[99] Zeno of Citium founded the Stoic School at Athens about the end of
the fourth century B.C.; see Ferguson: *Hellenistic Athens* (1911), p.
129. Cleanthes (331—c.233 B.C.) succeeded him as head of the school,
and was in turn succeeded by Chrysippus (281-78—208-5 B.C.). See
Hicks: *Stoic and Epicurean* (1910), pp. 4 ff.; the fragments of the early
Stoics are collected by Von Arnim: *Stoicorum veterum fragmenta*, 4
vols., 1921-4.

[100] Lucius Annaeus Seneca (c. 4 B.C.-65 A.D.) was perhaps the best
known of the Roman Stoics; see Dill: *Roman Society from Nero to
Marcus Aurelius* (1919), pp. 294 ff.; Arnold: *Roman Stoicism* (1911),
pp. 113 ff.

[101] The traditional date for the expulsion of the kings was 510 B.C.

LAELIUS: Yes, and a proud one, too.[102]

SCIPIO: How was it before his time?

LAELIUS: Before him there was a very just king, and so on back to Romulus, who was king six hundred years ago.

SCIPIO: Then it was not very long ago that even Romulus was king?

LAELIUS: Not at all. Greece was already growing old in his time.

SCIPIO: Tell me, now, surely Romulus was not a king of barbarians?

LAELIUS: If, as the Greeks say, every people is either Greek or barbarian, then I am afraid that he was a king of barbarians. But if we use the word to refer to manners rather than to language, then I deem the Romans to be no more barbarians than the Greeks.

SCIPIO: For the purpose in hand, we are interested not in their race but in their natural capacities. For if these men, who were both intelligent and comparatively modern, were willing to have kings, then the witnesses on whom I rely are neither too ancient nor uncivilized and barbarous.

XXXVIII. LAELIUS: I see, Scipio, that you are ready enough with your authorities; but for my part I, like any good judge, am more influenced by proofs than by witnesses.

SCIPIO: Very well, Laelius, take this proof drawn from your own feelings.

LAELIUS: What feelings?

SCIPIO: Those which you experienced if by any chance or at any time you felt yourself in a passion with someone.

LAELIUS: I have had that experience oftener than I should have liked.

SCIPIO: And when you are angry, do you let anger master your whole mind?

LAELIUS: No, I assure you. On the contrary, I imitate the famous Archytas of Tarentum, who, having gone to his country estate and having found that everything had been done contrary to his orders, said to his steward: "You good-for-

---

[102] This refers to Lucius Tarquinius Superbus. The just king mentioned below is Servius Tullius. See Cic. de rep. 2. 21; 25, below.

nothing fellow! I should have beaten the life out of you, if I were not so angry."[103]

SCIPIO: Excellent! Then Archytas rightly regarded anger —which is, of course, at odds with intelligence—as a sort of insurrection in the soul, and wished to quell it by reason. Now if to anger you add greed, the love of power and fame, and the lusts of the flesh, you see that, if there is a kind of royal power in the souls of men, it will be the dominion exercised by this one element, namely, reason. For reason is the best part of the soul; and so long as it is lord, there is no place for the lusts, for anger, or for any irrational impulse.[104]

LAELIUS: That is true.

SCIPIO: Do you then approve of a soul so regulated?

LAELIUS: There is indeed nothing of which I approve more.

SCIPIO: Then you would not approve, if the lusts of the flesh, which are without number, or the angry passions, should drive out reason and possess the entire soul?

LAELIUS: On the contrary, I should think that nothing was more wretched than such a soul or a man who had such a soul.

SCIPIO: Then you approve, if all the parts of the soul are subject to kingly rule, and if reason is their king?[105]

LAELIUS: Yes, such an arrangement I approve.

SCIPIO: Why, then, are you in doubt as to your conclusion about the state? If political power should be divided among several persons, you can immediately see that there will be no commanding authority, for an authority which is not a unit cannot exist.[106]

---

[103] This story is repeated in Cic. *Tusc.* 4. 36. 78, and Valerius Maximus: 4. 1. 1. It was a commonplace, for it was told also of Plato (Plutarch: *de liberis educandis*, 14. 10 d; Diog. L. 3. 39), and of Socrates (Seneca: *de ira*, 1. 15. 3).

[104] The analogy between the state and the soul is elaborately developed by Plato in the *Republic;* see especially 441 e ff., where reason is called the ruling part of the soul, as the wise are the natural rulers of the state. The analogy is implicit also in Stoic psychology, in which reason was often called king over the seven subordinate parts, and the perturbations were defined as movements of soul contrary to reason; see Diog. L. 7. 110; Cic. *Tusc.* 3. 11. 24; 4. 6. 11; 4. 21. 47; Arnold: *Roman Stoicism* (1911), ch. 11.

[105] See Aristotle: *Politics*, 1254 b 4 f., where it is said that reason rules the appetites with a royal rule.

[106] This sentence is apparently to be interpreted as an argument for

XXXIX. LAELIUS: But what difference, pray, is there between a single ruler or several, if justice exists in the several?

SCIPIO: Since I have found that the witnesses whom I have called do not influence you greatly, Laelius, I shall continue to use you as a witness in order to prove my case.

LAELIUS: Me? How will you do that?

SCIPIO: Not long ago when we were on your estate at Formiae, I noticed that you strictly charged your slaves to take their orders from one person only.

LAELIUS: Of course, from the steward.

SCIPIO: Well, now, when you are at home, do several persons manage your affairs?

LAELIUS: No; only one person manages my affairs.

SCIPIO: Surely no one except yourself rules your household?

LAELIUS: Of course not.

SCIPIO: Then do you not agree that in the state also the rule of an individual, provided it be just, is the best?

LAELIUS: You almost force me to agree with you.

XL. SCIPIO: You will be more ready to agree, Laelius, if I leave out of account such analogies as, for example, the fact that it is better to put a ship in charge of one pilot, or a sick man under the care of one physician, supposing, of course, that these men are worthy of their callings, than to entrust such matters to several persons, and if I go on to more important considerations.[107]

LAELIUS: What are the more important considerations that you refer to?

SCIPIO: Why, you see, do you not, that it was the insolence

---

monarchy as the best of the three simple forms of state. If Cicero discussed the division of authority in the composite state, which, following Polybius, he holds to be better than any of the simple forms and also exemplified by the Roman constitution, the passage has been lost. For a discussion of authority in general see Cic. *de leg.* 3. 1. 2 ff.

[107]As Cicero implies, such analogies were exceedingly common. They were probably derived mainly from Plato. For the analogy of the physician, see Plato: *Statesman*, 293 b; 295 c; 296 b; *Laws*, 720 a ff.; and Aristotle: *Politics*, 1324 b 29 ff. For that of the pilot see Plato: *Republic*, 488 a ff.; *Statesman*, 296 e ff.

and arrogance of one man, namely Tarquinius, which brought the name of king into detestation among the Romans? [108]

LAELIUS: I do indeed see it.

SCIPIO: Then you also see—and this is a topic which I think I shall elaborate in the course of the discussion—that, after the expulsion of Tarquinius, the people ran riot in an astonishing orgy of license. At that time innocent persons were driven into exile; the estates of many were confiscated; the consuls were established, holding office for only a year; the fasces were lowered before the people as a token of respect; appeals to the centuries were granted for all sorts of cases; the plebs seceded; and finally everything was so conducted that all power was in the hands of the people.

LAELIUS: It is exactly as you say.

SCIPIO: This condition, however, holds only in time of peace and quiet. For you may play the fool as long as you have nothing to fear, as on a ship [in calm weather] and often even in disease if it is not critical. But the passenger calls for a single skilled pilot when the seas begin suddenly to rise; and the invalid calls for a single doctor when his illness takes a turn for the worse. In the same way, our people in the peaceful course of civil affairs command and threaten the magistrates themselves, obstruct them, seek the aid of one against another, or carry an appeal from their decision to the centuries.[109] But in war the people obey their magistrates as if they were kings, for then their safety is of more moment than their mere whim.[110] In really serious wars, indeed, our people have decided that all military power should be in the hands of an officer who has no colleague and whose very name signifies the extent of his power. The word dictator is derived, indeed, from the fact that this magistrate is ap-

[108]Cicero deals at length with the expulsion of the Tarquinii and the ensuing constitutional changes in *de rep.* 2. 25 ff.

[109]For the significance of *appellatio* and *provocatio*, the two constitutional practices here alluded to, see Mommsen: *Röm. Staatsrecht*, 1 (1887) pp. 274 ff.; 3. 1 (1887), pp. 351 ff.; Cic. *de rep.* 2. 31, below.

[110]See Polybius:6.18.1-3. This extension of the magistrate's authority in time of war Cicero regards as essential to a good constitution; see *de leg.* 3. 3. 8.

pointed, but in our records you see, Laelius, that he is called the master of the people.[111]

LAELIUS: I see.

SCIPIO: Wisely, therefore, did our ancestors [provide for the appointment of such an officer].........

(The eighth leaf of the twelfth quaternion is missing)

XLI. SCIPIO: ....when a people has been deprived of a just king, "longing possesses their divine hearts," as Ennius says [when describing the people's feelings] after the death of an excellent king:

> Among themselves
> Thus men communed: O Romulus, O Romulus divine,
> How excellently didst thou, whom gods begot, guard
>   thy country!
> O father, O ancestor, O scion sprung from the gods!

Lord and master are names which the people never applied to those rulers whom they had justly obeyed; nor did they call them even kings. They called them guardians of their country or fathers or gods.[112] And not without reason, either, if we consider the next words of their apostrophe:

> Thou didst guide us onwards into the shores of light.

Life, renown, and glory, according to the people, were procured for them by the justice of the king. The same affectionate regard for kings would have continued in the hearts of subsequent generations, if the kings had retained the truly royal character. But you see that one king's injustice caused the total ruin of that form of commonwealth.

LAELIUS: I see indeed; and I am eager to learn the cycles of political change, both as they affect our state and as they affect every state.

---

[111] I.e., *dictator* from *dicitur*. Cicero *(de leg.* 3. 3. 9) says of the appointment of the dictator: "When there shall be a serious war or a civil uprising, if the senate so decree, one magistrate shall possess for not more than six months all the authority which the two consuls normally possess. He shall be appointed with favorable auspices and shall be the master of the people. To command the cavalry he shall have an inferior colleague with authority corresponding to that of the praetor." See Mommsen: *Röm. Staatsrecht*, 2. 1 (1887), pp. 141 ff.; Greenidge: *Roman Public Life* (1911), pp. 191 ff.

[112] Aristotle attributed the primitive kingship to the pre-eminent virtue of one man; see *Politics*, 1285 b 4 ff. See also Polybius: 6. 5. 7-8.

XLII. SCIPIO: After I have set forth my views about the form of state that I consider the best, I must certainly discuss with considerable care the revolutions that occur in governments,[113] though I do not think that my favorite type of mixed government will readily be subject to them.

In a kingdom, however, the first and most certain change is that which occurred under Tarquinius: when the king ceases to rule justly, the royal form of government is straightway destroyed. The king becomes a tyrant; and tyranny, though closest to the best type, is the worst of all states. If, as is usually the case, the tyrant is crushed by the leading citizens, the commonwealth enjoys the second of the three forms of government I mentioned. For there is a certain regal or paternal element in the council of chief men who study to serve well the people's needs. If, on the other hand, the people themselves have slain or driven out the tyrant, they govern with considerable restraint so long as they are prudent and wise. Taking pride in their achievement, they are willing to guard the commonwealth which they have established. But let us suppose that the people have revolted against a just king or have deprived such a ruler of his royal power, or again let us suppose—what more frequently happens—that they have even tasted the blood of the foremost citizens and have made the whole state subserve their lust. If this happens—and, believe me, there is no sea so hard to calm and no fire so hard to check as the vengeance of the unrestrained mob—then that condition exists which Plato vividly describes. I wish that I could render it adequately into Latin. It is hard to do, but I shall try it.

XLIII. "Once the insatiable gullet of the people is parched with a thirst for freedom[114] and once the thirsty populace has been led by its bad servants to drain draughts, not of decently blended, but of undiluted freedom, they are continually cen-

---

[113] See Cic. *de rep.* 2. 25 ff., below. The most important parallel passages on the cycle of constitutions are Plato: *Republic*, 545 ff.; Aristotle: *Politics*, 1304 b 17 ff.; Polybius: 6. 5. 4 ff.: See Introduction, pp. 57 ff.

[114] This passage, which purports to be a translation, is really a paraphrase of Plato: *Republic*, 562 c ff.

suring and accusing and incriminating their magistrates and leaders; and unless the latter supinely yield and grant freedom in generous measure, the people call them masters, kings, and tyrants." I feel sure that you are familiar with this passage.

LAELIUS: Perfectly familiar.

SCIPIO: Then Plato continues: "Those who obey their leaders are harassed by such a democracy and reproached with being willing slaves. Magistrates who are willing to perform their public duties as if they were merely private citizens, and those private citizens who would do away with all distinctions which mark off the magistrates, are extolled to the skies and rewarded with honors. Thus, it inevitably comes about that under such a government everything is full of liberty. No authority is exercised in any private home, and the evil extends even to the dumb animals, until finally the father fears his son, the son slights his father, and every feeling of respect is gone. Thus men are indeed free. There is no distinction between citizen and foreigner; teachers fear their pupils and flatter them; pupils scorn their teachers; the young affect the gravity of age; and old men revert to youthful pranks in order not to be tiresome and displeasing to the young. Even slaves conduct themselves with undue freedom; and wives enjoy the same rights as their husbands. And even the dogs and the horses and the asses live in such an atmosphere of freedom that they run on us and make us give them the right of way. From this boundless license," Plato continues, "the following result inevitably follows: so sensitive and effeminate do the feelings of the citizens become that, if the least restraint is applied to them, they are enraged and cannot endure it. Then they begin to ignore the laws also, and so are completely without any master."

XLIV. LAELIUS: You have exactly rendered Plato's words.

SCIPIO: This extreme of license, which is their only idea of freedom—to return now to Plato[115]—is a sort of root from which the tyrant springs and, if I may say so, is born. Even

---

[115]"In the following paragraph Cicero paraphrases several sentences from Plato: *Republic*, 563 e—566 b.

as the extreme power of the aristocracy brings about the downfall of the aristocracy, so freedom itself punishes with slavery a people whose freedom has no bounds. Thus, every extreme—in climate, in fertility, or in health—which has been too pleasant, passes generally into the opposite extreme. This happens especially in the case of states, where the extreme of freedom becomes, both for peoples and for individuals, the extreme of slavery. Thus, from perfect freedom arises the tyrant, bringing with him arbitrary and oppressive subjection.[116] Out of the untamed, or better still, the bestial populace, there is generally chosen a champion to guide them against their former leaders, who by this time have been overwhelmed and driven from their positions of authority. Overreaching and vicious, such a champion wantonly assails men who have often earned the gratitude of the state. He curries favor with the people by giving them the property of others as well as his own. Because he is still a private citizen, and because the insecurity of his position makes him afraid, great powers are granted him and are never resigned; and, as happened with Peisistratus at Athens, his person is protected even by armed guards.[117] The final stage is reached when the tyrant tyrannizes over the very citizens who have elevated him to his tyranny.

If the tyrant is overthrown by citizens with aristocratic leanings, as often happens, constitutional government is revived. If, on the other hand, political adventurers cause his downfall, there develops that turbulent oligarchy which is merely another form of tyranny. This kind of oligarchical state often arises also from the good form of aristocracy, when some lack of rectitude has corrupted the leaders themselves. The government is thus bandied about like a ball: tyrants re-

---

[116] See Cic. de rep. 2. 26, below. Cicero's treatment of the tyrant, transmitted through Isidore of Seville (etym. 9. 3; sent. 3. 47 ff.), exerted a profound influence upon mediaeval political theory; see John of Salisbury: policraticus, 4. 1; 8. 17 (ed. Webb. pp. 513 b ff.; 777 c ff.); Carlyle: Mediaeval Political Theory, 1(1903), p. 172; 3(1915), p. 126.

[117] For Peisistratus see Herodotus:1. 59-64; Thucydides: 6. 53. 3 ff.; Aristotle: Const. of the Athenians, 14-16; Beloch: Gr. Gesch. 1. 1 (1924), pp. 368 ff.; Busolt: Gr. Gesch. 2 (1895), pp. 295 ff.; Grote: History of Greece, 4(1870), pp. 29 ff.

ceive it from kings; from tyrants it passes either to aristocrats or to the people; and from the people to oligarchs or tyrants. The same form of government is never long retained.[118]

XLV. In view of these facts, monarchy is, in my judgment, far the best of the three simple types of state. But even monarchy will be excelled by the kind of state that is formed by an equal balancing and blending of the three unmixed types. For I hold it desirable, first, that there should be a dominant and royal element in the commonwealth; second, that some powers should be granted and assigned to the influence of the aristocracy; and third, that certain matters should be reserved to the people for decision and judgment. Such a government insures at once an element of equality, without which the people can hardly be free, and an element of strength. For, whereas the three forms of simple state which we mentioned first readily lapse into the perverted forms opposed to their respective virtues—tyranny arising from monarchy, oligarchy from aristocracy, and turbulent ochlocracy from democracy— and whereas the types themselves are often discarded for new ones, this instability can hardly occur in the mixed and judiciously blended form of state, unless its leaders fall into exceptional degradation. There is, indeed, no cause for change when each individual is firmly set in his proper place, and when there is no inferior position into which he may rapidly decline.

XLVI. But I am afraid, Laelius and my other wise and gracious friends, that if I continue longer in this strain you will find my discourse more after the manner of a dogmatic pedagogue than in the spirit of a fellow-student of politics. I shall accordingly enter at once into a discussion of those topics which are familiar ground to all of you but about which questions were put to me some time ago. It is, indeed, my judgment, opinion, and conviction that of all forms of government there is none which for organization, distribution of power, and respect for authority is to be compared with that constitution which our fathers received from their ancestors

---

[118] On the cycle of constitutions see Introduction, pp. 57 ff.

and have bequeathed to us. If you approve this course, I shall comply with the wish, which you really expressed, to hear from me facts which you knew yourselves; and I shall show at once the character and supreme excellence of our state. The Roman commonwealth will be the model; and to it I shall apply, if I can, all that I must say about the perfect state. If I can persevere in this course to the end, I feel that I shall have more than completely performed the task which Laelius assigned me.

XLVII. LAELIUS: Your task it is, Scipio, and yours alone. Who, in fact, could speak better than you either about the customs of our ancestors—since your own ancestors were so distinguished—or about the best form of state—in which, if we ever get it, no one indeed could play a more distinguished rôle than you play even now—or about policies aimed to meet the future—since you have banished the two terrors that threatened our city and have provided for its future welfare?[119]

FRAGMENTS OF BOOK I THAT CANNOT BE PLACED

1. [I do not write] for the most learned.
I do not wish Manius Persius to read these lines,
But I do desire Junius Congus to read them.[120]

2. Thus, since our country confers more benefits upon us and is a more venerable parent than he who has begot us, assuredly the gratitude we owe her is greater than the debt we owe a father.[121]

---

[119] Scipio destroyed Carthage in 146 B.C., and brought the Numantine War to a successful close in 133 B.C.; see Cic. de rep. 1. 11, above, and note; de am. 3. 11.

[120] Pliny: hist. nat., praef. 7. We have omitted the remarks of Pliny which Ziegler prints. The words translated are a corrupt quotation from Lucilius which Pliny, in a passage of incomparable inanity, says was used by Cicero in his work on the Commonwealth. We may perhaps infer that Cicero borrowed the verses because he desired to show that his work was designed primarily not for scholars but for men of affairs. Congus was the author of a work on law; see Cichorius: Untersuchungen zu Lucilius (1908), pp. 121 ff. Gaius Lucilius (c. 180-103 B.C.) is very important in the history of satire. See Duff: Literary History of Rome (1914), pp. 234 ff.; Schanz: Gesch. d. röm. Lit. 1. 1 (1907), pp. 203 ff.

[121] Nonius, p. 426. 9. Cf. Cic. de rep. 1. 4, above, for the obligations of the individual to the state.

3. Nor would Carthage have possessed such power for almost six hundred years if she had been without wisdom in counsel and training in citizenship.[122]

4. Learn by all means, said he, this custom, interest, and mode of speech.[123]

5. Certainly, though all the discussions of philosophers contain abundant sources of excellence and knowledge, nevertheless I fear that, if their arguments be compared with the acts and accomplishments [of statesmen,] they will seem to have brought less profit to men's serious concerns than delight to their leisure.[124]

6. From which they were calling [him] away.[125]

---

[122] Nonius, p. 526. 8. For the Carthaginian constitution see Cic. *de rep.* 2. 23, below, and note.

[123] Nonius, p. 276. 6.

[124] Lactantius: *inst.* 3. 16. 5. See Cic. *de rep.* 1. 1 and 2, above.

[125] Arusianus Messius: *gram. Lat.* ed. Keil, 7.457.14. See Cic. *de rep.* 1. 2 (end), above.

BOOK II

I. [When he saw that they were all] eager to hear him, Scipio continued as follows:[1] The view that I am going to present to you is that of Cato the Elder. He was, as you know, a man whom I especially loved and greatly admired, and to whom I devoted myself implicitly in my youth, both because of the esteem in which he was held by my father and adoptive father, and also because of my own affection for him. Of his discourse I could never weary, so rich was his experience in public life, in which he had long engaged with conspicuous ability both at home and abroad; and so complete was the propriety of his speech and the charm and dignity of his manner. He displayed also the highest enthusiasm both for teaching and for learning. His life was in close accord with his mode of speech.

He often said that the form of our government excelled that of all other states because in the latter there had usually been individual law-givers each of whom had given laws and institutions to his own particular commonwealth. Thus there had been Minos in Crete, Lycurgus at Sparta, and at Athens, where the government had gone through many changes, there had been first Theseus, then Draco, then Solon, then Cleisthenes, then many others down to the skilled Demetrius of Phalerum, who had revived the state when it was in an exhausted and prostrate condition.[2] Our commonwealth, on the

---

[1]This book has no introduction in which Cicero spoke in his own person. The amount lost in the lacuna is only about thirty letters. We translate Mai's supplement.

[2]According to tradition Minos was the founder of the Cretan constitution (Schoemann: *Gr. Alt.* 1, 1897, p. 303; Beloch: *Gr. Gesch.* 1. 2, 1913, p. 258), and of the first sea-power in western Europe (Thucydides: 1.4.1). For Lycurgus, the reputed founder of the Spartan constitution, see Schoemann: *op. cit.*, pp. 227 ff.; Busolt: *Gr. Gesch.* 1 (1893), pp. 569 ff. Theseus, the mythical king of Athens, was reputed to have united the hamlets of Attica into the city-state; see Thucydides: 2. 15. 1; Aristotle: *Const. of the Athenians*, fr. 2; Beloch: *op. cit.* 1. 1 (1924), pp. 206 ff. Draco (c. 621 B.C.) first reduced the laws to writing; see Aristotle: *op. cit.* 41. 2, a passage of doubtful authenticity; Beloch: *op. cit.* pp. 351 ff. A constitutional system is falsely attributed to him; see Aristotle:

other hand, was the product not of one genius but of many;
it was not established within the lifetime of one man but was
the work of several men in several generations.[3] For, as Cato
said, there had never been a genius great enough to comprehend everything, and all the ability in the world, if concen-
trated in a single person, could not at one time possess such
insight as to anticipate all future needs, without the knowledge conferred by experience and age.

Accordingly, I shall now follow Cato's custom and rehearse
the "origins" of the Roman people, for I am glad to employ his
very word.[4] And I shall more easily accomplish the task set me,
if I picture our commonwealth at the moment of its birth, in
the course of its development, and then in the strength and
vigor of its maturity,[5] instead of arbitrarily creating an
imaginary state, as Socrates does in Plato's "Republic."

II. When they had all expressed their approval, Scipio
continued: Can we mention any state ever established which
has had a beginning so famous and well-known as the founding
of our state by Romulus? He was the son of Mars—for we
may grant so much to tradition, especially since it is a belief

op. cit. 4. 2 ff. Solon, archon in 594 B.C., reconstructed the Athenian
state both economically and politically; see Aristotle: op. cit. 5-12; Beloch: op. cit. pp. 363 ff. Cleisthenes remodeled the government in 508
B.C. and the year following by introducing a system of ten tribes, by
instituting the generalship, and by transforming the council into a body
representative of the demes; see Aristotle: op. cit. 20-22; Beloch: op. cit.
pp. 395 ff. Demetrius of Phalerum was the Macedonian regent from
318-317 to 308-307 B.C.; he reorganized the state on the basis of a
property qualification; see Ferguson: Hellenistic Athens (1911), pp. 39 ff.
[3]This is an interesting exception to the usual tendency of antiquity
to attribute institutions to a specific law-giver. It cannot be said, however, that Cicero's adoption of a more historical point of view had much
effect upon his theory. See Introduction, pp. 63 f., above.
[4]A reference to Cato's origines; see Cic. de rep. 1. 1, above, and note.
[5] Since the history of the kings belongs chiefly to the realm of myth,
and since Cicero's narrative is the earliest consecutive version extant,
there is no need to do more than indicate the later accounts. In Livy
(59 B.C.-17 A.D.) the topic is covered in Book 1; see Duff: Literary
History of Rome (1914), p. 637. In Dionysius of Halicarnassus, who
came to Rome in 30 B.C., it occurs in books 1-4 of the antiquitates
Romanae; see Christ-Schmid: Gesch. d. gr. Lit. 2. 1(1920), pp. 466;
472 ff. In Diodorus Siculus, who also lived under Augustus, it is in
book 8, fr. 2-6; 14-15; 25-26; 31; and in book 10, fr. 1-2; 20-22. For
the general question of early Roman history see Mommsen: Röm. Gesch.
1(1912), pp. 464 ff. (Eng. trans. 1, pp. 457 ff.)

both sanctioned by age and also wisely fostered by our ancestors, that men who have deserved well of their country should be regarded as of the race of the gods and not merely of godlike powers.[6] Let us then grant that Romulus was descended from Mars. According to the story, he was exposed with his brother Remus on the banks of the Tiber at the command of Amulius, king of Alba, who feared for the security of his kingdom. Near the Tiber he was suckled by a beast of the forest, was nurtured by shepherds, and was reared in the toilsome labor of the countryside. When he had grown to man's estate, he so far excelled all of his fellows, both in bodily strength and in courage, that all who then inhabited the region where the city now stands were willing and content to obey him.[7] When he had made himself leader of their forces—to come now from legend to fact—he is said to have conquered Alba Longa, a strong and powerful city of those days, and to have slain King Amulius.

III. After winning this glory he is said to have first conceived the idea of founding a city, sanctioned by divine omens, and of establishing a powerful commonwealth. The location that he chose for the city—and this must always be a principal concern to anyone who aims to found an enduring state —was unbelievably favorable. For he did not move his city down to the coast, a step very easy for him to take with the forces at his command, either by invading the territory of the Rutuli or of the Aborigines,[8] or by himself founding a city at the mouth of the Tiber, where King Ancus many years later located a colony.[9] But with singular foresight Romulus saw and divined that a location upon the seaboard was not the most advantageous for cities intended to enjoy permanence and imperial sway, chiefly because maritime cities are exposed

---

[6] On the pious falsehood as part of the legislator's duty see Plato: *Republic*, 389 b; 414 b; 459 c; *Laws*, 663 d.

[7] Cf. Polybius: 6. 5. 7 ff., where the origin of the kingship is described in the same way.

[8] The Rutuli occupied a portion of the coast of Latium about the town of Ardea. The Aborigines were a mythical people supposed to have settled in Latium; see Dion. Hal. *ant. Rom.* 1. 9. 3 f.

[9] This is a reference to the founding of Ostia; see Cic. *de rep.* 2. 18, below; Polybius: 6. 11 a. b; Festus: s. v. *quaeso* and *Ostiam.*

to dangers both numerous and impossible to foresee.[10] A city surrounded on all sides by land receives many warnings of an enemy's approach, whether his coming be anticipated or not, such as the crashing [of the forest] and even the noise [of marching troops]. No enemy, in fact, can arrive by land without enabling us to know both his hostile intent and who he is and whence he comes. On the contrary, an enemy who comes by ships over the sea may arrive before anyone can suspect his coming; and indeed, when he appears, he does not show by any signs who he is, whence he comes, or even what he wants. Finally, there is no mark by which it is possible to judge and determine whether such a stranger is friend or foe.

IV. In addition, cities located on the sea are subject to certain corrupting influences and to moral decline, for they are affected by alien forms of speech and by alien standards of conduct. Not only foreign merchandise is imported but also foreign codes of morals, with the result that nothing in the ancestral customs of a maritime people can remain unchanged. The inhabitants of the seaboard do not remain at home but are tempted far from their cities by the hope and dream of swiftly gained wealth; and even when they remain at home in body, they are exiles and wanderers in spirit. Nothing, in fact, contributed more to the gradual decline and final overthrow of Carthage and Corinth than this tendency of their citizens to wander over the face of the earth, and the greed for maritime trade which had caused them to abandon the pursuits of agriculture and war.[11] Furthermore, many temp-

---

[10]With Cicero's treatment of the disadvantages of a maritime situation compare the similar discussion in Plato: *Laws*, 704 b ff., where Plato argues that the city must be at least eighty stadia from the sea; and in Aristotle: *Politics*, 1327 a 10 ff., where the disadvantages rather than the advantages of a location on the sea are stressed. The conclusions of these philosophers are probably colored by the fact that the Piraeus at Athens and the Athenian navy were strongly inclined towards democracy; see Pseud. Xen. *Ath. pol.* 1. 2; Aristotle: *Politics*, 1303 b 10; Thucydides: 8. 72; 74-78.

[11]This explanation is not correct. It is probable that Cicero accepts this theory because of his desire to dissuade the Romans from devoting themselves to commerce and consequently neglecting the service of the state. For the causes leading to the fall of Carthage see Rostovtzeff: *Social and Economic History of the Roman Empire* (1926), pp. 21 f.; Mommsen: *Röm. Gesch.* 2 (1908), pp. 22 ff. (Eng. trans. 3, pp. 22 ff.);

tations to luxurious living, ruinous to states, are offered by the sea, either in the form of piracy or of trade. And even the very charm of a situation on the sea brings with it the snares of many extravagant and enervating desires.

What I have said of Corinth may probably be said with perfect truth of all Greece. Indeed, practically all of the Peloponnesus is on the seaboard, and there is no people, except the Phliasians, whose territory does not touch the sea.[12] And outside the Peloponnesus, the Aenianes, the Dorians, and the Dolopians are the only peoples that live inland.[13] Why need I mention the Greek islands? They are surrounded by the sea and almost float—a description which applies no less to the customs and institutions of the states which existed on them. This, as I said above, is the condition in the mother land of Greece. In the case of the colonies which the Greeks founded in Asia, Thrace, Italy, Sicily, and Africa, is there a single one, except Magnesia,[14] that is not washed by the sea?[15] Thus it appears that the coast of Greece formed, as it were, a fringe about the territory of the barbarians, while of the barbarians

---

Heitland: *Roman Republic* (1909), sect. 589 ff.; Frank: *Roman Imperialism* (1914), pp. 234; 285. In the case of Corinth see Mommsen: *op. cit.* p. 49 (Eng. trans. 3, pp. 47 f.); Ferguson: *Hellenistic Athens* (1911), p. 329.

[12] The Phliasians were the inhabitants of Phlius, a small tract in the Peloponnesus southwest of Corinth. For his information concerning the topography of the Peloponnesus Cicero relied on Dicaearchus (c. 285 B.C.); see Cic. *ad Att.* 6. 2. 3; Hinze: *Quos scriptores Graecos Cicero in libris de re publica componendis adhibuerit* (1900), pp. 23 ff.

[13] Aenianes: the inhabitants of Aeniania, an inland district west of the Malian Gulf. Dorians: the inhabitants of Doris, a small inland tract, lying about one-third of the distance from the Malian Gulf to the Gulf of Crisa, with its northern boundary about five miles from Thermopylae. Dolopians: the inhabitants of Dolopia, a section of country bounded on the north and north-east by Thessaly, on the south-east and south by Aeniania, on the south-west by Aetolia, and on the west by Amphilochia.

[14] There were two cities in Asia Minor named Magnesia, one near the Meander River half way between Miletus and Ephesus, and the other on the Hermus River northeast of Smyrna.

[15] For the general topic of early Greek colonization, which occurred in the period from the twelfth to the ninth centuries B.C., see Busolt: *Gr. Gesch.* 1 (1893), pp. 262 ff.; Beloch: *Gr. Gesch.* 1. 1 (1924), pp. 133 ff. Cicero seems to have no knowledge of the great colonizing movement which developed under Alexander the Great, in the course of which countless cities were founded in inland locations. It is surprising that Cicero has so little knowledge of Alexander; see p. 162, below.

themselves, none was a seagoing people in ancient times except the Etruscans and the Carthaginians,[16] of whom the former sailed the sea for piracy and the latter for trade. Thus the obvious cause of the misfortunes and revolutions that befell Greece lies in the weaknesses inherent in maritime cities which I merely touched upon a moment ago.[17] There is, nevertheless, a great advantage which accompanies these weaknesses: a maritime situation permits you to import all the fruits of the earth into your city, and in turn you can export the products of your own city into whatever lands you wish.

V. How, then, could Romulus with a more divine insight have made use of the advantages of a situation on the sea, while avoiding its disadvantages, than by placing his city on the banks of a river that flows throughout the year with an even current and empties into the sea through a wide mouth? Thus, the city could receive by sea the products it needed and also dispose of its superfluous commodities. By the river the city could bring up from the sea[18] the necessaries of a civilized life as well as bring them down from the interior. Accordingly, it seems to me that even then Romulus foresaw that this city would sometime be the seat and home of supreme dominion. For practically no city situated in any other part of Italy could have been better able to command such economic advantages.

VI. Is there, moreover, anyone so unobservant as not to have marked and clearly appraised the natural defenses of our city? Romulus and the other kings planned the extent and lo-

---

[16] For the Etruscans see Beloch: *Gr. Gesch.* 1. 1 (1924), p. 244; for the Carthaginians see E. Meyer: *Gesch. d. Alt.* 3 (1915), p. 689. Cicero perhaps used the term *Poeni* as a generic name for the Phoenicians.

[17] Neither Thucydides (3. 82-83) nor Aristotle (*Politics*, 1302 a 16 ff.) mentions specifically a maritime location as one of the predisposing causes of factional strife.

[18] We read, with Niebuhr, *a mari subveheret.* It is interesting to observe that, in Cicero's eyes, the commercial importance of the Tiber is derived solely from the traffic passing up and down the stream. He does not mention the island and the bridge on the site of Rome which facilitated trade between the north and south of Italy. In the words of M. Homo (*L'Italie primitive et les debuts de l' imperialisme romain*, 1925, p. 102), "à ce point de contact du Tibre, où s' affrontaient depuis deux siècles les avant-gardes des peuples latin et étrusque, s'était constitué un centre de trafic important."

cation of the city's wall with such wisdom that it followed everywhere the brink of high steep hills; that the only access, between the Esquiline and the Quirinal, was blocked by a great rampart and girt with a deep ditch; and that the citadel, thus fortified, rose from an ascent steep on every side and above a precipitous cliff.[19] As a result, even at the terrible time when the Gauls attacked us, the citadel remained safe and uncaptured.[20] In addition, the location which he chose is plentifully watered with streams; and although in an unhealthful region, the site is healthful because of hills, which are themselves cooled by the breezes and which also give shade to the valleys.

VII. All this Romulus accomplished very quickly. He not only founded a city, which he commanded to be named Rome after himself, but he also followed out a plan for strengthening the new state which was novel and somewhat boorish, but which, in so far as it aimed to protect the resources of his kingdom and people, was the mark of a great man who even then looked far into the future. Romulus had decided to hold certain games at the time of the festival in honor of Consus.[21] They were to be celebrated in the circus in commemoration of the city's first anniversary. The young Sabine women of good family who had come to Rome to witness these games he ordered to be seized and given in marriage to the men of the best Roman families—an act which caused the Sabines to declare war against the Romans. After varying fortunes of war had made the outcome of the battle doubtful, Romulus made a treaty with Titus Tatius, king of the Sabines, upon the intercession of the very women who had been abducted. By the terms of this treaty he enrolled the Sabines in the state, allowed them to take part in the religious ceremonies, and shared his throne with their king.

---

[19] The citadel was the Capitoline, and the precipitous cliff was the Tarpeian Rock.

[20] In 387 B.C.; see Polybius: 1. 6. 2; 2. 18. 2; Boak: *History of Rome to 565 A.D.* (1922), p. 35; Mommsen: *Röm. Gesch.* 1(1912), pp. 331 ff. (Eng. trans. 1, pp. 329 ff.).

[21] Consus was an ancient rural divinity of fruitfulness, whose festivals, the Consualia, came on the twenty-first of August and the fifteenth of December; see Wissowa: *Religion und Kultus der Römer* (1912), pp. 201 ff.

VIII. After the death of Tatius, all authority reverted to Romulus. Acting in concert with Tatius, he had chosen for his royal council the chief men of the state, who were called "fathers" because of the affection in which they were held. He had also divided the people into three tribes[22]—named after himself, Tatius, and Lucumo, a comrade who had been killed in the battle with the Sabines—and into thirty curiae, named after the Sabine women who had been abducted and had afterward acted as mediators in the treaty of peace. These arrangements, to be sure, had been made during the lifetime of Tatius, but after his death Romulus went even farther in governing according to the advice and authority of the senate.

IX. As a result of this policy, he first came to see and accept the same fact which Lycurgus at Sparta had perceived a little while before, namely, that the individual authority inherent in monarchy is more successful in directing and ruling states when the king's prerogative is supplemented by the sanction of all the leading citizens.[23] Accordingly, Romulus was supported and protected by this council, which I may call the senate, and waged many wars with signal success against neighboring peoples. Though he brought back no plunder for himself, he did not fail to enrich his fellow citizens. Moreover, Romulus placed chief dependence upon the auspices—a procedure which continues even at the present day to contribute greatly to the safety of the state.[24] For he himself not only

---

[22]The Rhamnes, from Romulus; Titienses, from Tatius; and Luceres, from Lucumo. Livy (1. 13) regards these as divisions of the knights, a view implied also by Cicero: de rep. 2. 20, below. In fact, these tribes, if they ever existed, were obsolete so far as political function is concerned before Roman history begins. A threefold division, suggested by the word tribus and carried out in the thirty curiae and three hundred senators, appears to have had some significance in early Roman history; see Botsford: Roman Assemblies (1909), pp. 2 ff.

[23]This seems to be an allusion to the fact that at Sparta the kings were bound by the council's advice. For the Spartan constitution see Cic. de rep. 2. 28, below, and note.

[24]Every important act of Roman life, both public and private, was conceived to depend upon preserving a right relation with the gods, and this right relation was manifested by favorable auspices. Accordingly, the auspicia and the imperium were inseparably connected as the divine and human side of every magistrate's authority. The right to take the auspices was an essential element of the constitutional competence of a Roman magistrate and an indispensable part of every function of govern-

founded the city after consulting the auspices—which was the beginning of the state—but he also chose one augur from each tribe to be his partner in taking the auspices at the initiation of all public business. He divided the common people among the leading men of the state as clients—a policy the great value of which I shall consider later.[25] Finally, he kept order not by inflicting corporal punishment but by imposing fines in sheep and cattle. For property then consisted in possession of herds or land—a condition which gave rise to the usual words for wealthy.[26]

X. Romulus reigned for thirty-seven years and set up these two important buttresses of the state, the auspices and the senate. Accordingly, his achievements were so great that, when he did not reappear after a sudden eclipse of the sun, he was thought to have been translated to the gods. Such fame no mortal could ever have attained if he had not been reputed to possess qualities of unusual excellence. And it is the more surprising in the case of Romulus, because all the other men who are said to have become gods lived in times when men were less well-informed, when the making of myths was easy, and when the ignorant were readily induced to believe in them.[27] Romulus, on the contrary, lived less than six hundred years ago, at a time when, as we see, letters and learning had already been long established and had banished barbarism and primitive delusions from the lives of men. For if, as is shown by the annals of the Greeks, Rome was founded in the second

ment; see Cic. de leg. 3. 3. 10; 3. 4. 11; see also Fowler: *Religious Experience of the Roman People* (1911), pp. 300 ff.; Botsford: *Roman Assemblies* (1909), ch. 5.

[25] In the extant portions of his work Cicero does not revert to the clients. For the nature of clientship see the various explanations in Mommsen: *Röm. Staatsrecht*, 3.1(1887), pp. 54 ff.; Pauly-Wissowa: *Realencyclopädie*, s. v *clientes*, esp. p. 24, line 51 ff.; Bouché-Leclercq: *Manuel des inst. romaines* (1886), pp. 8 ff.

[26] That is, *pecuniosi* from *pecus* (flock) and *locupletes* from *locus*.

[27] From what Cicero says here, we may infer that he was wholly ignorant of the deification of Alexander the Great, an event that did not occur in a benighted age; see Ferguson: "Legalized Absolutism en Route from Greece to Rome," *American Historical Review*, vol. 18 (1912), pp. 31 ff.; *Cambridge Ancient History*, 6(1927), pp. 398 ff.; 419 f.; 432 f.

year of the seventh Olympiad,[28] the life of Romulus falls within a period when Greece was already filled with poets and artists and when less credence was accorded myths unless the subjects were old. The first Olympiad was dated one hundred and eight years after Lycurgus began to draft his laws, though a confusion of names has led some to believe that the legislator was the same Lycurgus who established the Olympiads. Now Homer is placed some thirty years before the time of Lycurgus, even by those who make the shortest interval between them. It may thus be seen that Homer preceded Romulus by a great many years, so that there was hardly any longer an opportunity for myth-making, since by this time men were educated and the age itself was well-informed. In ancient times, indeed, quite crude myths sometimes passed for the truth; but the age of Romulus, of which I speak, was already so sophisticated that it rejected with mockery every impossible tale.[29]

[It is perfectly clear, moreover, that Hesiod,[30] though living many years after Homer, nevertheless antedated Romulus, since Stesichor]us,[31] who, according to some, was the son of Hesiod's daughter, was born a few years after the founding of the city. Stesichorus died the same year that Simonides[32] was born, namely, during the fifty-sixth Olympiad.

Thus it may be easily understood that the belief in the deification of Romulus obtained currency at a time when civilization had already been long established and when civilized ways

---

[28] That is, 751 B.C.; see Polybius:6. 11 a 2. Varro gives the date as 753 B.C. The confusion between King Lycurgus and the founder of the Olympiads, mentioned in the next sentence, goes back at least to Aristotle; see Plutarch: *Lycurgus*, 1.

[29] The Vatican manuscript is badly mutilated at this point. The last sentence of this paragraph has been recovered from Augustine: *de civ.* 22. 6. The first sentence in the following paragraph was suggested by Mommsen (*Rhein. Mus.* 15, 1860, pp. 165 ff.) and the two sentences after it were reconstructed by Niebuhr.

[30] For Hesiod of Ascra in Boeotia (c. 700 B. C.), the earliest of the Greek didactic poets and noted chiefly as the author of the *Works and Days* and the *Theogony*, see Christ-Schmid: *Gesch. d. gr. Lit.* 1 (1912), pp. 109 ff.

[31] Stesichorus of Mataurus in Sicily (c. 640-555 B. C.) was one of the chief Greek lyric poets; see Christ-Schmid: *op. cit.* pp. 210 ff.

[32] Simonides of Ceos (556-468 B.C.) also was one of the chief lyric poets; see Christ-Schmid: *op. cit.* pp. 217 ff.

were practiced and known. Yet Romulus truly possessed such powers of mind and character that men accepted the story told by Proculus Julius, a mere rustic, although for many generations before they had refused to accept similar stories told about any other human being. For Proculus, at the instigation of the senators, who wished thus to free themselves from the imputation of having caused the death of Romulus, is said to have declared in a public meeting that he had himself seen Romulus on the hill now called the Quirinal, that Romulus had commanded him to lay a proposal before the people for building a shrine in his honor on the Hill, and that he had said that he was a god and was called Quirinus.[33]

XI. Do you perceive, then, that one man by his wisdom founded a new people, and not leaving it like an infant mewling in the cradle, raised it to boyhood and almost to manhood's estate?

LAELIUS: In truth we do perceive it, and we perceive also that you have begun the discussion in accordance with a new principle which is not to be found anywhere in the works of the Greeks. For Plato, the prince of philosophers, who has no superior as a writer, chose his own ground that he might construct a commonwealth according to his fancy. His was a noble state, no doubt, but incongruous with human life and customs.[34] The other Greek philosophers discussed the kinds of states and their principles but failed to treat any concrete example and type of the commonwealth.[35] You, it seems to me, are likely to combine the concrete with the general. You have so begun the discussion that you prefer attributing

---

[33] In reality Quirinus was a member of the original triune divinities (Jupiter, Mars, and Quirinus) and the identification of the deified Romulus with him was late; see Wissowa: *Religion und Kultus der Römer* (1912), pp. 153 ff.

[34] This suggests Aristotle's statement that Plato's two forms of state, described respectively in the *Republic* and the *Laws*, depart farther from actual practice than the ideal constitutions proposed by any other writer on the subject; see *Politics*, 1266 a 31.

[35] Cicero apparently disregards the numerous studies in the history and functioning of Greek constitutions made by Aristotle and his pupils. There are said to have been one hundred and fifty-eight such studies, of which the *Constitution of the Athenians* is the only considerable example extant; see Christ-Schmid: *Gesch. d. gr. Lit.* 1 (1912), p. 751.

your own discoveries to others instead of setting them forth in your own person, as Socrates does in Plato's "Republic." Moreover, with respect to the location of the city, you show the principle behind the measures which Romulus adopted either by accident or necessity. Your discussion, in fine, does not wander but deals with one commonwealth alone. Go on, therefore, as you have begun. Already, indeed, I seem to see what may be called a perfect state unfolding as you discuss the rest of the kings.

XII. SCIPIO: Very well, then. The senate which Romulus established was composed of leading citizens to whom the king himself had made such concessions that he was willing for them to be called "fathers" and their children "patricians."[36] After his death, when the senate attempted by itself to rule the city without a king, the people did not tolerate the usurpation, but because of their sorrow at the loss of Romulus continued to demand a king. Then the leaders of the state in their wisdom devised the scheme of instituting an interregnum.[37] The object of this plan, which was new and unknown to any other people, was that the city should not be without a king and yet that no one should be king for long, until a permanent king should be chosen. Thus no one could become entrenched in office and so be too slow in laying down authority, or too favorably situated for usurping it.

At this period in its career the Roman people, though newly founded, still perceived a fact which escaped the attention of Lycurgus at Sparta. Lycurgus thought that the king should

---

[36] That is, patricii from patres.

[37] The interregnum, contrary to Cicero's statement, was not exclusively a Roman institution, since it existed also in some Latin communities; see Mommsen: Röm. Staatsrecht, 1 (1887), pp. 647 ff. The term refers to the period between the death of the king (or, in the republican era, of an entire college of the higher magistrates) and the nomination of a successor. During this time, the right of consulting the auspices reverted to the totality of the patrician senators, who chose by lot one of their own members to perform this duty. This ad interim ruler, called the interrex, held office for not more than five days. A nomination of a new king could be made by any interrex except the first. When such a nomination had been ratified by the comitia curiata, the interregnum ended. See Cic. de leg. 3. 3. 9; Mommsen: loc. cit.; Bouché-Leclercq: Manuel des inst. romaines (1886), pp. 15 ff.; Greenidge: Roman Public Life (1911), pp. 47 ff.

not be elected—if, indeed, this question could have fallen within the province of Lycurgus—but that any descendant in the line of Hercules, irrespective of his qualifications, should succeed to the kingship.[38]   On the other hand, our yeomen even of that remote age saw that the requirements for a king should be excellence and wisdom rather than mere descent.

XIII. Since it was generally acknowledged that Numa Pompilius excelled in these qualities, the people themselves passed over their own fellow-citizens and, with the consent of the senate, made him their king, though he was foreign born, summoning him from his native Sabine city of Cures to rule at Rome.   Although the people had already voted in the assembly of the curiae[39] that he should be king, nevertheless after arriving in Rome Numa proposed a curiate statute conferring royal authority upon him.   Moreover, since he saw that the precepts of Romulus had inspired the Romans with a love of war, he thought that some restraint should be placed upon their incessant fighting.

XIV. His first step was to divide among the citizens individually the lands which Romulus had taken in war, and to teach them that agriculture could abundantly supply them with all commodities, without resorting to pillage and plunder. He inspired them with the love of peace and quiet—conditions which are especially adapted to strengthen justice and good faith and which, above all things, serve to protect the cultivation of the fields and the harvesting of crops.   Numa like-

---

[38] On the Spartan kingship see Gilbert: *Gr. Staatsalt.* 1 (1893), p. 46; Schoemann: *Gr. Alt.* 1 (1897), p. 230; Busolt: *Gr. Staatskunde,* 2 (1926), pp. 671 ff.; Cic. *de rep.* 2. 28, below, and note.

[39] The assembly of the thirty *curiae (comitia curiata)* was the most primitive of the Roman popular assemblies. The *curia* was an organization united by a supposed common ancestry and by common religious rites. It is probable that this assembly was never a legislative body, and in historical times its sole political function was the passage of the *lex curiata de imperio.* In origin, this was an act ratifying the nomination of a new king. Under the Republic it formally conferred *imperium* on any of the higher magistrates, though these were elected by the *comitia centuriata.* The *lex de imperio* supplied the ground for the juristic theory that the authority of the *princeps* or emperor was delegated to him by the people. See Mommsen: *Röm. Staatsrecht,* 1 (1887), pp. 609 ff.; Bouché-Leclercq: *Manuel des inst. romaines* (1886), pp. 18 ff.; Greenidge: *Roman Public Life* (1911), pp. 250 ff.· 343; Heitland: *Roman Republic* (1909), sect. 79; Botsford: *Roman Assemblies* (1909), ch. 9.

wise founded the higher class of auspices, adding two augurs to the original number, and also put the religious rites into the charge of five priests drawn from the foremost men of the state.[40] By the laws which he promulgated and which we have preserved in our collections,[41] he used the rites of religion to temper the customary ardor of the people for war. He established also the flamens, the Salian priests, and the Vestals.[42] All the forms of religious worship he drew up in a most scrupulous and pious spirit. It was his desire that the performance of the rites themselves should require minute attention to details, but that the means for performing them should be easily accessible to all. Hence, he established numerous rites, which had to be thoroughly learned and observed, but which involved no expense.[43] In this way he made the performance of religious obligations laborious but inexpensive. Numa provided also for market places and games and all the occasions which bring men together in numbers. Such were the measures by which he recalled to a humane and civilized

[40] According to tradition there had originally been three augurs, one from each tribe; see Cic. *de rep.* 2. 9, above. The higher class of auspices were those taken by the consuls, praetors, and censors, as distinguished from the lesser auspices taken by inferior magistrates. The difference depended on the importance of the occasion. See Greenidge: *Roman Public Life* (1911), p. 165. For the number of the priests (*pontifices*) see Wissowa: *Religion und Kultus der Römer* (1912), p. 503.

[41] The word which we translate by "collections" is *monumenta*. Since it is known that Manius Manilius, one of the interlocutors in this dialogue, composed a work bearing the name *Monumenta* on the laws which Numa was supposed to have drawn up, it is probable that Scipio is here alluding to that work. See Schanz: *Gesch. d. röm. Lit.* 1. 1 (1907), pp. 339 ff. The body of extant laws purporting to date from the kings (*leges regiae*) may be found in Bruns: *Fontes iuris Romani antiqui* (1909), pp. 1 ff., and in Girard: *Textes de droit romain* (1923), pp. 3 ff. A discussion of them may be found in Girard: *Manuel de droit romain* (1924), p. 17.

[42] For these various religious bodies see Wissowa: *Religion und Kultus der Römer* (1912), pp. 504; 555; Introduction, p. 72, above.

[43] On Roman religion in its early stages see Wissowa: *Religion und Kultus der Römer* (1912), pp. 34 ff.; Boissier: *La religion romaine d' Auguste aux Antonins* (7th ed.), 1, pp. 12 ff.; Fowler: *The Religious Experience of the Roman People* (1911), pp. 103-104 and *passim*. Further light is thrown upon its formalism by a comparison with early Roman legal procedure, when *ius*, or secular law, had not supplanted *fas*, or religious law; see Gaius: *inst.* (ed. Poste), 1904, pp. xiv ff., and as an example of this formalism, *ibid.* 4. 13 ff., where the *actio sacramenti* is described.

life men whose minds had long been rendered wild and untamed by the love of fighting. So after reigning in the greatest peace and harmony for thirty-nine years—let us accord
preference to the conclusions of our friend Polybius, since no
one has been more accurate than he in investigating questions
of chronology—Numa died, having made two signal contribu-
tions to the permanence of the commonwealth, the code of
religious observances and the spirit of humanity.

XV. When Scipio had finished, Manilius said: Is there a
tradition, Africanus, that King Numa, of whom you have been
speaking, was a pupil of Pythagoras himself or, at any rate, a
Pythagorean? Certainly we have often heard this report from
our ancestors and we know that it is the current belief, although we clearly see that it is not sufficiently attested by
authentic public records.

SCIPIO: The reason for this, Manilius, is that the whole tale
is false; in fact, it is not only a fiction but a stupid and absurd
fiction as well. A falsehood is indeed quite intolerable when
we perceive that it is not merely false but actually impossible.
Thus, we find that it was not until the fourth year of the reign
of Lucius Tarquinius Superbus that Pythagoras came to
Sybaris and Crotona and the adjacent parts of Italy. For it
was the sixty-second Olympiad that marked both the beginning of the reign of Superbus and the coming of Pythagoras.[44]
From this fact it may be seen, when the period of the monarchy is computed, that Pythagoras first came to Italy approximately one hundred and forty years after Numa's death,
nor has this fact ever been open to question among careful
students of chronology.

MANILIUS: Heavens, what a blunder, and how long it has
lasted! Still, I am glad that our civilization was not brought

---

[44] Pythagoras was born in Samos, whence he migrated to Crotona in
southern Italy. His school, which appears to have been as much a
religious and political society as a school of philosophy, flourished in the
Greek cities of Magna Graecia until it was dispersed by popular uprisings
against its aristocratic tendencies, perhaps about the middle of the fifth
century B. C., or even later. The date given by Cicero is quite uncertain.
The ancient evidence on this point is canvassed by Zeller: *Phil. d. Griech.*
1. 1 (1923), p. 381, n. 1; see esp. *Cambridge Ancient History*, 4 (1926),
pp. 544 ff.

from across the sea but grew from our own native excellences.

XVI. SCIPIO: You will see the truth of what you say still more clearly when you observe the state progressing and coming to its perfect form by a course of development natural to itself. You will conclude, in fact, that the wisdom of our ancestors deserves praise even for the many institutions which, as you will find, they adopted from other states and made much better in our state than they had been in the places where they originated and whence they were derived. And you will also learn that the Roman people, although favored by fortune, became strong not through chance but through wisdom and self-discipline.

XVII. After the death of King Numa, the people, upon the proposal of the interrex, elected Tullus Hostilius king in the assembly of the curiae. Following the example of Numa, he solicited the suffrages of the people in the curiae in support of his own authority. His glory in war was surpassing and his warlike exploits were great. He built and enclosed the comitium and the senate house out of the spoils of war. He devised and prescribed the ritual according to which wars were declared, and invested this just procedure with the ceremonial of the Fetial College.[45] Accordingly every war that had not been announced and declared prior to the opening of hostilities was adjudged unjust and unholy.

Now observe how wisely our kings, even at this early period, understood the need of granting certain powers to the people—a point about which I shall be obliged to speak at length. For Tullus did not presume to use even the royal insignia[46] until the people had so commanded. In order that

---

[45] The Fetial College, composed of twenty (or fifteen) members, was a religious body charged with the administration of the *ius fetiale*. This was a code of formal procedure which had to be followed in declaring war, making peace, and concluding treaties. The origin of the college is variously ascribed to Numa and to Ancus Martius as well as to Tullus Hostilius. For the subject see Cic. *de rep.* 3. 23, below; *de leg.* 2. 9. 21; Livy: 1. 24 and 32; Aulus Gellius: *noct. Att.* 16. 4. 1, and modern treatments in Wissowa: *Religion und Kultus der Römer* (1912), pp. 550 ff.; Frank: *Roman Imperialism* (1914), pp. 145 ff.

[46] These included, according to tradition, the lictors with the fasces, robes of colors appropriate for the several functions of the king, "the eagle-headed scepter, the golden crown, the throne, and the chariot within

he might be allowed to have twelve lictors precede him with the fasces.[47]. . . . .

(The third leaf of the seventeenth quaternion is missing)

Cicero refers also to Tullus Hostilius, the second king after Romulus, who was likewise killed by lightning, and in the same work affirms that the manner of his death did not create the belief that he had been translated to the gods. The reason was perhaps that the Romans did not wish to accord indiscriminately—and thus to cheapen by granting it readily also to another—the deification which was proved, that is, believed, to have been Romulus' reward.   Augustine: *de civ.* 3. 15

XVIII. LAELIUS?: . . . as your discourse develops, the commonwealth assumes its perfect form not haltingly but by leaps and bounds.

SCIPIO: After Tullus, Ancus Martius, the son of Numa's daughter, was made king by the people; he likewise caused a curiate statute to be passed confirming his authority. After crushing the Latins in war, he enrolled them in the state. He also added the Aventine and Caelian hills to the city, divided among the citizens the territory which he had captured, and made public property of all forests which he had seized along the coast.[48] He founded near the mouth of the Tiber a city which he strengthened by sending there a body of colonists.[49] And so he died, having reigned twenty-three years.

LAELIUS: The king whom you mention is indeed worthy of praise, but truly the annals of Rome are obscure, if we know the mother of this king but not the father.

SCIPIO: That is true, but of this period scarcely more has been brought to light than the names of the kings.

XIX. It was apparently at this time that intellectual inter-

---

the walls, from which the curule chair (*sella curulis*) was believed to be derived"; see Greenidge: *Roman Public Life* (1911), p. 44; Mommsen: *Röm. Staatsrecht*, 2. 1 (1887), pp. 5 ff.

[47] For the lictors and fasces see Mommsen: *Röm. Staatsrecht*, 1 (1887), pp. 373 ff.; Cic. *de rep.* 2. 31, below.

[48] This is perhaps an allusion to the seizure of the *silva Mesia*, a wooded tract belonging to Veii and located on the right bank of the Tiber; see Livy: 1. 33.

[49] See Cic. *de rep.* 2. 3, above, and note.

ests became, as it were, engrafted upon the state and caused its
first cultural growth. Greek learning and arts now flowed into
Rome not like an insignificant rill but like a river in flood.[50] It
is the tradition that there lived in Corinth a certain Demaratus
who was without question the first man of the state in fame,
prestige, and wealth. Since he could not endure the Corinthian
tyrant Cypselus,[51] the story goes that he fled, taking with him
ample means, and came to Tarquinii, the most prosperous city
of Etruria. When he heard that the rule of Cypselus was firmly established, this free and brave man became an exile from
his country. He was given citizenship by the inhabitants of
Tarquinii and there set up his home and dwelling place. When
his wife, a native of Tarquinii, had borne him two sons, he
trained them in all the arts, after the manner of Greek education.........

(The sixth leaf of the seventeenth quaternion is missing)

XX. SCIPIO: [After Lucumo, the son of Demaratus],[52] had
readily secured admission to the [Roman] state, his culture
and learning caused him to become so intimate a friend of King
Ancus that he was regarded as the sharer of all his plans and
almost as his partner in the kingdom. Moreover, he possessed
extreme affability of manner and also extreme generosity in
placing his resources, his services, his facilities for protection,
and even financial aid at the disposal of all the citizens. Consequently, after the death of Ancus, the people unanimously
elected him king, with the name of Lucius Tarquinius—for
Lucumo had taken this name in place of his Greek name in
order that he might appear to follow the custom of our people
in every way.[53] After he proposed a law confirming his

---

[50] It is a fact that the expansion of Greek commerce in the sixth
century reached and affected Latium and Etruria; see Beloch: *Gr. Gesch.*
1. 1 (1924), pp. 273-274.

[51] Cypselus became tyrant of Corinth after expelling the Bacchiadae, in
the seventh century B. C. See Busolt: *Gr. Gesch.* 1 (1893), pp. 637 ff.;
Beloch: *Gr. Gesch.* 1. 1 (1924), pp. 361 ff.; Gilbert: *Gr. Staatsalt.* 2
(1885), p. 89; *Cambridge Ancient History,* 3 (1925), pp. 550 ff.; 764 ff.

[52] That the following refers to the son of Demaratus is clear from Livy:
1. 34; Dion. Hal. *ant. Rom.* 3. 46-48; Polybius: 11 a 7 ff. Cicero refers
to the legend, *de leg.* 1. 1. 4.

[53] Cicero apparently regards Lucius as a Latinized form of Lucumo,
a name which is of Etruscan, and not, as he supposes, of Greek origin.

authority, his first step was to double the existing number of senators. The original senators he described as coming from the principal families, and he called upon these to give their votes first; the additional senators whom he had himself enrolled he named the members of the lesser families. His next step was to organize the knights in the fashion that has persisted to this day. But he failed to change the names of the Titienses, the Rhamnes, and the Luceres, though he desired to do so, because a highly renowned augur, Attus Navius,[54] would not assent to the proposal. In passing, I note that the Corinthians also at one time took care to create and maintain an equestrian order at public expense, raising the money by taxes levied on the estates of orphans and widows.[55] At all events, Tarquinius duplicated the existing units of the knights. Thus, he formed a body of eighteen hundred, which was double the original number.[56] Later he conquered the Aequi, a great and warlike people which threatened the Roman state. After he had driven the Sabines from before the walls of the city, he scattered them with his cavalry and completely defeated them. We are told also that he founded the most important of the games, now called the Roman Games,[57] and that while actually

---

[54] For Attus Navius see Pease's notes on Cic. *de div.* 1. 17. 31 ff.

[55] According to Curtius ("Studien zur Geschichte von Korinth," *Hermes,* 10, 1876, p. 227), this is the chief passage which points to the existence of a thoroughly timocratic constitution at Corinth.

[56] Cicero's account of the origin and development of the equestrian order is obscure, and the same may be said of the accounts in the other sources. The evidence is analyzed by Mommsen: *Röm. Staatsrecht,* 3. 1 (1887), p. 107, n. 3; 254, n. 1. The relevant passages in Cicero state that Romulus founded three tribes, meaning apparently three centuries of knights (2. 8), that Tarquinius doubled the number and gave the order its final organization (this passage), and a fragment of a sentence in the account of the Servian constitution which shows that Servius made eighteen centuries (2. 22). These statements are inconsistent with accounts given by other sources but can be made self-consistent if we suppose that the original three centuries had been raised to 300 men each, that Tarquinius made six centuries of this size, and that Servius merely increased the number of centuries without changing the total number of knights. But this hypothesis fails to explain the traditionally patrician character of the six original centuries (*sex suffragia*; Cic. *de rep.* 2. 22), which is the most probable part of the whole legend.

[57] Games formed an important part of Roman worship. They were of two classes, one specifically religious and conducted by priests, the other given by magistrates. The Roman Games were of the second kind and are supposed to have been instituted in the sixth century B.C.; see Wis-

fighting in the Sabine War, he vowed to build a temple to Jupiter the Most High, on the Capitoline Hill, and that he died after he had reigned thirty-eight years.

XXI. LAELIUS: Now the truth of Cato's saying becomes more clearly established, that the founding of the state is not the work of one man or of one time. For it is obvious how important an addition of good and useful institutions was made under each monarch. In my opinion, however, it is the king after Lucius Tarquinius who had the clearest insight into politics of them all.

SCIPIO: That is true. Servius Tullius, who followed Lucius Tarquinius, was the first king, according to tradition, who ruled without the sanction of the people. It is said that his mother was one of Tarquinius' slaves, while his father was one of the king's clients. Although he was reared among slaves and served the king's table, the spark of genius, which even then was evident in the boy, was not obscured, so intelligent he proved himself in every word he said and in every service he performed. And although Tarquinius then had children who were quite young, he loved Servius so deeply that the latter was commonly reputed to be his son. Moreover, he took the utmost care to instruct Servius, according to the finest patterns of Greek education, in all the arts which he himself had learned. After Tarquinius was treacherously murdered by the sons of Ancus, Servius began his reign, as I said before, not by the command of the citizens but with their leave and approval. For when it was falsely said that Tarquinius had been sick from a wound but was still living, Servius assumed the royal insignia, administered justice, and relieved debtors out of his own purse. By the great affability of his manner he convinced the citizens that he was pronouncing judgments by the command of Tarquinius. He did not lay before the senate the question of his succession but, after Tarquinius was buried, brought the matter in person before the people. When they directed him to be king, he proposed the curiate statute conferring upon him his authority. His

sowa: *Religion und Kultus der Römer* (1912), pp. 449 ff.; Marquardt: *Röm. Staatsverwaltung*, 3 (1885), p. 497.

first act was to avenge in war the wrongs committed by the Etruscans; as a result of which..........

(The third leaf of the eighteenth quaternion is missing)

XXII. SCIPIO: [Servius organized the equestrian order in] eighteen [centuries, drawn from the citizens] having the highest property assessment. After he had set off this large group of knights from the main body of the people, he next divided the rest of the population into five classes, each of which he further subdivided into seniors and juniors.[58] This division was so carried out that the voting strength lay in the hands of the wealthy, rather than in the hands of the majority. Thus, he guarded against giving power to mere numbers—a point to be avoided in any commonwealth. If you were not already familiar with this scheme of distribution, I should explain it to you. As it is, you see that the plan is such that the [eighteen] centuries of knights, including the six original centuries, added to the centuries of the first class and supplemented by the smiths and carpenters, who were organized as a special century because of their importance to the city, make up altogether eight-nine centuries.[59] Thus, if only eight of the remaining hundred and four centuries have been added to the

---

[58] The *comitia centuriata* was chronologically the second of the Roman popular assemblies. It was military in origin, the century being the voting unit. Its functions included the election of certain magistrates, declarations of war, jurisdiction (until the rise of *quaestiones perpetuae*) in criminal cases that involved the life or civil status of a citizen, and an undefined legislative competence. Owing to its organization and its mode of transacting business, it was wholly subject to patrician control. Partly for this reason and partly because of its unwieldiness, it was superseded as a legislative body by the *comitia tributa*. See Bouché-Leclercq: *Manuel des inst. romaines* (1886), pp. 109 ff.; Mommsen: *Röm. Staatsrecht*, 3. 1 (1887), pp. 245 ff.; Botsford: *Roman Assemblies* (1909), chs. 10 and 11.

[59] When compared with the accounts preserved by Livy (1. 43) and Dionysius (*ant. Rom.* 4. 16 ff.; 7. 59), Cicero's figures present certain difficulties. In all of these authors the total number of centuries is given as one hundred and ninety-three or one hundred and ninety-four. Whereas Livy and Dionysius both assign eighty centuries to the first class, this figure cannot be made to fit Cicero's total of eighty-nine centuries for the knights, the first class, and one century of artizans. Cicero's total is explicable, if we assume the first class to have consisted of seventy centuries, the number assigned to each of the classes after the reform of the third century B. C. (Botsford: *Roman Assemblies*, 1909, pp. 211 ff.). This fact led Mommsen (*Röm. Staatsrecht*, 3. 1, 1887, pp. 270 ff.) to the conclusion that Cicero is really describing the *comitia*

eighty-nine, a voting majority of the entire people has been constituted. By this plan the remaining ninety-six centuries, which included a far greater number of citizens, would not be deprived of their votes, for fear that such a step might be overbearing; and they would not possess too much power, for fear that this would be dangerous.

Servius provided carefully even for the very terminology to accompany this scheme. On the wealthy he conferred the name "assidui" because they contributed money; then he called those "proletarii" who either had not entered in their census returns more than fifteen hundred asses worth of property or had made no return at all except of their civil status.[60] He chose this name in order that it might appear that they were expected to provide what we may call the progeny, that is, the offspring, of the state. In a single one of the ninety-six centuries there were, then, almost more citizens enrolled than in the entire first class. Thus no one was deprived of the right to vote, and yet the chief weight was attached to the votes of those who had the chief interest in the well-being of their country. Furthermore, to the groups of citizens called "accensi," "velati," "cornices," "proletarii".........[61]

(The sixth and seventh leaves of the eighteenth
quaternion are missing)

XXIII. [SCIPIO:] I hold that the best constituted state is one which is formed by the due combination of the three simple

---

centuriata as it existed in its modified form. It would appear either that Cicero is in error or that he has confused the tradition which Livy and Dionysius followed with the arrangements of the reformed *comitia*.

[60] Cicero derives *assidui* from *ab asse dando* and *proletarii* from *proles*. The term *assidui* was certainly used of wealthy persons (Cic. *top.* 2. 10), but the origin of this meaning is obscure. Similarly, *proletarii* means the poor (Nonius, p. 155. 20); as Cicero suggests, it may well have meant those persons who had too little property to be included in any of the five classes. The words are of ancient usage, being contrasted in the Twelve Tables: 1. 4 (Girard: *Textes de droit romain*, 1923, p. 12, and Bruns: *Fontes iuris Romani antiqui*, 1909, p. 18, in which citations most of the evidence for their meaning is collected).

[61] *Accensi* were citizens whose property did not entitle them either to membership in the cavalry or in any of the five classes but who were used for replacing losses in the army (Festus: s. v. *accensi*). *Velati* were unarmed followers of the army, used also for replacements (Festus: s. v. *velati*). *Cornices* were musicians attached to the army, probably in the capacity of signalers. See Mommsen: *Röm. Staatsrecht*, 3. 1 (1887), pp. 288 ff.; Greenidge: *Roman Public Life* (1911), pp. 71 ff.

types, monarchy, aristocracy, and democracy, and which does not arouse a wild and untamed spirit [in its citizens] by punishing[62]..........

SCIPIO: ....[Carthage was][63] sixty-[five] years older [than Rome], for it was founded thirty-nine years before the first Olympiad. And Lycurgus was the earliest to come to nearly the same conclusion. Accordingly, the even balance of governmental elements in the composite form of state which we have been discussing appears to me to have been common to the Roman constitution and to these other governments. But the peculiar and incomparable excellence of our government in its present form I shall analyze, if I can, in greater detail. It will be found to consist in a quality the like of which can be discovered in no other state. The elements which I have been hitherto explaining were blended in the Roman monarchy, at Sparta,[64] and at Carthage,[65] but so blended that the balance between them was not maintained. For in a state in which one man holds perpetual power—and especially if his power be royal— his authority predominates; and such a

---

[62] Nonius, p. 342, 39.

[63] We translate Mai's supplement.

[64] Cicero seems to be following the account of the Spartan constitution given by Polybius (6. 10). Plato (*Laws*, 691 e ff.) also cites Sparta as an example of the balanced form of government, which is a mean between democracy and monarchy. On the Spartan constitution see Cic. *de rep.* 2. 28, below, and note.

[65] The Carthaginian constitution was an aristocracy of the balanced type, much admired by ancient thinkers and compared by them to the constitution of Sparta. The royal element consisted of two annual magistrates, named *suffetes*, who resembled the Roman consuls. The aristocratic and dominant element was the senate of three hundred members, which habitually functioned through a committee of thirty and which met in plenary session only on important occasions. The popular element was the assembly, composed of the citizen body and possessing little real power. It met only when the *suffetes* and senate failed to agree. At a later date power passed largely into the hands of a board of one hundred and four members, which corresponded in a general way to the ephors at Sparta and the tribunes of the plebs at Rome, their function being to protect the people against the *suffetes* as the ephors checked the kings and as the tribunes the consuls. See Heitland: *Roman Republic* (1909), sects. 236-7; Newman: *Politics of Aristotle*, 2 (1887), Appendix B; E. Meyer: *Gesch. des Alt.* 3 (1915), pp. 685 ff.; Gsell: *Hist. ancienne de l' Afrique du Nord*, 2 (1918), pp. 183 ff. Cicero's statement that the royal power predominated in the Spartan and the Carthaginian governments is incorrect; at Sparta the ephors predominated and at Carthage the board of one hundred and four.

commonwealth cannot fail to be a monarchy both in fact and name, even if there is also a senate, as was the case at Rome under the kings or at Sparta under the laws of Lycurgus, or if the people themselves possess a certain degree of authority, as was the case in the Roman monarchy. Moreover, the monarchical form of government is particularly unstable because failure on the part of a single individual easily sweeps it headlong to utter ruin. In itself monarchy is not only unobjectionable but, if I were to give my approval to any simple type of state, is probably far preferable to either of the other two simple types, as long as it preserves its own proper nature. Still, it is inherent in the nature of monarchy that the permanent authority, the sense of justice, and the wisdom of a single[66] individual control the safety, the political equality, and the peace of the citizens. A people who live under a monarchy are wholly deprived of many blessings. The first of these is liberty, which consists not in being subject to a lawful master but in being subject to no master at all[67]..........

(The second leaf of the nineteenth quaternion is missing)

XXIV. ....they endured.[68] For this arbitrary and cruel tyrant was long blessed by fortune in his public acts. He conquered all Latium in war and captured and sacked Suessa Pometia,[69] a wealthy and populous city. Having thus enriched himself with a great treasure of gold and silver, he redeemed his father's vow by building the temple to Jupiter on the Capitoline. He also founded colonies, and in accordance with the custom of the people from whom he had sprung, he

---

[66] For *omneque* we read *uniusque*, perhaps the ms. reading according to Ziegler.

[67] Unless it was qualified in the lacuna, this sentence is strangely at odds with Cicero's usual view, that freedom depends upon law; cf. the famous saying, "We are slaves of the laws in order that we may be free" (*pro Cluent.* 53. 146). The view of liberty given in the text represents the characteristic usually assigned to bad democracy; see Plato: *Republic*, 557 b; Aristotle: *Politics*, 1310 a 28 ff.

[68] This lacuna, or possibly the preceding one, must have included the murder of **Servius by Lucius Tarquinius** Superbus and the usurpation of the throne by the latter; see Livy: 1. 48.

[69] An ancient city of Latium, the precise location of which is not known; see E. Meyer: *Gesch. des Alt.* 5 (1902), p. 138.

sent splendid gifts, the first-fruits of his spoils, to Apollo at Delphi.

XXV.   In these circumstances there will occur a change in the political cycle, the natural course and revolution of which you must learn to recognize in their beginnings.   The highest achievement of political wisdom, with which all our discussion deals, is to perceive the tortuous path followed by public affairs, in order that we may know the tendency of each change and thus be able to retard the movement or forestall it.   Now the king of whom I speak, polluted first by the murder of an excellent ruler, was not sound of mind.   Since he himself feared the extreme punishment merited by his crime, he desired to be feared by others.   Moreover, relying upon his victories and his wealth, he took delight in lawless violence, and could not control either his own conduct or the lusts of his kindred.   The result was that his elder son violated Lucretia, the daughter of Tricipitinus and the wife of Collatinus, and the modest and well-born woman slew herself because of this assault.   Then Lucius Brutus, a man distinguished both for his ability and for his character, lifted from the shoulders of his fellow-citizens the unjust yoke of oppressive servitude. Though Brutus held no public office, he upheld the whole common weal.   Thus he was the first man in our commonwealth to teach the lesson that, when it is a question of preserving the liberty of the citizens, there is no such thing as private station.   He began and led a revolution, and as a consequence of the fresh charge brought by the father and kindred of Lucretia, added to the memory of the arrogance of Tarquinius and the many wrongs committed by him and his sons, the state decreed the exile of the king himself, his children, and the whole line of the Tarquinii.

XXVI.   Do you see, then, how a king developed into a tyrant and how a defect on the part of one man turned the state from a good form into a thoroughly bad one?   In Tarquinius we see a master of the people such as the Greeks call a tyrant.   A king, on the other hand, they define as one who cherishes the interests of his people like a parent, and who preserves his

subjects in the best possible mode of life.[70] Monarchy is undoubtedly a good type of state, as I have said, but it nevertheless has a tendency or, as I might say, a leaning towards the
worst type. For once the king has adopted a form of rule
which is unjust and arbitrary, he becomes forthwith a tyrant,
than whom no creature more foul, or loathsome, or detestable
to gods or men can be imagined. Though he is formed in
the image of man, the monstrous ferocity of his character sur-
passes that of the wildest of beasts. Who can justly give the
title of human being to one who, in his dealings with his fellow
citizens and indeed with the entire human race, does not desire
the bond of a common law and the relationships involved in
civilized life? But this topic will engage us at another and
more suitable time,[71] when the development of our subject
prompts us to criticise those who have sought to set up tyrannical power even in a state already free.

XXVII. Such is the first origin of the tyrant, for this was
the name which the Greeks applied to an arbitrary ruler. The
Romans have used the word "king" to mean all who held absolute and perpetual authority over their people. Thus, it has
been said that Spurius Cassius, Marcus Manlius, and Spurius
Maelius desired to set up a "kingdom,"[72] and recently [the
same charge was made against Tiberius Gracchus].[73]

(The seventh leaf of the nineteenth quaternion is missing)

XXVIII. [The senators] at Sparta [Lycurgus] called
["elders"].[74] In number they were far too few, being only
twenty-eight. In their hands he desired the chief deliberative

---

[70] Plato defines the king, in contrast with the tyrant, as one who rules
over voluntary subjects (*Statesman*, 291 e) ; and this distinction is retained by Aristotle (*Politics*, 1285 a 27). Cf. also the Pythagorean fragments on the king cited in the Introduction, pp. 95 f.

[71] The later passage referred to has been lost.

[72] For the probable hypothesis that these legends preserve the record
of three unsuccessful attempts on the part of patricians to set up a
tyranny, see Boak: *History of Rome to 565* A.D. (1922), p. 53.

[73] Here and at the beginning of ch. 28 we translate Mai's supplement.

[74] Broadly considered, the Spartan government consisted of four elements: a dual kingship; a body of elders called the *gerusia*; a popular
assembly known as the *apella*; and the ephors. (1) The kingship was
hereditary. The powers of the office were mainly religious and military;
the kings had no effective control over the *gerusia* or the *apella* and no
important judicial powers. (2) The *gerusia* had twenty-eight members

power to rest, whereas the king exercised the chief military and executive authority. Our statesmen adopted from him the same arrangement and, translating his terms, gave the name senate to the body of those whom he had called elders.[75] Romulus, as we have already said, pursued the same course when the senators were chosen. Nevertheless, the power, authority, and title of king predominate. Suppose that you grant some authority to the people also, as both Lycurgus and Romulus did; you will not thereby satisfy their desire for liberty, but you will fire them with the love of liberty by giving them an opportunity merely to taste it. The fear will always hang over them that the king may become an arbitrary ruler, as generally happens.[76] Precarious, therefore, is the lot of a people which is dependent, as I have previously said, on the caprice or character of a single man.

XXIX. Accordingly, let this be the first type, form, and origin of the tyrant. We have found it in the government which Romulus established after consulting the auspices, and not in that commonwealth which, according to the version written by Plato, Socrates himself sketched in the famous dialogue on the state.[77] We have found how a man like Tarquin-

---

elected for life. It advised the kings in matters of legislation, exercised judicial functions, and prepared measures for the consideration of the popular assembly. Its powers were diminished by the ephorate but still remained considerable in the fourth century B. C. (3) The *apella* included the whole body of Spartans. Though it had the power to pass laws, to declare war, and to conclude treaties, it never became a democratic institution, since its acts were largely under the control of the *gerusia* and the ephors. (4) The ephorate was of later date than the institutions already mentioned, being established, according to tradition, in 753 B. C. The ephors were five in number, representing the five villages composing the Spartan state, and held office for one year. They were the most powerful element in the government, checking the powers of the kings and *gerusia*, directing the *apella*, conducting foreign affairs, and controlling finance. See Busolt: *Gr. Staatskunde*, 2 (1926), pp. 671 ff.; Schoemann: *Gr. Alt.* 1 (1897), pp. 230 ff.; Gilbert: *Gr. Staatsalt.* 1 (1893), pp. 46 ff.; Kahrstedt: *Gr. Staatsrecht*, 1 (1922), pp. 119 ff.; 237 ff.; 246 ff.; 255 ff.

[75] That is, *senatus* from *senes*.

[76] The Spartans feared this change so greatly that they subjected their kings to a monthly oath by which they bound themselves to rule according to the laws; see Busolt: *Gr. Staatskunde*, 2 (1926), p. 677.

[77] It will be seen from the Introduction (pp. 57 ff.) that Cicero explains the origin of tyranny in two ways. In the present passage he derives it from monarchy, while in *de rep.* 1. 44, above, he derives it from the extreme form of democracy.

ius completely subverted monarchy, not by usurping new
authority but by using arbitrarily the authority which he had.
Now let us imagine the antithesis of this tyrant, a ruler who
is good and wise and versed in all that contributes to the advantage and prestige of the state; who is, as it were, the guardian and steward of the commonwealth, for so we should call
anyone who directs and pilots the state.[78] You should bend
all your efforts to recognize such a man, since it is he who can
protect the state by his wisdom and services. Since I have
said little as yet about this man, and since I shall be obliged to
refer to him frequently in the remainder of my discussion....

(The six inside leaves of the twentieth quaternion are missing)

XXX......... [Plato] sought......... and he created a
state which must be regarded as an impractical ideal rather
than one whose realization can be expected. It was drawn in
the smallest dimensions possible; and while it could not exist,
it was one in which the theory of political relations could be
fully understood.[79] On the other hand, if I can at all accomplish my purpose, I shall strive to follow the same principles
which Plato perceived, and to illustrate them, not in an unreal
and shadowy state, but in our own glorious commonwealth. I
shall do this, in order to place my finger, as it were, upon the
cause of every good and evil in the state.

The period of royal government, together with the inter-
regna, occupied a little more than two hundred and forty years.
After the expulsion of Tarquinius, the Roman people hated

---

[78] Cicero developed the conception of the ideal statesman at length in
the fifth book; see *de rep.* 5. 6 and 7; also 2. 40 and 42; 6. 1; Introduction, pp. 93 ff., above. Cf. Plato's contrast of the king and the tyrant
(*Republic*, 576 d; *Statesman*, 301 ff.).

[79] The reference appears to be to the account of the formation of a
new state, or the purgation and reconstitution of a corrupt state, in
Plato's *Laws* (735 a ff.), where the number of citizens is limited to five
thousand and forty. In this lacuna and in the one following ch. 30,
Cicero must have dealt with the expulsion from Rome of the partizans
of the Tarquinii, the establishment of the consulate, and the development of the power of the people; see *de rep.* 1. 40, above. The parallel
sources for early Roman history after the expulsion of the kings and
before the passage of the Twelve Tables, with which Cicero's historical
account practically ceases (*de rep.* 2. 36, below), are as follows: Livy:
2. 1 to 3. 57; Dion. Hal. *ant. Rom.* 5. 1 to 10. 60; Diodorus Siculus: 10.
20-22; 11. 40; 68; 12. 23 to 26.

the name of king as intensely as they had loved it after the death or, as we should say, departure of Romulus. Thus, whereas at the earlier time they could not be without a king, after the expulsion of Tarquinius they could not abide the title of king. Under these circumstances the power.........

(All eight leaves of the twenty-first quaternion are missing)

XXXI. Thus, after that celebrated form of government set up by Romulus had stood firm for about two hundred and forty years[80].........

Hence, because they would not bear the rule of kings, they made the chief magistracy annual and created two magistrates with military authority.[81] These were called consuls from the verb meaning to consult, not kings from the verb to reign, or masters from the verb to dominate.[82]

Augustine: *de civ.* 5. 12.

SCIPIO: ....that whole law was abrogated.[83] As a result of this feeling our ancestors then exiled Collatinus, innocent though he was, because they were suspicious of his kinship with Tarquinius, and they banished the rest of the Tarquinii because of the hostility felt toward their name. Because of the same feeling Publius Valerius first ordered the fasces to be lowered after he had begun to speak in a formal gathering of the citizens.[84] He also moved his house down to

---

[80] Nonius, p. 526. 10.

[81] For the constitutional significance of the change from kings to consuls, see Greenidge: *Roman Public Life* (1911), pp. 78 ff.

[82] This passage contains four plays on words: *imperia* and *imperatores*; *consules* from *consulere*; *reges* from *regnare*; and *domini* from *dominare*. Compare Mommsen's well-known but not generally accepted derivation of *consulere* from *con* and *salio*, referring to some primitive religious dance; see *Röm. Staatsrecht*, 2. 1 (1887), p. 77, n. 3.

[83] Mai acutely suggests that this lacuna contained an account of the Athenian practice of ostracism. On this constitutional device see Aristotle: *Const. of the Athenians*, 22. 1 ff.; Beloch: *Gr. Gesch.* 1. 2 (1913), p. 332; 2. 1 (1914), p. 30; Busolt: *Gr. Staatskunde*, 2 (1926), pp. 884 ff.; R. J. Bonner: "The Minimum Vote in Ostracism," *Classical Phil.* 8 (1913), pp. 223-5.

[84] The lowering of the fasces was a mark of submission to the people. The meeting referred to was a *contio*, that is, an assemblage called by a magistrate for any purpose such as the reading of an edict or the presentation of a measure later to come before the *comitia*. The Roman law recognized no right on the part of the people to assemble peaceably and of their own volition, and there was no debate in the *comitia* itself. Hence it was customary to hold a *contio* before meetings of the assembly. The

the foot of Mount Velia, after he noticed that the people's suspicions were aroused by his beginning to build at a higher point on the hill, just where King Tullus had lived. But the act by which Valerius especially showed himself a friend of the people was the proposal of a law—the first passed in the assembly of the centuries—prohibiting any magistrate from executing or flogging a Roman citizen without permitting an appeal to the centuries.[85] Even in the time of the kings there had existed the right to appeal from their decisions, as our pontifical books assert and as the augural records also show. Moreover, it is clear from many provisions of the Twelve Tables that an appeal was permitted from every conviction on a criminal charge. And the tradition that there was no right of appeal from the decision of the Decemvirs, who reduced the law to writing, is itself sufficient evidence that an appeal would lie from decisions of the other magistrates. The law of the consuls Lucius Valerius Potitus and Marcus Horatius Barbatus, men who were wisely democratic in the interest of harmony, enacted that no magistrate should be constituted from whose decisions an appeal would not lie. Finally, the three Porcian Laws, which, as you know, are named for the three Porcii, really added nothing new except the clause setting the penalty for violation.

To resume then: After the passage of the law we have mentioned on the right of appeal, Publicola at once ordered the axes to be withdrawn from the fasces,[86] and on the following day he secured the election of Spurius Lucretius as his col-

---

magistrate presented and explained measures which were to be proposed in the assembly and at his own discretion could permit discussion. The *contio* did not vote. See Botsford: *Roman Assemblies* (1909), ch. 7.

[85] For this right of appeal, which was regarded among Romans much as the principle of *habeas corpus* is held among English-speaking peoples, see Greenidge: *Legal Procedure of Cicero's Time* (1901), pp. 311 ff.; Botsford: *Roman Assemblies* (1909), pp. 240 ff.; Bouché-Leclercq: *Manuel des inst. romaines* (1886), pp. 60 ff.; 122 ff.; 444, note 7.

[86] This signified that the magistrate no longer had summary power over the lives of citizens; see Cic. *de rep.* 2. 17, above, and note. The presence or absence of the axes symbolized the legal distinction of *imperium militiae* and *imperium domi*; see Bouché-Leclercq: *Manuel des inst. romaines* (1886), p. 36; Mommsen: *Röm. Staatsrecht*, 1 (1887), pp. 379-380.

league,[87] and commanded his lictors to be transferred to Lucretius because he was the elder. He was the first also to establish the rule that the lictors should precede each consul in alternate months.[88] The design of this plan was that there should not be more symbols of authority in a free people than there had been under the monarchy. Publicola, I should certainly judge, was a man of no mean ability, since he made it easier to maintain the authority of the nobility by giving freedom in moderation to the people. It is not without reason that I now descant upon these events, which you find so ancient and out of date. On the contrary, I use notable personalities and periods to mark out such types of men and achievement as the remainder of my discussion will treat.

XXXII. Accordingly, at this period the senate maintained the commonwealth in the following condition: the people, though free, performed few functions by themselves; the senate carried on the greater share of public business by virtue of its prestige and customary authority; and the consuls possessed a power which, though annual in duration, was royal in its legal nature. The provision which was really the chief factor in preserving the ascendancy of the nobility was rigidly maintained, namely, that enactments by the people were not binding unless they had received the sanction of the senate.[89] It was also at this same period, about ten years after the establishment of the consulate, that the first dictator,[90] Titus Larcius, was appointed. This form of authority was a strange

---

[87] That is, to replace Brutus after the latter was killed in battle by Arruns Tarquinius (Livy: 2. 6. 9; 2. 8. 4).

[88] This was an automatic way of indicating which of the consuls occupied the higher position. Though the principle *par maiorve potestas* generally prevailed, responsibility, at least in unimportant and routine matters, was fixed by rotation, as here, by lot, or by mutual agreement. Julius Caesar revived this practice in 59 B.C.; see Suetonius: *Iulius*, 20; Greenidge: *Roman Public Life* (1911), p. 198; Festus: s. v. *maiorem consulem*.

[89] Though in theory an advisory body, the senate in fact exercised in historical times an authority over the magistrates and popular assemblies far beyond its strict legal competence. On the powers of the senate see Mommsen: *Röm. Staatsrecht*, 3. 2 (1888), pp. 1022 ff.; Greenidge: *Roman Public Life* (1911), pp. 261 ff.; Introduction, pp. 83 ff., above.

[90] For the dictator see Mommsen: *Röm. Staatsrecht*, 2. 1 (1887), pp. 141 ff.; Greenidge: *Roman Public Life* (1911), pp. 191 ff.; Introduction, pp. 81 f., above.

phenomenon and seemed a close approximation to kingship; nevertheless, all the chief powers of government were then wielded by the senate with full authority granted by the people. Great were the exploits in war performed in those ages by brave men invested with the supreme military command, either as dictators or consuls.

XXXIII. In the very nature of things, however, it was inevitable that the people, once they were freed from the kings, should demand for themselves a greater degree of authority. This enlargement of their power they attained, after a brief interval of about sixteen years, in the consulate of Postumus Cominius and Spurius Cassius. There was perhaps no element of design in this change, but there is a principle of growth inherent in public affairs which often overrides design. For you should master the principle which I laid down at the beginning: Unless there is in the state such an equal distribution of legal rights, functions, and duties that the magistrates possess an adequate power, the council of the chief men an adequate influence, and the people an adequate measure of liberty, the balance of the commonwealth cannot be preserved unchanged. Thus, when the question of debt had thrown the state into disorder, the common people seized first the Sacred Mountain and later the Aventine.[91] Not even Lycurgus, for all his discipline, reined back the Greeks from constitutional change. For even at Sparta, in the kingship of Theopompus, there were set up five magistrates called ephors,[92] while in Crete there were ten officials named kosmoi,[93] whose duty was to limit the power of the kings, just as at Rome the tribunes of

---

[91] The traditional date of the first secession of the plebs and the establishment of the tribunate is 494 B. C. According to the sounder tradition preserved in Diodorus the year was 466 B.C. Cicero, developing his theory of the unmixed forms of government, considers the question of debt merely as a pretext or occasion for the revolution. The true cause, according to him, is the tendency of any element in the state, if uncontrolled, to usurp tyrannical powers and so bring about the revolt of the oppressed classes; see Introduction, pp. 57 ff.

[92] The traditional date for the establishment of the ephorate is 754-3 B. C.; see Busolt: *Gr. Staatskunde*, 2 (1926), pp. 677; 683; Cic. *de rep.* 2. 28, above, and note.

[93] For the *kosmoi*, whom Aristotle (*Politics*, 1272 a 5) equates with the Spartan ephors, see Busolt: *Gr. Staatskunde*, 2 (1926), pp. 747 ff.

the plebs were established to limit the authority of the consuls.[94]

XXXIV. Our ancestors[95] had perhaps a plan for the relief of debtors similar to the scheme which had occurred to Solon of Athens a short time before,[96] and which at a later date suggested itself to our own senate, when the lustful act of a single individual caused the cancellation of all contracts by which the person of a citizen was pledged for debt, a kind of contract never subsequently permitted.[97] It was always the practice in such emergencies, when the common people were suffering from expenses incident to a public misfortune, to seek some remedy and alleviation in the interest of general safety. On the occasion which we are discussing, however, this policy was neglected, and accordingly the people were given a motive for resorting to civil strife. The result was that the power and prestige of the senate were limited by the creation of two tribunes of the plebs. Still, the senate's authority remained weighty and extensive, since the men who guarded the state by their prowess and their wisdom were the wisest and bravest of their country. The prestige of these senators was very great, because, though they were inferior to other men in the luxury

---

[94] Cicero's account of the origin of the tribunate is historically unreliable. The best ancient source is Diodorus (11. 68. 8) and an excellent modern account is supplied by E. Meyer: *Gesch. des Alt.* 5 (1902), pp. 141 ff. For other modern accounts see Mommsen: *Röm. Gesch.* 1 (1912), pp. 270 ff. (Eng. trans. 1, pp. 270 ff.) ; *Röm. Staatsrecht*, 2. 1 (1887), pp. 272 ff.; Heitland: *Roman Republic* (1909), sect. 64; Greenidge: *Roman Public Life* (1911), pp. 93 ff.; 233 ff.; Bouché-Leclercq: *Manuel des inst. romaines* (1886), pp. 68 ff.

[95] Most of the editors, including Ziegler, regard this sentence as corrupt.

[96] For Solon's legislation in relief of debtors see Aristotle: *Const. of the Athenians*, ed. Sandys (1912), 6. 1 ff., with commentary; Grote: *History of Greece*, 3 (1869), pp. 100 ff.; Busolt: *Gr. Gesch.* 2 (1895), pp. 258 ff.; Beloch: *Gr. Gesch.* 1. 1 (1924), pp. 363 ff.; Zimmern: *Greek Commonwealth* (1915), p. 128.

[97] The story of Lucius Papirius and his debtor Gaius Publilius is related in Livy: 8. 28; cf. Dion. Hal. *ant. Rom.* 16. 5 (9) ; Val. Max. 6. 1. 9. A form of contract (*nexum*) which reduced debtors to a sort of slavery apparently existed in early Roman law (see tab. 3 of the Twelve Tables in Girard: *Textes de droit romain*, 1923, p. 13), but it was obsolete long before the time of the classical law. It seems to have been abolished by a *Lex Poetelia*, passed a short time prior to 300 B. C., but the precise terms of this statute are unknown. For various views see Buckland: *Text-book of Roman Law* (1921), p. 426.

of their establishments and hardly superior to them in wealth, they far surpassed them in distinction. And their excellent qualities exerted a wider influence in public life, because in private affairs they assiduously protected individual citizens by their exertions, their counsel, and their wealth.

XXXV. While this form of government prevailed, Spurius Cassius, a man of the greatest influence among the people, was charged by a quaestor with attempting to seize royal power. As you have heard, after his father had declared that he had found him guilty of the charge, he inflicted the death penalty with the permission of the people. About fifty-four years after the establishment of the consulate, the consuls Spurius Tarpeius and Aulus Aternius secured the passage in the assembly of the centuries of the popular statute on fines and judicial wagers. Twenty years later, because the censors Lucius Papirius and Publius Pinarius had imposed fines diverting to the state countless flocks belonging to private citizens, Gaius Julius and Publius Papirius, the consuls, proposed a statute establishing a reasonable money equivalent for cattle and sheep.[98]

XXXVI. Some years before, however, while the chief power was vested in the senate and the people still submissively tolerated their rule, a plan was initiated whereby both the consuls and the tribunes of the plebs were to resign from office, and ten men were to be elected with absolute power, from whose decisions no appeal should lie. It was intended that they should possess supreme authority and should reduce the laws to writing.[99] After they had drawn up a legal code of

---

[98] The traditional views of these laws may be found in Botsford: *Roman Assemblies* (1909), p. 269; Greenidge: *Legal Procedure of Cicero's Time* (1901), p. 335. They appear to be mentioned by Cicero as landmarks in the growth of popular power, though it is not clear what relation he supposed the *Lex Aternia Tarpeia* bore to judicial wager (*sacramentum*). The latter is described by Buckland: *Text-book of Roman Law* (1921), pp. 605 ff.

[99] According to Diodorus (12. 23-26), the date of the law of the Twelve Tables was 444-442 B. C.; see Boak: *History of Rome to 565 A. D.* (1922), p. 54. According to Livy (3. 9-57) and Dionysius (*ant. Rom.* 10. 1-60), the decemvirs were first appointed in 451. The date given by Diodorus is questionable but the more probable of the two. The literature on the Twelve Tables would "clothe the walls of spacious libraries." For the general topic see Gibbon: *Decline and Fall* (ed. Bury, 1914), 4, pp. 473 ff.; Mommsen: *Röm. Gesch.* 1 (1912), pp. 280 ff. (Eng. trans. 1,

Ten Tables, marked by the highest justice and wisdom, they nominated other decemvirs for the following years, whose good faith and justice have not been equally esteemed. Nevertheless, Gaius Julius, one of the members of this latter group, is accorded the highest praise. It happened that a corpse had been disinterred in the bed chamber of a certain nobleman, Lucius Sestius, and that Gaius actually witnessed this occurrence. In spite of the fact that Gaius had supreme authority and as a decemvir was competent to give decisions from which there was no appeal, he nevertheless admitted Lucius to bail, because, as he said, he would not disregard the excellent law which forbade a decision affecting the life of a Roman citizen to be passed anywhere except in the assembly of the centuries.

XXXVII. There followed a third year in which the same decemvirs still held office and refused to appoint successors. In such a form of commonwealth—which, as I have already frequently remarked, could not be permanent, because it was not fair to the different classes in the state—all political authority was in the hands of the aristocracy. Their leaders, the decemvirs, were members of the most important families; their power was not checked by tribunes of the plebs; no other magistrates were associated with them; and there was no appeal to the people in cases of capital punishment and flogging. Consequently, the injustice of their rule suddenly caused a tremendous upheaval and revolution involving the entire commonwealth. For they had added two tables of inequitable laws which forbade marriage between plebeians and patricians—a monstrous provision, since the right of intermarriage is usually granted even to citizens of different states. The prohibition was subsequently repealed by the Canuleian plebiscite.[100]

---

pp. 279 ff.) ; Heitland: *Roman Republic* (1909), ch. 10. For texts of the surviving fragments see Schoell: *Legis duodecim tabularum reliquiae* (1866) ; Bruns: *Fontes iuris Romani antiqui* (1909), pp. 15 ff.; Girard: *Textes de droit romain* (1923), pp. 9 ff., with the literature mentioned in the introductions to the two works last mentioned. There is no satisfactory edition in English.

[100] The traditional date of this measure is 445 B. C. The usual view, taken from Livy (4. 1; 6), is that the Lex Canuleia first legalized marriages between patricians and plebeians; see Buckland: *Text-book of Roman Law* (1921), p. 115, n. 1.

The decemvirs wantonly overrode the authority of every magistracy, and ruled the people in a harsh and mercenary fashion. The outcome is well known, of course, and has frequently been treated in literature. A certain Decimus Verginius with his own hand killed his unmarried daughter in the forum because of the license of one of the decemvirs, and fled in tears to the army, which was then at Algidus. Then the soldiers abandoned the war in which they were engaged and occupied first the Sacred Mount, as had been done before in a similar case, and then the Aventine[101].........

(The four inside leaves of the twenty-third quaternion are missing)

So, let who will be vexed.[102] I will face it all. For right is on my side, especially since I have given bail, with the six books of the "Commonwealth" for sureties, as it were. I am glad you approve them so heartily. In connection with them, however, you raise an historical question concerning Gnaeus Flavius, the son of Annius. His date was not earlier than the decemvirs, since he was curule aedile, a magistracy founded many years after their time. What, then, you ask, did he accomplish by publishing the fasti? The common view is that this portion of the Twelve Tables was at one time kept secret, in order that the proper days for the transaction of legal business might be obtained only from the few men [comprising the college of pontiffs.][103] There are many authorities who assert that Gnaeus Flavius, while he was the secretary of Appius

---

[101] The traditional date of the second secession of the plebs is 449 B. C.; see Livy: 3. 44 ff.; Greenidge: *Roman Public Life* (1911), pp. 107 ff. For a different account see Diodorus: 12. 24 ff., who ascribes the event to 443 B. C. and puts the episode of Verginia before the promulgation of the Twelve Tables.

[102] In this letter to his friend Atticus, dated 50 B. C., Cicero asserts that his actions in certain financial negotiations had been above reproach. He could not have acted otherwise than honorably, he adds, since he would not have dared to fall below the standard of conduct which he had set up in the *Commonwealth*. See Tyrrell and Purser: *The Correspondence of Cicero*, 3 (1890), no. 252. 8, and note.

[103] As Cicero suggests, there were two traditions among the Romans themselves about the origin of their law of judicial procedure. One of the theories was that this law formed an integral part of the Twelve Tables and had been published at the same time; see Schoell: *Legis duodecim tabularum reliquiae*, 1886, pp. 63 ff.; pp. 156 ff., where the *fasti* are included among the provisions of the eleventh *tabula*. The other theory, and the one supported by Cicero, was that the law of procedure

Claudius Caecus, published the fasti and drew up a summary of the forms of legal procedure. For I would not have you think that the story was invented by me, or rather by Africanus, since he is the speaker.   Cic. *ad Att.* 6. 1. 8.

Lucius Quinctius having been appointed dictator[104] . . . .

SCIPIO: . . . . I judge that our ancestors approved it in the highest degree and very wisely retained it.

XXXVIII. After Scipio had said this and while all were silently awaiting the rest of his remarks, Tubero spoke: Since the older men here have no questions to ask you, Africanus, I shall tell you what I fail to find in your presentation.

SCIPIO: Very well, I shall be glad to hear it.

TUBERO: In my opinion you have praised our state, although Laelius had asked you not about our state but about the state in general. And yet, I have not learned from your discussion what are the training, the customs, or the statutes by which we can preserve the very commonwealth which you praise.

XXXIX. SCIPIO: I think, Tubero, that we shall soon have a more suitable opportunity for discussing the founding and preservation of states. But in the matter of the best type of state I did think that I had given a sufficient answer to the question that Laelius had put to me. For in the first place I had defined the three kinds of good states and the three perverted forms opposed to them. In the second place I had showed that none of the simple forms is best, but that a state properly compounded of all three types is better than any one by itself. Moreover, my use of our own state as an example did not serve the purpose of defining the perfect state, for that

---

had not been revealed to the common people by the decemviral commission but had been kept as the secret possession of the privileged classes until Gnaeus Flavius published it in 304 B.C. An essential part of the rules of procedure (*legis actiones*) which he made known was the *fasti*, or the calendar of the days on which it was permissible to transact legal business. So long as the law retained a highly sacramental character, i. e., so long as it was colored by *fas*, the monopoly of such knowledge by a narrow circle of initiated and *quasi* priestly personages was an important element in patrician power. See Greenidge: *Legal Procedure of Cicero's Time* (1901), pp. 26 ff.; Gaius: *inst.* ed. Poste (1904), p. xxiii; Girard: *Manuel de droit romain* (1924), pp. 46 ff.

[104] Servius (ed. Thilo et Hagen): *ad georg.* 3. 125.

could have been done without any example. My purpose was rather to illustrate empirically, in the greatest of states, the nature of that which I was describing theoretically. But if you ask for the type of state which is best in itself, without the example of any specific people, we must use the model which nature suggests, since you [regard] our chosen model of the Roman city and people [as too restricted..........]¹⁰⁵

(Probably the first or the first two leaves of the twenty-fourth quaternion are missing)

XL. SCIPIO: ....that man whom I have long been seeking and whom I desire to find.

LAELIUS: You are seeking the wise man, perhaps.

SCIPIO: The very same.

LAELIUS: You have a good choice among those present— for example, you might begin with yourself.

SCIPIO: Would that there were an equal proportion of wise men in the senate! And yet, he is a wise man who, seated upon a huge and savage elephant—we have often seen the like in Africa—guides and directs the beast wherever he will and turns him aside with a touch or with a gentle command.

LAELIUS: I understand, and I often saw what you describe when I was a legate on your staff.

SCIPIO: Well then, the Indian or Carthaginian controls only one monster, and that a docile one, who has been trained to the ways of men. But that hidden element in men's souls which is called intelligence bridles and masters not one monster only, or one easy to subdue, supposing—what rarely happens—that

---

¹⁰⁵ The supplement is Mai's. At this point Cicero apparently began the transition to Scipio's eulogy of justice which, as we know from Augustine (see ch. 43, below), closed the second book and introduced the longer discussion of this subject in the third book. We may conjecture that the main heads of the discourse were somewhat as follows: (1) In principle human society is based upon the rational nature in man which is akin to universal reason (cf. *de off.* 1. 4. 11 ff.; 1. 16. 50 f.; *de fin.* 2. 14. 45; 3. 19. 63; 4. 2. 4); (2) reason in the wise man has dominion over the passions and perturbations of the soul which are like wild beasts when uncontrolled; (3) the wise man who has reduced his own soul to harmony is the only fit ruler of the state; (4) as the soul is a harmony when ruled by reason, so the state is a harmony of its various classes united by justice.

it ever accomplishes this. And that wild [appetite in man] must be restrained[106] . . . .

(Either two or four inside leaves of the twenty-fourth quaternion are missing)

XLI. . . . . which is nourished on blood and which so exults in every form of cruelty that it is scarcely sated by the merciless slaughter of men.[107]

To a man greedy, avaricious, lustful, and wallowing in pleasures.[108]

And the fourth [form of perturbation] is depression of mind which inclines toward melancholy and is always weeping and indulging in self-torture.[109]

---

[106] In the following lacuna Cicero dealt with the violent passions which reason has to subdue, and from the quotations given by Nonius, it may be inferred that he followed the outline of the Stoic theory of perturbations. These are defined, following Zeno, as "violent movements of soul contrary to right reason and against nature" (*Tusc.* 4. 6. 11). All are forms of false judgment and they are four in number: (1) false opinion about a present good, or undue exaltation (*voluptas, laetitia*), that is, a lack of soberness in enjoying pleasure, including malice and ostentation; (2) false opinion of a future good, or greed (*libido, cupiditas*), that is, a lack of soberness in pursuing advantages, including greed of money or power, anger (undue pursuit of revenge), and hate; (3) false opinion of future ill, or fear (*metus, formido*) ; (4) false opinion about a present evil, or grief (*aegritudo*), that is, a lack of fortitude in bearing pain and disappointment, including envy, fretfulness, bitterness, worry, undue pity, and mourning. See *Tusc.* 3. 11. 24-25; 4. 7. 14-16; *de fin.* 3. 10. 35; Arnold: *Roman Stoicism* (1911), ch. 14. Since Cicero has in mind especially the character of the statesman, it is probable that he followed much the same line of argument as in *de off.* 1. 20. 66 ff.

[107] Nonius, p. 300. 29. This fragment refers to anger (*iracundia*) and may possibly have formed part of a more general treatment of the perturbation *libido*. Cicero defines anger as the "lust for vengeance" (*Tusc.* 3. 5. 11). The question whether anger is a vice was a moot point between the Stoics and Peripatetics. The latter followed Aristotle in recognizing the righteousness of anger under proper circumstances (*Nic. Eth.* 1125 b 26 ff.). Cicero takes the Stoic position (*de off.* 1. 38. 136) and refers to anger as a vice especially to be avoided by statesmen (*ibid.* 1. 26. 88-89; *Tusc.* 4. 22. 49-50).

[108] Nonius, p. 491. 16. This fragment seems to have formed part of a treatment of the perturbation *voluptas* or *laetitia*; see *Tusc.* 4. 9. 20-22.

[109] Nonius, p. 72. 34. The perturbations are mentioned by Cicero in different orders, but it is clear that the fourth in this passage is *aegritudo* (*Tusc.* 4. 7. 16). The word *anxitudo*, not elsewhere used in Cicero's philosophical works, is here taken as an alternative translation for the Greek *lupe*. *Aegritudo* is defined as a "casting down or drooping of the spirit" (*ibid.* 4. 7. 14).

But these are vexations if a man is afflicted with wretchedness or cast down by fear or sloth.[110]

As an unskilled charioteer is dragged from his car, is run over, is torn to bits, is crushed to death.[111]

XLII. [SCIPIO:] .... it might be said.

LAELIUS: I see now what duty and function you assign to the man whom I was looking for.

SCIPIO: He has in fact scarcely more than this single duty—for it includes nearly everything else—that he should never abandon the study and contemplation of himself; that he should challenge others to imitate him; and that by the nobility of his mind and conduct he should hold himself up to his fellow citizens as a model.[112] For, as in the music of lyre and flute and as even in singing and spoken discourse[113] there is a certain melody which must be preserved in the different sounds—and if this is altered or discordant it becomes intolerable to the ears of a connoisseur—and as this melody is made concordant and harmonious in spite of the dissimilar sounds of which it is composed, so the state achieves harmony by the agreement[114] of unlike individuals, when there is a wise blending of the highest, the lowest, and the intervening middle classes in the manner of tones. And what musicians call harmony in song is concord in a state. It is the closest and the

---

[110] Nonius, p. 228. 19. We read *adflictus aut abiectus* with Gerlach. The text is obviously corrupt. The fragment seems to belong to an account of fear (*metus*), of which *timiditas* and *ignavia* are forms; see *Tusc.* 5. 17. 52. *Angor* and *miseria*, however, belong to *aegritudo; ibid.* 4. 7. 16; 4. 38. 83.

[111] Nonius, p. 292. 38. This fragment suggests that Cicero used Plato's myth of the charioteer (*Phaedrus*, 246 a ff.) to typify the opposition of reason and passion in the soul; cf. *Tusc.* 4. 5. 10. This opposition was introduced into Stoicism by Panaetius' adoption of Plato's threefold division of the soul. The older Stoa had regarded the soul as wholly rational. See Introduction, p. 30, above.

[112] Cf. Cic. *de leg.* 1. 22. 58-62.

[113] That a certain melody was desired in speaking may be seen from the custom of Gaius Gracchus, who had a slave stand near him when he spoke. The slave was equipped with a pitch-pipe and would blow upon it when Gracchus' voice became harsh in order to recall him to more pleasing tones; see Greenidge: *History of Rome,* 1 (1904), p. 192.

[114] This paragraph, from "agreement" to the end, is supplied from Augustine: *de civ.* 2. 21. In the comparison of "concord" in the state to "harmony" in music Cicero is combining three notions. First, he is apparently alluding to the heptachord lyre, used by the Pythagoreans in

best bond of security that can be found in any commonwealth, and without justice it cannot exist at all.

(From ten to twelve leaves of the twenty-fourth, the twenty-fifth, and the twenty-sixth quaterions are missing)

XLIII. *And then, after Scipio had showed at greater length and in more detail how great were the advantages which justice conferred on a state and how serious the loss if it were absent, Philus, who was one of those present at the discussion, took up the argument and asked that this question be considered more carefully, and that justice be discussed more at length, because of the prevalent belief that injustice was necessarily inherent in the government of a commonwealth.*

Augustine: *de civ.* 2. 21.

XLIV. PHILUS: ....is full of justice.

SCIPIO: I agree with what you say, and I declare that no importance is to be attached to anything which, as we suppose, has hitherto been established about the state, and that no further advance is possible, unless we shall prove both the falsity of the view which regards injustice as a necessary part of government, and the truth of the view which regards a high degree of justice as essential if the state is to function at all. But, if you please, this is enough for today. What remains—and there is much yet to be said—let us defer until to-morrow.

They approved this suggestion and the discussion ended for that day.

---

their attempts to determine the numerical ratios that produced "concord." (Concord meant tuning or fitting successive tones into a scale.) On this instrument the highest string—"highest" referring to position and not to pitch—was called *hypate* and corresponded to *summus ordo* in Cicero's text; the middle was named *mese*, the equivalent of *medius ordo;* and the lowest was termed *nete*, the counterpart of Cicero's *infimus ordo*. See Burnet: *Greek Philosophy*, 1 (1914), pp. 45 ff. Second, Cicero seems to refer, in a less exact manner, to the harmony produced by the spheres, and suggested perhaps by the Vision of Er in Plato's *Republic* (617 b, with Adam's notes). There were eight circles (see Cic. *de rep.* 6. 17, below, for a somewhat similar arrangement): the Fixed Stars gave the note *nete*; the Sun, Venus, and Mercury *mese*; while Saturn corresponded to the string named *hypate*. Note, however, that Heath (*Aristarchus of Samos*, 1913, p. 110, n. 1) understands Plato to assign the note *hypate* to the Moon, as Cicero does, *de rep.* 6. 18, below. Third, Cicero probably had in mind the passage in Plato's *Republic* (443 d), where justice is defined as an inner harmony whereby the three parts of the soul are in perfect attunement.

BOOK III

*The discussion of justice and its place in the state had been
postponed until the following day, and accordingly in the third
book the question was debated sharply between the two opposing points of view. Thus, Philus himself undertook to set
forth the views of those who believed that the state cannot be
conducted without injustice,[1] though he earnestly disclaimed
any belief in this view himself. He developed fully the case
for injustice as against justice, as if he were seeking to show
by plausible arguments and examples that injustice is advantageous to the state and justice disadvantageous. Then Laelius, at the request of all present, addressed himself to the task
of defending justice.[2] He did all in his power to show that
nothing is so antagonistic to the state as injustice, and that the
commonwealth cannot function or exist at all, unless justice
strongly marks its activities. When this question had been
discussed apparently to the satisfaction of all, Scipio returned
from the digression to the main argument.[3] He reconsidered
his brief definition of a commonwealth and offered it for the
approval of his hearers. The commonwealth he had defined as
the people's affair, and the people, in turn, not as any group
composed of a considerable number of men, but as the coming
together of persons who are united by a common agreement
about law and rights and by the desire to participate in mutual
advantages. He then showed how greatly definitions aid argument, and inferred from his own definitions that there is no
commonwealth—that is, nothing which is the people's affair—
unless the state is conducted in accordance with rectitude and
justice, whether it be ruled by a monarch, a small number of
aristocrats, or the people collectively. A king, indeed, may
defy the law, in which case Scipio, using Greek terminology,*

---

[1] This begins at ch. 5.
[2] This begins at ch. 21.
[3] Scipio returns to the argument in ch. 30.

called him a tyrant. Similarly, the aristocrats may govern arbitrarily, and their agreement to violate the law makes them, he said, an oligarchy. Or again, the people may themselves transgress the law, and for such a government Scipio did not find any accepted term but called it also a tyranny. These forms of government, he now concluded, are not perverted types of commonwealth, as he had said in the discussion of the preceding day, but are not really types of commonwealth at all, as he proved by inference from his definitions of the commonwealth and the people. The reason for this was that there is no affair of the people when a tyrant or an oligarchy controls a government. The people itself, moreover, is no longer a people when it oversteps the bounds of law, for then it no longer satisfies the definition of being a considerable number of individuals united by a common agreement about law and rights and by the desire to participate in mutual advantages.

Augustine: *de civ.* 2. 21.

I. *In the third book of his treatise on the Commonwealth Cicero likewise declares that nature, which has brought men into being, is less like a mother than a step-mother.*[4] *Their bodies are naked, frail, and weak.*[5] *Their minds are vexed by trouble, bowed down by fears, incapable of enduring toil, and inclined toward lust. Nevertheless, there lies hidden in them a divine spark of intelligence and reason.*

Augustine: *contra Iulianum,* 4. 12. 60; ed. Ben. 10, p. 612.

Although man is born frail and weak, he is nevertheless safe from the attack of all the dumb brutes. And all those creatures

---

[4] The dialogue of the second day, contained in Books 3 and 4, was preceded by an introduction (chs. 1-4) in which Cicero speaks in his own person. The chief heads of this introduction appear to have been somewhat as follows: (1) Man is born weaker than other animals but the possession of reason makes him their superior (ch. 1; cf. *de leg.* 2. 7. 16). (2) Reason gives man speech and the arts and sciences (ch. 2; cf. *de n. d.* 2. 59. 147 ff.; 2. 61. 153; Lactantius: *de opif. dei,* 3. 4). (3) Reason and speech give rise to law and society (cf. *de n. d.* 2. 61. 153; *de off.* 1. 4. 12; 1. 16. 50-51; *de fin.* 2. 14. 45; 3. 19. 63; 4. 2. 4). (4) Wisdom has two branches, the arts and sciences and law and government, but the summit of human excellence is reached by the man who can combine scholarly tastes and practical achievement (chs. 3 and 4; cf. *de am.* 5. 18 f.).

[5] This is perhaps an echo of Lucretius: 5. 222 ff.

*which are by nature stronger than man, though they endure
bravely the struggle with the elements, are still unable to save
themselves from the attacks of men. Thus, reason confers
more upon man than instinct confers upon the brutes, for
neither the greatness of their strength nor the power of their
bodies can save them from being killed or domesticated by man
........I presume it was to refute these ingrates [who enlarge upon human weakness] that Plato thanked nature for
being born a man.*[6]   Lactantius: *de opif. dei,* 3. 16; 17; 19.

(Either two or four leaves of the twenty-sixth quaternion are missing)

II.   [Reason enabled man to domesticate the animals and
thus to make use of][7] vehicles to aid his slowness.   And when
[reason] found men employing uncouth sounds and using ut-
terance imperfect and confused, she distinguished and classi-
fied these inarticulate sounds and assigned certain words to
certain things as their symbols.   Thus, with the most agreeable tie of speech she bound together men who had hitherto
been solitary.   Likewise, reason discovered a few letters by
which all the apparently infinite variety of sounds might be
indicated and expressed, that men might communicate with
their absent fellows, express their wishes, and preserve the
records of their past.   Next followed the discovery of number,
which is necessary to life and is also the only thing unchangeable and eternal.   Likewise it was number which first moved
men to look up into the heavens and to contemplate intelligently the movements of the stars and [to determine the length
of the year] by counting nights and days[8].......

(The last leaf, or the last two leaves, of the twenty-sixth
quaternion, and the first three leaves of the
twenty-seventh quaternion, are missing)

III.   [By such studies] their minds were uplifted, and they
could accomplish or design something worthy of that which I

[6] See also Plutarch: *Marius,* 46; Lactantius: *inst.* 3. 19. 17, where the
same statement about Plato is made.
[7] This supplement is added from Cic. *de n. d.* 2. 60. 151.
[8] Cf. Cic. *de n. d.* 2. 61. 153, where he continues: "By contemplating
such subjects [i. e., the heavenly bodies], the mind arrives at a knowledge of the gods, and from this arises a sense of duty toward gods and
men *(pietas)* to which justice and the other virtues are akin."

have called the gift of the gods. For this reason let us count those who treat the philosophy of life as great men—as indeed they are—let us count them as scholars and as teachers of truth and excellence. But at the same time let us admit the existence of an art—whether discovered by statesmen who have faced the vicissitudes of public life or studied even by your philosophers in scholarly retirement—an art which comprises the theory of politics and the government of peoples and which, in truth, is by no means to be despised. This art, when added to great natural abilities, produces, as it has often done in the past, a type of character extraordinary and divine. And when men have felt, as did the participants in this dialogue, that, to the powers of mind received from nature and developed by experience in public affairs, they should add also scholarly interests and a richer acquaintance with life, such men must be universally conceded to be superior to all others. What, indeed, can be more glorious than the union of practical experience in great affairs with an intelligent enthusiasm for the liberal arts?[9] Can anything be imagined more perfect than the distinction of a Publius Scipio, a Gaius Laelius, or a Lucius Philus,[10] men who, in order not to neglect anything which might bring the highest glory to illustrious men, united the rules of conduct which they learned at home and inherited from their ancestors even with a foreign philosophy derived from Socrates?[11] Hence I hold that a man who has been able and willing to combine these two interests, and has disciplined himself both in the ways of his ancestors and in liberal culture, has attained everything that entitles a man to praise. But if it should happen that we must make a choice between these two paths of wisdom, though some will feel that a tranquil life spent in the pursuit of literature and the liberal arts is the more delightful, still a political career is assuredly more

---

[9] This sentence may be said, without much exaggeration, to sum up the ideal of the statesman's character from Cicero's time down to that great school of English statesmanship, the course at Oxford in *litterae humaniores.*

[10] For a similar eulogy of these three men see Cic. *de or.* 2. 37. 154; *pro Arch.* 7. 16.

[11] Cf. Cic. *acad. post.* 1. 1. 3.

praiseworthy and honorable. It was this manner of life that brought honor to the greatest men, like Manius Curius,

> Whom steel could not subdue nor gold corrupt,[12]

or..........

(The three last leaves of the twenty-seventh quaternion are missing)

IV. [Either course] was a part of philosophy, but still there was this difference between the methods proposed by the two classes [of thinkers.][13] The one fostered the innate powers of man by means of training in rhetorical science, the other by means of training in law and political institutions. In fact, the Roman state has itself produced more men who, if not themselves philosophers—for this term is narrowly restricted by [those who advocate rhetorical training]—are at all events worthy of the greatest honor for having put into practice the teachings and discoveries of philosophers. Now there have been, and there still are, many states deserving praise, and it is a work of the highest wisdom in the world to found a state that can endure.[14] If, then, we count a single lawgiver to each of these states, how great a number of eminent men shall we find! If we choose to confine our observation to Italy, and consider Latium, or the Sabine and Volscian peoples, or Samnium, or Etruria, or renowned Magna Graecia; if we consider then the Assyrians, or the Persians, or the Carthaginians; if these[15]

....

(The six inside leaves of the twenty-eighth quaternion are missing)

V. ....counselors.[16]

PHILUS: Truly, a noble task you assign me when you would have me undertake the defense of wickedness!

---

[12] This is a line from Ennius: *ann.* (Vahlen, 2nd ed.), line 373.

[13] The fragmentary condition of the text prevents our knowing what thinkers are here contrasted. We put forward the tentative suggestion that Cicero is here comparing either the methods of instruction adopted respectively by Isocrates and Plato, or the forms of political instruction accepted respectively by the Greeks and the Romans.

[14] Cf. Plato: *Symposium*, 209 a; *Republic*, 428 a; *Laws*, 714 b ff.

[15] Cicero probably went on to enumerate a long list of Roman statesmen, such as that in *de n. d.* 2. 66. 155.

[16] We adopt Mai's suggestion. In the lacuna the dialogue has recommenced. The question proposed at the end of the second book is about to be debated, viz., Does the state depend upon justice or does it thrive by injustice? Philus presents the case for injustice.

LAELIUS: Still, in presenting the customary arguments against justice, you need not fear that you will be thought to hold such views yourself. For you are, as we may say, a unique example of ancient uprightness and good faith; and it is well known that you are in the habit of marshaling the arguments on both sides of a question, since you believe that in this way the truth is most readily elicited.

PHILUS: Very well, then, I shall comply with your request and knowingly defile myself. Men who hunt gold do not think that they should spare themselves trouble; and we who seek justice, a thing much more precious than all the gold in the world, surely ought not to shun any inconvenience.[17] As the arguments which I shall use are another's, I would that I might speak with the mouth of another. But as matters stand, I, Lucius Furius Philus, must set forth the arguments by which Carneades,[18] who was a Greek and accustomed to propound any view that suited his purpose, [attempted to overthrow justice].

(The first two leaves of the twenty-ninth quaternion are missing)

[I advance these views merely] that you may controvert the arguments of Carneades, who frequently uses clever quibbles to make sport of worthy topics.[19]

VI. *Carneades was a philosopher of the Academy. Anyone who does not know his force in argument, his eloquence, and his shrewdness will understand them from the commendation given him by Cicero and Lucilius. For the latter represents Neptune as discussing a difficult question and as showing that the matter cannot be explained,*

Not even if Hades should send back Carneades himself.[20]

---

[17] This closely parallels Plato: *Republic*, 336 e.

[18] On the philosophy of Carneades, and especially its influence upon Stoicism in the period to which Cicero attributes his dialogue, see Introduction, pp. 26 f.

[19] Nonius, p. 263. 8.

[20] Lucilius (ed. Marx): 1. 31. Cicero (*de or.* 1. 11. 45) says of Carneades that, according to report, he was "the shrewdest and most eloquent of all speakers"; cf. *ibid.* 2. 38. 161; 3. 18. 68; Polybius: 12. 26 c; 33. 2. Admiration of his eloquence and logical power was universal among the ancients; many references will be found in Zeller: *Phil. d. Griech.* 3. 1 (1923), p. 517, n. 3.

It was Carneades whom the Athenians sent to Rome on an embassy[21] *and who discoursed eloquently on justice in the hearing of Galba and Cato the Censor, the most important orators of the age. But the next day Carneades refuted his former arguments and overthrew justice, which he had eulogized the day before. His performance was somewhat beneath the dignity of a philosopher, whose views should be fixed and unvarying. It was rather a kind of rhetorical exercise in arguing on both sides of a question*[22]—*a practice he regularly followed in order to refute other speakers, no matter what views they supported. His refutation of justice is reproduced in Cicero's work by Lucius Furius Philus. Cicero's purpose in his discussion of the state, as I suppose, was to include a defense and eulogy of justice, which he regarded as a necessary element in government. Carneades, on the other hand, because he wished to refute Plato and Aristotle, who were the champions of justice, brought together in his first speech all the arguments which they used in support of it. His purpose was to be in a position to overthrow justice [in his second speech], and as a matter of fact he did it.*[23]   Lactantius: *inst.* 5. 14. 3-5.

VII. *Many philosophers, but especially Plato and Aristotle, have had much to say about justice. It was this virtue which they esteemed and praised most highly, because it gives to every man his own and preserves fair dealing in all human*

---

[21] This embassy, consisting of Carneades, the Stoic Diogenes, and the Peripatetic Critolaus, came to Rome in 156-5 B. C. to obtain the release of Athens from a fine imposed for attempting to seize the town of Oropos. The embassy has generally been regarded by both ancient and modern writers as a landmark in the process of introducing Greek education at Rome; see Ferguson: *Hellenistic Athens* (1911), ch. 8, especially pp. 325 ff.; 333 ff.

[22] This was a common practice of skeptical philosophers and part of the device by which they sought to show the uncertainty of all knowledge. Cicero frequently refers to it as characteristic of the critical method of the Academy; see *acad. prior.* (ed. Reid), note to 2. 3. 7; *de div.* 2. 72. 150, with Pease's commentary, where references to other passages in Cicero will be found.

[23] This and the following extract are colored by the views of Lactantius himself. He is following the text, "The wisdom of this world is foolishness with God." Hence philosophy without revelation is "empty and false" (*inst.* 3. 2) and the virtues, without the rewards and punishments of a future life, are "the most useless and stupid things in human existence" (*ibid.* 5. 19).

relationships. And while all other virtues are, so to speak, silent and self-centered, justice is the only one, they said, which does not exist for itself alone and is not secret, but exerts its influence wholly abroad and tends to do good and thus to benefit the greatest possible number of persons. As if, in truth, justice were required only of judges and those in authority, and not of all men! For there is in fact no man, not even the humblest beggar, who is not concerned with justice. But because Plato and Aristotle did not understand the nature of justice, or its source, or its function, they attributed to a few that supreme virtue which is the common good of all mankind. Moreover, they said that justice seeks no selfish advantage but considers solely the interests of others. Quite reasonably, therefore, Carneades, who was a man of great ability and shrewdness, came forward to refute their arguments and overturn a view of justice which was without firm foundation. He was led to do this, not because he believed that justice deserved to be assailed, but in order to show that the defenders of justice urged nothing in its behalf that was indisputable or well proved. Lactantius: *epit.* 50 (55). 5-8.

Justice turns its gaze abroad; it is wholly directed toward interests outside the individual and rises above selfish considerations.[24]

This virtue more than any other devotes and dedicates itself to the interests of others.[25]

VIII. PHILUS: [In the "Republic" Plato formulated an ideal commonwealth in order to] discover justice and defend it, while [Aristotle][26] devoted four good-sized books to justice itself. From Chrysippus[27] I expected nothing significant or

---

[24] Nonius, p. 373. 30.

[25] Nonius, p. 299. 30.

[26] The passages from Lactantius in the two preceding chapters make it clear that the reference is to Plato and Aristotle. For Plato's object in constructing an ideal state see *Republic,* 368 c ff. Aristotle's work on justice was one of his earlier writings, probably in dialogue form; see Zeller: *Phil. d. Griech.* 2. 2 (1921), p. 58, n. 3. The extant fragments are in Rose: *Arist. fragmenta* (1886), pp. 86 ff.

[27] The charge of verbalism was universally brought against Chrysippus in antiquity. For references see Zeller: *Phil. d. Griech.* 3. 1 (1923), p. 44, n. 1, and the testimonia on his life and writings in von Arnim:

elevating, for it was characteristic of him to investigate all questions rather by examining the meanings of words than by weighing the facts at issue. It was the task of Plato and Aristotle, the princes of philosophy, to awaken justice and raise her from her lowly place to that divine throne only a little below philosophy itself. For justice—assuming that it exists— is the only virtue pre-eminently unselfish and generous, and [only a man who is inspired by justice] prefers the interests of all men to his own and is born to serve others rather than himself.[28] Certainly Plato and Aristotle did not lack the inclination to extol justice, for this was the only motive or design that prompted them to write about it at all; nor were they lacking in genius, for in this they excelled all men. And yet their inclination and resources were defeated by the weakness of their cause. For the justice which forms the object of our investigation pertains to society but not at all to nature.[29] If it were a part of nature, justice and injustice, like heat and cold or bitterness and sweetness, would be the same for all men.

IX. Suppose now that we could ride in Pacuvius' chariot drawn by winged serpents[30] and, looking down, could survey the many races and cities of men. We should perceive, first, that the Egyptians, though they retain an unexampled simplicity of life and possess written records covering the events of many ages, nevertheless regard a bull as a god and call him Apis. We should perceive also that they have enrolled among the gods many other strange monsters and beasts of every

Stoicorum veterum fragmenta, 2 (1923), pp. 1 ff. Chrysippus was the author of a work on justice, the extant fragments of which, so far as they can be assigned to this work, are listed by von Arnim: *ibid.* 3 (1923), p. 195.

[28] This view of justice is assigned to Plato, perhaps on the strength of his contention that doing injury, even to enemies, can never be just (*Republic*, 335 b ff.). The definition of justice as rendering to every man his own is not Platonic but Stoic. See the references in von Arnim: *Stoicorum veterum fragmenta*, 4 (1924), Index, s. v. *dikaiosune*. This definition developed no doubt from the conception of proportional justice in Plato and Aristotle; see note to *de rep.* 1. 27, above.

[29] On the distinction of nature and convention, see Introduction, pp. 14 ff.

[30] A reference to a chariot used in one of Pacuvius' plays, perhaps, as Mai suggests, one in which Medea was a character. For the idea see Cic. *Tusc.* 1. 45. 108.

kind. If we should pass next to Greece, we should observe there, as at Rome, splendid temples dedicated to gods in human form. This practice the Persians regarded as impious and it is said that Xerxes ordered the Athenian temples to be burned solely because he thought it wicked for gods to be shut in and confined by walls, when their home is this entire world.[31] And yet, somewhat later, Philip planned a war against the Persians and Alexander carried it out, alleging as their motive the desire to avenge the shrines of Greece. Moreover, the Greeks thought that their temples should not even be rebuilt, in order that posterity might have eternally before its eyes a reminder of the crimes committed by the Persians.[32] How many peoples have there been, like the Taurians on the shores of the Euxine Sea, like the Egyptian King Busiris, and like the Gauls and the Carthaginians, who have thought that it was right and pleasing in the sight of the immortal gods to offer human sacrifices![33]

Manners of life are in fact so diverse that the Cretans and Aetolians consider brigandage an honorable calling,[34] and the Lacedaemonians asserted that they owned all the territories which could touch with the dart.[35] The Athenians even had the custom of taking public oath that every land which bore grain or the olive belonged to them.[36] The Gauls hold it to be ignominious to raise grain by their own labor; hence they go forth in armed bands and appropriate the grain in other

---

[31] See Cic. *de leg.* 2. 10. 26; Herodotus: 1. 131; 8. 109; cf. Augustine: *de civ.* 4. 9; 31; 6. 10.

[32] For the refusal to rebuild the temples see Pausanias: 10. 35.

[33] For human sacrifice among the Taurians see Euripides: *Iphigeneia in Tauris*, hypothesis; Pomponius Mela: 2. 1. 11. For King Busiris see Vergil: *georg.* 3. 5. For the Gauls see Caesar: *de bell. Gall.* 6. 16; Diodorus: 5. 31. For the Carthaginians see Plato: *Minos*, 315 b ff.; Diodorus: 20. 14; Augustine: *de civ.* 7. 19.

[34] In Polybius (4. 3; 18. 4) the Aetolians are represented as being habitually engaged in brigandage; and in the same author (6. 46) a general charge of greed, wrongfully satisfied, is brought against the Cretans.

[35] See Plutarch: *apophth. Lac.* 28; *quaest. Rom.* 15.

[36] This was a part of the ephebic oath taken by young men on attaining their eighteenth year. See Plutarch: *Alcib.* 15; the phrase does not occur in Lycurgus: *contra Leocr.* 77, where the oath is given; Gilbert: *Gr. Staatsalt.* 1 (1893), pp. 347 ff.; Schoemann: *Gr. Alt.* 1 (1897), p. 379; Busolt: *Gr. Staatskunde*, 2 (1926), p. 1190.

men's fields.[37]   We Romans are strongly moved by considerations of justice, and yet, in order that the products of our own vineyards and olive groves may bring us a larger return, we do not permit the races beyond the Alps to plant the vine and the olive.[38]   In this policy we are said to act prudently but not justly.   From this fact you may perceive that justice and wisdom are not identical.   Finally, Lycurgus, who devised excellent statutes and a notably just code of laws, made the common people cultivate the lands of the wealthy, just as though they were slaves.[39]

X.   Now if I cared to enumerate the different kinds of laws, institutions, customs, and practices, I might show not only that they differ in different races, but that even in a single city—our own, for example—they have undergone a thousand changes.   Thus our friend Manilius here, in his capacity of jurisconsult, advises those who ask his opinion that the law governing legacies and inheritances by women is different now from what it was when he gave his opinion as a younger man, before the Voconian Law[40] was passed.   This is a statute

---

[37] See Diodorus: 5. 32.

[38] In the era preceding the Gracchi, due in part to incessant warfare, there had been a general increase of pasture land worked by slaves at the expense of tilled soil managed by freemen. The dangerous consequences of this economic decline had been realized. One of the measures passed to aid the small farmers of Italy in raising the vine and the olive, products for which that country, or at least parts of it, was admirably adapted, was the law mentioned in the text. See Columella: 3. 3. 11; Greenidge: *History of Rome*, 1 (1904), pp. 79 ff.; 269; Rostovtzeff: *Social and Economic History of the Roman Empire* (1926), p. 22. A similar provision seems to have been in force in the time of Domitian (81-96 A. D.); see Suetonius: *Domit.* 7.

[39] For the Helots, who are referred to here, see Gilbert: *Gr. Staatsalt.* 1 (1893), pp. 32 ff.; Busolt: *Gr. Staatskunde*, 2 (1926), pp. 667 ff.

[40] The *Lex Voconia* (169 or 168 B. C.), passed with the intention of repressing luxury and immorality among women, forbade a woman to be instituted heiress by a citizen whose property exceeded one hundred thousand sesterces, and also enacted that the amount taken by a legatee (not the heir) should not be more than that taken by the heirs. Thus, a testator with one heir could not make a legacy of more than one-half his property to a woman, or of one-third if he had two heirs, etc. If the woman were an only child (*filia unica*), as Philus supposes in the case of Crassus' daughter, she might take the whole estate as heiress, if her father died intestate—an uncommon occurrence among the Romans. See Gaius: *inst.* ed. Poste (1904), p. 239; Heitland: *Roman Republic* (1909), sects. 634; 651; Girard: *Manuel de droit romain* (1924), pp. 866 ff.

enacted in the interests of men but fraught with injustice toward women. For why should a woman not have money [on the same terms as a man]? Why may a Vestal bequeath property and her mother not?[41] Or again, granting that the amount of property which a woman can receive must be limited, why should the daughter of Publius Crassus, if she be his only child, be permitted to inherit a hundred million sesterces without violating the law, while my daughter cannot inherit three million?. . . . .

(The seventh leaf of the twenty-ninth quaternion is missing)

XI. PHILUS: [If justice were natural, then nature] would have laid down our laws; all peoples would be subject to the same laws; and the same people would not be subject to different laws at different times. Now I put the question to you:[42] If it be the duty of a just man and a good citizen to obey the laws, what laws should he obey? Shall he obey any laws that happen to prevail? But surely rectitude does not admit of inconsistency, and nature does not permit different standards of conduct. Laws, therefore, are obeyed because of the penalties they may inflict and not because of our sense of justice. Consequently, the law has no sanction in nature. It follows, then, that men are not just by nature. Or do they mean that, while there is diversity in human legislation, good men follow true justice rather than that which is merely thought to be just?[43] For rendering unto everything its deserts is said to be the mark of a good and just man. But in the first place, then, what shall we render to dumb animals? Thus, Pythagoras and Empedocles, men of no ordinary attainments but scholars of the first rank, assert that there is a

---

[41] Until the time of Hadrian a woman could not make a will, but the Vestals were an exception; see Buckland: *Text-book of Roman Law* (1921), p. 287.

[42] The argument is a dilemma: A just man either obeys the law or renders to everything its deserts. If he obeys the law, which varies from place to place, he cannot follow a universal sense of justice; and if he renders to everything its deserts, he must sometimes go counter to law and usage. On the two definitions of justice see Aristotle: *Nic. Eth.* 1129 a 31 ff.

[43] Compare Cic. *de leg.* 1. 18. 48.

single legal status belonging to all living creatures.[44] They proclaim, moreover, that everlasting punishment awaits those who have wronged anything that lives. It is a crime, accordingly, to injure an animal, and he who presumes to commit this offense[45]. . . .

(Of the next eighty leaves, composing quaternions thirty to thirty-nine, all but four are missing and these four cannot be precisely placed)

XII. *If a man wishes to act in accordance with justice, and yet is ignorant of the divine law, he will honor the enactments of his own people as if they were the true law, although they are in general the product, not of justice, but of self-interest. Why indeed have diverse and unlike codes of law been established among all peoples? Is it not because each people has enacted for itself such provisions as it thought to be useful in its own conditions of life? But how wide is the divergence between justice and utility[46] may be learned from the case of the Roman people itself. By using the Fetial College in their declarations of war, they gave acts of aggression the color of law. Thus, they constantly coveted and seized the possessions of others and so made themselves the masters of the whole world.*
Lactantius: inst. 6. 9. 2-4.

For unless I am mistaken, every kingdom or empire is acquired by war and extended by victory, and furthermore, the chief element in war and victory is the capture and overthrow of cities. Such acts are impossible without doing injury

---

[44] This is a reference to the transmigration of souls, the only teaching that can be ascribed with certainty to Pythagoras himself; see Burnet: *Early Greek Philosophy*, 1908, pp. 101 ff. For Empedocles see fragments 135-7 in Diels: *Vorsokratiker*, 1 (1912), p. 274 ff.; Burnet: *op. cit.* p. 289.

[45] This does not represent Cicero's own view; see *de leg.* 1. 8. 25, where animals are said to have been created for man, and among the uses to which they may be put is that of food.

[46] The argument now turns upon the discrepancy between self-interest and the interests of others. Prudence, or intelligence, dictates the former; justice the latter. Consequently, justice must always be stupid. The argument applies both to the dealings of individuals with each other and to those of states with other states. All large states have been built up by conquest, and the extension of a people's power is commonly counted as a virtue in its rulers. Yet this achievement is possible only when statesmen and peoples disregard justice—that is, rendering unto each his own—and follow the dictates of intelligent self-interest.

to the gods, for the destruction of the city's walls is likewise the destruction of its temples; the murder of its citizens involves likewise the murder of its priests; and the plundering of secular wealth includes also the plunder of sacred treasures. Hence, the irreligious acts of the Roman people equal the number of its trophies; every triumph over a people is a triumph over its gods; the collections of booty equal in number the surviving images of captive gods.[47]

Tertullian: *apol.* 25; ed. Mayor, p. 90.

Therefore, since the arguments of the philosophers were weak, Carneades made bold to refute them because he knew that they could be refuted. The heads of his discourse were as follows. Men have established laws to serve their own advantages. These laws, of course, were different to suit the different characters of peoples, and even in the same people they were often modified to accord with changing conditions. On the other hand, there is no natural law. All human beings as well as all other living creatures are led by nature to consult their own self-interest. Hence, either there is no such thing as justice, or, if there is, it is the height of folly, since a person would do injury to himself by consulting the interests of others. And Carneades brought forward the following proof. All peoples who built up empires — including the Romans themselves, who became masters of the world[48]— would be obliged to return to huts and live in wretched poverty if they wished to be just, that is, if they should restore all that is not their own.

Lactantius: *inst.* 5. 16. 2-4.

Ever to count your country's welfare first [49]

is an utterly meaningless verse if you banish the discord that prevails among men. What, I ask, are the advantages of your country if they be not the disadvantages of another state or race? For it is to the advantage of your country to extend its

---

[47] Tertullian is disproving the claim of the Romans to signal piety, and the contention that their empire was extended through the favor of the gods. See Cic. *de rep.* 3. 14 ff., below.

[48] See the fragments of the Vatican manuscript in Cic. *de rep.* 3. 15, below.

[49] Lucilius (ed. Marx), 1337.

boundaries by forcibly appropriating the territories of others,
to enlarge the sphere of its power, and to increase its revenues.
......When, therefore, a man has won for his country these
goods, as his countrymen call them; that is, when he has over-
thrown states, destroyed peoples, filled the exchequer with
their wealth, taken their territory, and enriched his fellow-
citizens, he is extolled to the skies. In him a consummate and
perfect excellence is supposed to reside. This is a mistake not
only of the common people and the ignorant, but of philos-
ophers as well, for the latter also supply lessons in injustice,
that folly and wrong-doing may not lack the authority that
comes from education. Lactantius: *inst.* 6. 6. 19 and 23.

XIII. PHILUS: [50] .... for all those who have the power of
life and death over a people are tyrants, but they prefer to
take the name which belongs to Jupiter the Most High and to
call themselves kings. And when a group of men controls the
commonwealth by virtue of their wealth, their birth, or any advantages they happen to possess, they form an oligarchy, but
they call themselves leading citizens. And again, if the people
have the supreme power and if all public business is carried on
at their pleasure, we have what is called liberty, but what in
fact is license.[51] Now when the citizens fear each other, when
man fears man and class fears class, no one feels secure; and
as a result, a contract, as we may call it, is made by the commons and those who have power. From this agreement there
arises the composite form of state which Scipio was praising.[52]

---

[50] In the long lacuna beginning at ch. 12 and running to ch. 29, only
chs. 13, 15-18 are in the Vatican manuscript.

[51] This passage depends clearly on the view put forward by Thrasymachus in Plato's *Republic* (337 a—344 c), that justice is really the
interest of the most powerful class in the state. Cf. also Plato: *Gorgias*,
483 b ff.

[52] As an explanation of the composite state, this seems to be unique,
though the contractual theory of the state was well known in antiquity.
It appears among the Sophists, e. g., Lycophron; see Aristotle: *Politics*,
1280 b 10; cf. also Plato: *Republic*, 358 e ff.; *Laws*, 683 c ff.; Barker:
Greek Political Theory, Plato and his Predecessors (1918), pp. 123; 159
ff.; 309, n. 1. It was also the theory of the Epicureans; see Usener;
Epicurea (1887), p. 78, *Golden Maxims*, nos. 31-33. No doubt also Roman
political practice led to the belief "that true social order was the issue of
conflicting claims pushed to their breaking point until a temporary compromise was agreed upon by the weary combatants" (Greenidge: *History*

Thus, neither nature nor deliberate choice but weakness is the mother of justice. For since a man must choose one of three possibilities[53]—either to act unjustly without suffering injustice, or both to act unjustly and to suffer injustice, or neither to act unjustly nor to suffer injustice—the best choice is to act unjustly without suffering the consequences, if you can. The second choice is neither to act unjustly nor to suffer injustice. But the most wretched condition of all is an incessant warfare in which men both do and suffer injustice. Consequently, he who [cannot] attain the first choice [mentioned above, of doing without suffering injustice, must take the second choice, viz., neither doing nor suffering injustice].[54]

(Either two or four leaves are missing)

XIV. For when [a pirate] was asked what criminal impulse had led him to make the sea unsafe with a single little ship, he replied, "The same impulse which has led you, [Alexander], to make the whole world unsafe."[55]

XV. PHILUS: ...... prudence bids you to use every means to expand your influence, to increase your wealth, and to extend your boundaries. For how could the eulogy, "He extended the frontiers of the empire," have been inscribed upon the monuments of famous generals, if they had not added some territory which belonged to another people? Prudence also bids you to govern as many as you can, to enjoy pleasures, to have power, to rule, and to be the master of men. Justice, on the other hand, teaches you to spare all men, to consider the interests of the human race, to render to each his own, and

---

of Rome, 1, 1904, p. 2). Philus' argument is not to be confused with Cicero's own view; cf. *de rep.* 1. 25, above.
[53] Compare Plato: *Republic*, 359 a ff.; also the fragment of Antiphon the Sophist, text and translation in *Oxyrhynchus Papyri*, 11 (1915), no. 1364, pp. 92 ff., translation in Barker: *Greek Political Theory, Plato and his Predecessors* (1918), pp. 83 ff.
[54] We translate Mai's supplement.
[55] Nonius, p. 125. 12; 318. 18; 534. 15. Cf. Augustine: *de civ.* 4. 4, where the reference to Alexander the Great is clear. The fragment belongs to the same context as the extract from Tertullian in Cic. *de rep.* 3. 12, above, and illustrates the point that conquest is robbery and piracy on a large scale. In John of Salisbury: *policraticus* (ed. Webb), 508 a ff., this same story occurs in a form which suggests that the writer had access to a more complete text of Cicero than the Vatican ms. presents.

not to tamper with that which is sacred, that which is public, and that which belongs to another. What is gained, then, if we obey prudence? Both individuals and peoples gain wealth, power, influence, repute, dominion, and rule. But seeing that the commonwealth forms the topic of our discussion, we find these results more clearly illustrated in the activities of states. And since the principle of justice is the same for both persons and states, I feel that I must discuss prudence as the rule of a people's conduct. Our own nation, whose history Africanus traced from its beginnings in yesterday's discourse, now holds sway over the whole world. Saying nothing of other peoples, I ask you: Was it by justice or by prudence that our nation rose from the least among states [to be the greatest of all]?

(At least two leaves are missing)

PHILUS: .... except the Arcadians and Athenians,[56] who, I presume, feared that justice might sometime interpose her decree [against their further occupancy of land they had taken by force], and pretended, accordingly, that they had sprung from the earth, like the field mice we see here before us.[57]

XVI. Against these arguments the following answers are usually advanced, in the first place, by [the Epicureans],[58] for they are least disingenuous in presenting their case. Their

---

[56] For the antiquity of the Arcadians, who claimed that they were in existence even "before the moon was in the sky," see Scholiast on Aristophanes: *Clouds*, 398. For the claim of the Athenians that they were autochthonous, see Euripides: *Ion*, 29; 589; 737; Isocrates: 4. 24; 12. 124. For the "decree" which justice might interpose, see Cic. *de rep.* 1. 13, above, and note.

[57] The dialogue takes place in a meadow; see Cic. *de rep.* 1. 12, above. For the view that mice sprung directly from the earth see Diodorus: 1. 10. The belief that lower forms of life were spontaneously generated was common in antiquity; see Aristotle: *Metaph.* 1032 a 30; 1034 b 34 ff.; Ross: *Aristotle* (1924), pp. 117 ff.

[58] This clearly refers to the Epicureans, who taught that the evil in injustice is not intrinsic but due to the probability of detection and punishment; see *Golden Maxims*, no. 34, Usener:*Epicurea* (1887), p. 79, translated by Hicks: *Stoic and Epicurean* (1910), p. 178. An account of their social theories will be found in Zeller: *Phil. d. Griech.* 3. 1 (1923), pp. 471 ff.; Eng. trans., *Stoics, Epicureans, and Sceptics* (1892), pp. 490 ff.; Hicks: *op. cit.* pp. 174 ff. Philus introduces the Epicurean position as the strongest argument against the advantages of injustice, thus making the case against natural justice so much the stronger.

reasoning on the present question has the more weight because, in their inquiry about the good man, whom we would have to be a person of transparent genuineness of character, they are neither tricky, deceitful, nor insincere. Now [the Epicureans] assert that the wise man is good, not because he is pleased with goodness and justice in and for themselves, but because the lives of good men are free from fear, worry, anxiety, and danger. Wicked men, on the other hand, always have a certain uneasiness at the bottom of their hearts, and always have before their eyes the penalties of the law. But according to [the Epicureans], there is no profit and no reward gained by injustice great enough to repay a man for being always in fear, or for believing that some punishment is always at hand and hanging over him..............

(Either two or four leaves are missing, but nearly a page has been recovered from Lactantius: *inst.* 5. 12. 5-6)

XVII. PHILUS: I put the question to you:[59] Let us suppose that there are two men, one of whom is thoroughly upright and honorable, a man of consummate justice and unique integrity, while the other is a man of extraordinary depravity and shamelessness. And let us assume that the state in which they live is so misguided as to believe the good man a monster of unspeakable criminality, while, on the other hand, it considers the scoundrel to be a model of uprightness and good faith. Let us suppose further that, in conformity with this error on the part of all the citizens, the good man is persecuted, harassed, has his hands cut off and his eyes gouged out, is condemned, cast into chains, tortured by fire, exiled,[60] and reduced to destitution. Finally, let us assume that he is universally regarded as justly meriting his wretched condition. On the other hand, let us suppose that the evil man is praised, honored, and esteemed by all; that all sorts of offices, civil and military, and every form of influence and wealth are conferred upon him; and that he is universally held to be an excellent man, fully deserving the best gifts fortune can bestow. I ask

---

[59] This passage closely parallels Plato: *Republic*, 361 e ff.
[60] The Vatican ms. begins again at this point.

you then: Who under these circumstances will be so mad as to doubt which of the two lots he would prefer?

XVIII. What is true of individuals is true also of states. There is no country so stupid as not to prefer unjust dominion to just subjection. I shall not adduce remote examples. In my consulate, I presided over an inquiry into the treaty with Numantia, and you were members of my council. Every one knew that Quintus Pompey and Mancinus had both concluded treaties under similar circumstances. The latter of these men was of sterling character and even urged the passage of the law which I proposed in accordance with the senate's decree. while Pompey defended himself most stubbornly. If you wish an example of conscientiousness, integrity, and good faith, Mancinus displayed these qualities; if, on the other hand, you desire shrewdness, penetration, and prudence, Pompey carries off the prize.[61] Whether........

XIX. *Then Carneades abandoned the general question [of justice as against injustice] and went on to specific examples.[62] Let us suppose, he said, that a good man possesses a runaway slave or an insanitary and unhealthful house, and that he alone is aware of these defects. If, on this account, he offers the slave or the house for sale, will he declare that he is putting on the market a runaway slave or an unhealthful house, or will he conceal these defects from a purchaser? If he admits them, he will be considered honest in that he will not deceive, but he*

---

[61] In 140 B.C. Quintus Pompey, the consul, after a disastrous defeat, concluded a treaty with Numantia to save his army. Later both Pompey and the senate repudiated the treaty, but Pompey, by dexterity and influence, escaped the usual penalty for negotiating a treaty that failed of ratification. In 137 Gaius Hostilius Mancinus negotiated a treaty under similar circumstances and, after an investigation presided over by Philus, was surrendered to the Numantines. See Cic. *de off.* 3. 30. 109; Appian: *res Hisp.* 76-83; Mommsen: *Röm. Gesch.* 2 (1908), pp. 13 ff. (Eng. trans. 3, pp. 13 ff.); Greenidge: *History of Rome*, 1 (1904), pp. 108 f.; Heitland: *Roman Republic* (1909), sects. 604-6. This passage in the *Commonwealth* is the chief evidence for the power of the consuls to preside over special *quaestiones* concerning international affairs; see Mommsen: *Röm. Staatsrecht*, 2. 1 (1887), p. 112; Greenidge: *Roman Public Life* (1911), p. 199.

[62] Many of the examples given here occur also in Cic. *de off.* 3. 13. 54; 3. 23. 89. In the latter passage Cicero says that he derived them from the sixth book of Hecato's work *On Duty.* Hecato was a pupil of Panaetius.

will also be regarded as a fool, for he will either sell at a low price or he will not sell at all. If he conceals the defects, he will be prudent in that he considers his own interest, but he will be dishonest in that he deceives. Again let us suppose that a man finds a dealer who thinks he is selling copper, though it is really gold, or who thinks he is selling lead, when it is really silver. Will an honorable man keep silence in order to buy at a low price, or will he disclose the truth and pay a high price? Only a fool, it appears, would choose the latter course. By such examples Carneades would have it understood that the just and good man is a fool and that the prudent man is wicked, and yet that men may be content with poverty without being ruined.[63]

XX. *Carneades accordingly passed on to more important cases in which a man could not be just without endangering his life. For he said: Certainly justice requires us not to kill human beings and not in any way to touch another's property. What, then, will the just man do if he is in a shipwreck and someone weaker than himself has found a plank [on which to keep afloat]? Will he not push the weaker man off the plank, that he may get on it himself and thus make his escape, especially when there is no one in the middle of the sea to bear witness against him?*[64] *If he is prudent he will do this, for he will inevitably lose his own life if he does not. If, however, he would rather die than raise his hand against another man, he is indeed just but he is a fool, because in sparing another's life he fails to spare his own. Similarly, when the army in which he is fighting has been routed, and the enemy begin pursuit, if a man finds a wounded soldier mounted on a horse, will he spare the wounded man and be killed himself, or will he throw the other from the horse in order that he may himself escape the enemy? If he follows the latter course, he is prudent but also wicked; if he takes the former course, it necessarily follows that, though just, he is a fool. Accordingly, after Carneades had distinguished two kinds of justice, politi-*

---

[63] Some editors of Lactantius regard the last clause as an interpolation.
[64] Cf. Plato: *Republic*, 348 c ff., where the sophist Thrasymachus argues that justice is simplicity and injustice discretion.

cal and natural, he overthrew both, for political justice is in fact prudence and not justice, while natural justice, though it is really justice, is not prudence. Clearly these arguments are subtle and ensnaring; indeed, Cicero could not refute them. For though he makes Laelius answer Philus and present the case for justice, Cicero left all these objections unrefuted, as if they were mere traps. The result is that Laelius appears as the defender not of natural justice, which had been subjected to the charge of being mere stupidity, but rather of political justice, which Philus had admitted to be prudent, though it was not just.
                                        Lactantius: *inst.* 5. 16. 5-13.

XXI. PHILUS: I should not feel it burdensome [to continue the subject], Laelius, if I did not think that our friends here wished that you too should take some part in this discussion of ours, and if I myself did not desire it also, especially since you said yesterday that you would have even more to say than we should care to hear.   But, of course, that is impossible, and we all beg you not to disappoint us.[65]

LAELIUS: But our youth ought not to listen to [Carneades] at all.   For in fact, if he meant what he says, he is a scoundrel; if he believed otherwise, as I prefer to think, his discourse is nevertheless monstrous.[66]

XXII. LAELIUS: There is in fact a true law[67]—namely, right reason—which is in accordance with nature, applies to all men, and is unchangeable and eternal.   By its commands this law summons men to the performance of their duties; by its prohibitions it restrains them from doing wrong.   Its commands and prohibitions always influence good men, but are without effect upon the bad.   To invalidate this law by human

---

[65] Gellius: *noct. Att.* 1. 22. 8.   With ch. 20 Philus ends his defense of injustice, and with ch. 21 the presentation of the case for justice is begun by Laelius. See Augustine's summary at the beginning of Book 3.
[66] Nonius, p. 323. 18; 324. 15.
[67] The definition of true law (*vera lex*) is a Stoic commonplace, going back certainly to Chrysippus and perhaps to Zeno. See Introduction, p. 48, above, and compare Cic. *de leg.* 1. 6. 18, where he says, "Law is transcendent reason, implanted in nature, commanding what should be done, and forbidding what should not be done." A long list of Stoic parallels will be found in von Arnim: *Stoicorum veterum fragmenta,* 4 (1924), Index, s. v. *nomos.*

legislation is never morally right, nor is it permissible ever to restrict its operation, and to annul it wholly is impossible. Neither the senate[68] nor the people can absolve us from our obligation to obey this law, and it requires no Sextus Aelius[69] to expound and interpret it. It will not lay down one rule at Rome and another at Athens, nor will it be one rule today and another tomorrow. But there will be one law, eternal and unchangeable, binding at all times upon all peoples; and there will be, as it were, one common master and ruler of men, namely God, who is the author of this law, its interpreter, and its sponsor. The man who will not obey it will abandon his better self, and, in denying the true nature of a man, will thereby suffer the severest of penalties, though he has escaped all the other consequences which men call punishment.[70]

XXIII. *I know that in Cicero's work on the Commonwealth—in the third book, unless I am mistaken—there is a discussion of the proposition that* no war is undertaken by a well-conducted state except in defense of its honor or for its security.[71] *What he means by security, or what he would have his reader understand by a state that is secure, he shows in another passage:* From those penalties of which even the stupidest men are sensible—such as destitution, exile, chains, and stripes—private individuals often escape by adopting the proffered alternative of a speedy death. But for states death is itself a punishment, though for individual men it seems to be a deliverance from punishment. For the state ought to be so organized that it will endure forever. Hence, death is not

---

[68] While the Roman senate did not possess the right of legislation, it had the power to exempt persons from the operation of the law; see Greenidge: *Roman Public Life* (1911), pp. 275 ff. During the last century B. C. an attempt was made to deprive the senate of this right and to confer it solely upon the people. As a result of the agitation it was enacted that, when the senate granted such an exemption, there must be present at least two hundred senators; see Bouché-Leclercq: *Manuel des inst. romaines* (1886), pp. 104 ff.

[69] For Sextus Aelius see Cic. *de rep.* 1. 18, above, and note.

[70] Lactantius: *inst.* 6. 8. 6-9.

[71] Cf. Aristotle's view that war is justifiable in three cases: (1) for self-defense; (2) to establish political rule over those who would be benefited thereby; (3) to establish despotic rule over nations that deserve to be enslaved; see *Politics*, 1333 b 38 ff.; also Newman: *Politics of Aristotle*, 1 (1887), pp. 327 ff.

a natural end for the commonwealth as it is for a human being, whose death is not only necessary but frequently even desirable. But when a state is destroyed and wiped out and annihilated, it is somewhat as if—to compare small things with great—this whole world should perish and collapse.[72]

There are four kinds of wars, the lawful, the unlawful, civil wars, and foreign wars. A lawful war is one which is formally declared and which is waged either to secure restitution of property for which a claim has been made, or to repel an invader. An unlawful war is one that is begun from a mad impulse and without a legitimate cause. Of this kind of war Cicero says in his work on the Commonwealth: Wars are unlawful which are undertaken without a reason. For no war can be justly waged except for the purpose of redressing an injury or of driving out an invader. *And a little farther on Cicero adds:* No war is held to be lawful unless it is officially announced, unless it is declared, and unless a formal claim for satisfaction has been made.[73]

Our people, on the other hand, were by this time masters of the whole world because they defended their allies.[74]

XXIV. *To be sure, many spirited and powerful arguments are advanced in the same work on the commonwealth against injustice and in favor of justice. In the earlier part of the discussion, when the case for injustice and against justice was presented, and when it was urged that the commonwealth could not exist or expand without injustice, it was laid down as an irrefutable principle that it was always unjust for human*

---

[72] Augustine: *de civ.* 22. 6. We have translated the context from Augustine, which Ziegler prints in the apparatus criticus. Laelius clearly undertook to show that the expansion of states, and particularly of Rome, was not necessarily the result of unjust aggression. He adduced the procedure of the Fetial College (see 2. 17, above, and note) as constituting a sort of international law. Philus had asserted (3. 12, above) that it merely gave the color of law to injustice.

[73] Isidore: *etym.* 18. 1. 2 ff. Cf. Cic. *de off.* 1. 11. 36. We have combined the two passages given by Ziegler and have added the context in Isidore.

[74] Nonius, p. 498. 18. Laelius doubtless argued that Roman expansion had been incidental to a general policy of keeping faith with allies, possibly even that it was a reward of merit, for the Romans had a singular conceit of their own piety. See the extract from Tertullian, ch. 12, above, and the "backward nation" argument in ch. 24, below.

*beings to be the subjects and chattels of other human beings;
and yet, unless an imperial state—to which class the great
commonwealth belongs—should practice this kind of injustice,
it could not rule dependencies. In the argument on behalf of
justice the answer was accordingly made that subjection is
just because it is advantageous for a certain kind of men, and
that it serves the advantage of such men when it is brought
about in the right way—that is, when the power of doing
wrong is taken from wicked men, and when those who have
been conquered will be better off, inasmuch as they were worse
off when unconquered.*[75] *In support of this reasoning a notable
illustration was adduced, drawn as it were from nature, and
the following argument was advanced:* Do we not perceive
that the dominion which nature herself has given to the best
conduces in a high degree to the interests of the weak? Is it
not for this reason that God rules man, that the soul commands the body, and that reason governs desire, anger, and all
the other defective elements of the soul?[76]

XXV. We must recognize, however, that there are different kinds of rulership and subjection.[77] Thus, the soul is said
to rule the body and also the desires. But whereas it rules the
former as a king governs his subjects or a father his children,
it rules the desires as a master drives his slaves, since in this
case its rule is repressive and crushing. Similarly, the authority which kings, generals, magistrates, senates, and peoples
exert over citizens and allies resembles the rule of the soul over

[75] After justifying the expansion of Rome, Laelius lays down a general principle for imperialism, namely, that it is right for superior peoples
to rule backward nations. The argument is clearly derived from the
rooted conviction of the Greeks that non-Greek peoples are "slaves by
nature." See Aristotle: *Politics*, 1253 b 14 ff.; 1255 a 28 ff.; also Newman: *Politics of Aristotle*, 1 (1887), pp. 139 ff. Plato and Aristotle agree
on the principle that government rightly depends upon natural superiority, but Laelius' argument is not consistent with Cicero's strong assertion of equality; see Cic. *de leg.* 1. 10. 29; also Introduction, pp. 50 f.
[76] Augustine: *de civ.* 19. 21; the last two sentences are in part supplied from the same author's *contra Iulianum*, 4, 12. 61; ed. Ben. 10,
p. 613.
[77] On the different kinds of rule see, besides the references already
given, Plato: *Laws*, 690 a ff.; 714 e ff.; Aristotle: *Politics*, 1253 b 14 ff.;
1255 b 16 ff. (cf. Plato: *Statesman*, 258 e ff.) ; 1259 a 37 ff.; 1259 b 32 ff.;
1278 b 32 ff.; 1325 a 36 ff.; 1332 b 41 ff.

the body.[78] On the other hand, masters discipline their slaves
as the soul's best element, wisdom, disciplines the defective
and weaker elements of the same soul, such as the lusts, the
passions, and all other emotions.[79]

For there is a kind of subjection that is not just. It exists
when those who might be their own masters are subject to
another;[80] but when those are slaves [who cannot rule themselves, no injustice is done.][81]

XXVI. *If you know, says Carneades, that an asp is hidden
in a certain place, and that some careless person whose death
will be to your advantage is likely to sit upon it, you will do
wrong unless you warn him not to sit down, though you will
not thereby be liable to punishment.*[82] *For who can prove
that you knew about the asp? But we are multiplying instances needlessly, since it is obvious that no good man can
be found, if fair dealing, good faith, and justice do not spring
from nature but are all reduced to self-interest. Moreover,
this subject has been sufficiently discussed by Laelius in our
work on the commonwealth.*   Cicero: *de fin.* 2. 18. 59.

*And if, as you remind us, we have spoken correctly in that
work when we said that nothing is good except what is mor-*

---

[78] See Aristotle: *Politics*, 1254 b 4, where he says that the soul rules
the body with a despotic rule, whereas intelligence rules appetite with
a constitutional and kingly authority. Cicero gives a Stoic version of the
relation between reason and passion.
[79] This passage is preserved by Augustine; *contra Iulianum*, 4. 12. 61
(ed. Ben. 10, p. 613) ; cf. *de civ.* 14. 23.
[80] See Aristotle: *Politics*, 1252 a 31 ff.; 1254 b 6 ff.
[81] Nonius, p. 109. 2. The supplement is Mai's.
[82] This sentence refers to the disjunction developed by Philus between
justice, which consists in rendering to every man his own and is therefore unselfish, and prudence, which consists in intelligent self-interest;
cf. chs. 19 and 20, above. The answer, in general, is that it is impossible
to develop morality and the sense of duty merely from self-interest
(the Epicurean theory; cf. ch. 16, above). Hence, an innate sociability
must be assumed (cf. *de rep.* 1. 25, above), which is developed by reason
and language (*ratio et oratio; de off.* 1. 16. 50; 51; *de invent.* 1. 2. 2),
and thus becomes the basis of social and political life and of justice and
all the other virtues upon which the state depends. Some of the most
eloquent passages in Cicero's ethical works deal with this subject. See,
for example, his eulogy of disinterested virtue (*de fin.* 5. 22. 61 ff.) and
his description of the moral community (*de off.* 1. 7. 20 ff.; *de fin.* 2. 14.
45 ff.).

ally right, and nothing bad except what is morally base, surely both [Caesar and Pompey] are most wretched.[83] *For both of them have always regarded the safety and honor of their country as less important than their own ascendancy and personal interest.*

Cicero: *ad Att.* 10. 4. 4.

XXVII. *I am glad that you take pleasure in your little daughter and that you approve the view that parental affection is in accordance with nature.*[84] *For if it is not, there is no natural tie which unites a human being to his kind. And if this tie is taken away, then social life itself is abolished. "May luck go with it," says Carneades—a vicious way of speaking, to be sure, but still more sensible*[85] *than the opinions of our friend Lucius and of Patro.*[86] *For in referring all acts to self-interest they suppose that nothing is ever done for the sake of another, and in saying that a man ought to be good in order that he may escape evil and not because this is by nature the right thing to do, they do not perceive that they are talking about a cunning fellow and not about a good man. But I believe that these questions are treated in the work your praise of which has so greatly encouraged me.*

Cicero: *ad Att.* 7. 2. 4.

In these matters I agree that a worrisome and hazardous justice is not the part of a wise man.[87]

---

[83] We have translated the entire sentence of which Ziegler gives only the first clause.

[84] This sentence is a somewhat pointed allusion to Atticus' Epicureanism. Epicurus held that there is no inborn love between children and parents; see Usener: *Epicurea* (1887), p. 320, nos. 527 and 528.

[85] It is not clear what is referred to in this mention of Carneades. Accordingly, there is some doubt whether we should read *prudentius* (that is, "more sensible") with Ziegler and certain mss. or *pudentius* (that is, "more decent") with other mss.

[86] It is not clear who is meant by Lucius, but he is perhaps Lucius Manlius Torquatus, who speaks for the Epicureans in *de fin.* Patro was the head of the Epicurean School at Athens from 70 until after 51 B. C.; see Cic. *ad fam.* 13. 1. 2 ff.; *ad Att.* 5. 11. 6; 5. 19. 3; *ad Q. fr.* 1. 2. 4. 14.

[87] Priscian: 8. 6. 32; ed. Hertz, p. 399. 13. This fragment perhaps formed part of the refutation of Philus' argument that justice is sometimes dangerous (ch. 20, above). The general nature of Cicero's answer may probably be gathered from *de off.* 3. 20. 81, where he argues that in the end there can be no radical discrepancy between the expedient and the right.

XXVIII. *In Cicero's work the same champion of justice, Laelius, says:*[88] Virtue certainly[89] desires recognition, and it has no other reward. *But there is another reward, and one quite worthy of virtue, of which, Laelius, you could not have dreamed, for you had no knowledge of Holy Writ.* Though glad to receive praise, virtue does not harshly demand it. *Wrong you are, very wrong, if you think that human beings can render unto virtue its reward, for in another place you have truly asserted:* What riches will you offer to this [truly good] man? What great powers? What royal authority? Such external honors he considers to be of merely human origin, while the goods that he has within himself he judges to be divine. *Who, I ask, could regard you as wise, Laelius, when you utter such inconsistencies, and straightway strip virtue of all you gave her? But, of course, it is ignorance of the truth which makes your judgment unsure and faltering. And then what do you add?* But if either the ingratitude of a whole people, or the envy of many men, or the enmity of the powerful despoil virtue of its proper rewards—*Oh how weak, how vain a thing is the virtue you have brought before us, if it can be despoiled of its due rewards! If virtue regards its own goods as divine, as you said, what men can be so ungrateful, so envious, or so powerful as to be able to despoil virtue of those goods which have been divinely bestowed on her?* Truly, *Laelius says,* virtue enjoys many consolations and, in particular, it is sustained by its own peculiar glory.

Lactantius: inst. 5. 18. 4-8.

The bodies [of Hercules and Romulus] were not carried into the heavens, for nature would not permit that which came from earth to exist anywhere except on the earth.[90]

---

[88] This passage from Lactantius consists of short quotations from Cicero followed by Lactantius' criticisms of Laelius' views. We have translated the context, which Ziegler prints in the apparatus criticus.

[89] We read *plane* for *paene* with most of the editors.

[90] Augustine: *de civ.* 22. 4. The fragment is perhaps part of an argument setting forth the divine nature of the soul. There are numerous passages in Cicero to the same effect, though he is uncertain whether the soul is immaterial or only not grossly material; see Cic. *Tusc.* 1. 12. 26 ff.; 1. 25. 60; 1. 26. 65; 1. 28. 70; *de leg.* 1. 8. 24; Zeller: *Phil. d. Griech.* 3. 1 (1923), p. 691; Eng. trans., *Eclectics* (1883), p. 170.

The bravest never [fail to enjoy the fruits of] courage, energy, and endurance.[91]

Thus Fabricius rejected the bounty of Pyrrhus, or Curius rejected the money of the Samnites.[92]

When our hero Cato went to his house in the Sabine country, as he himself has told us, he used to visit the hearth of [Manius Curius], where [Curius] was seated when he had rejected the gifts of the Samnites, who had formerly been his enemies but who had now become his clients.[93]

(The fortieth quaternion begins here)

XXIX. LAELIUS: .....Asia.....Tiberius Gracchus. He devoted his efforts to the interests of the citizens, but he disregarded the treaty-rights of our allies and of the Latin League.[94] If this habitual disregard of our engagements should begin to spread too widely, and should transform our empire from a government based on law to one based on force, the result would be that peoples which have hitherto obeyed us of their own free will would be ruled by fear. In such an eventuality, although we at our age have kept the state nearly to the end of our watch, yet I fear for our children and for the continuance of the commonwealth, which might last for-

---

[91] Nonius, p. 125. 18. The supplement is Mai's.

[92] Nonius, p. 132. 17. This and the following fragment doubtless formed part of a eulogy of the disinterested and incorruptible statesman. That Cicero's work contained such a passage appears from the letter to Atticus included in *de rep.* 2. 37, above.

[93] Nonius, p. 522, 26. Curius' name is supplied from Cic. *de sen.* 16. 55, from which the sense of this passage may be gathered.

[94] The first words of the chapter probably refer to the bequest of his kingdom to the Roman people by Attalus III of Pergamum in 133 B. C. Tiberius Gracchus proposed to use the treasure of Attalus to carry out his agrarian law, a measure which would have destroyed the senate's power over finance and provincial administration. See Mommsen: *Röm. Gesch.* 2 (1908), pp. 53; 89 (Eng. trans. 3, pp. 51 f.; 87 f.); Greenidge: *History of Rome*, 1 (1904), pp. 129 ff.; Heitland: *Roman Republic* (1909), *sects.* 699-700. In the criticism of Tiberius' policy which follows Cicero seems to be in error. As Greenidge (*op. cit.* p. 136, n. 2) says: "Cicero is perhaps stating the result, rather than the intention, of the Gracchan legislation ... No point in the Gracchan agrarian law is more remarkable than its strict, perhaps inequitable, legality. That its author consciously violated treaty relations is improbable."

ever if its life were in accordance with the institutions and customs of our fathers.[95]

XXX. When Laelius had finished speaking, all who were present showed that they had been greatly pleased by what he had said, but Scipio was, as it were, carried away with delight more than all the rest.[96]

SCIPIO: You have defended many cases, Laelius, with such skill that I [should not hesitate to compare] you with my colleague, Servius Galba,[97] whom you considered the best of all the orators of his time, or even with any of the Attic orators, either for charm or . . . .

(The six inside leaves of the fortieth quaternion are missing)

[He said that] he lacked two things, self-confidence and a strong voice, by which he was prevented from speaking publicly or in the market-place[98] . . . .

---

[95] For Cicero's object in writing this work see Introduction, pp. 46 f. Here it is implied that a tenacious adherence to the principles of the "fathers" was necessary if the state were to endure. To represent the persons of the dialogue as anxious for the future of Rome was not an anachronism but a dramatic device which was historically justified. Polybius (6. 57) hints at a possible decline and, in an eloquent and memorable passage (*ibid.* 38. 21-22), Scipio is represented as expressing his fears to Polybius while they watch the destruction of Carthage, and as quoting the words of Homer:
    A day shall come when holy Ilium will fall,
    And Priam and the folk of Priam of the stout ashen spear.
See also Greenidge: *History of Rome*, 1 (1904), pp. 99 ff.

[96] At this point Scipio resumes the thread of the argument; see Augustine's summary at the opening of the third book. He takes up first the three so-called perverted forms of unmixed state and shows that none really constitutes a group of men united by the possession of a common law. His account of tyranny is in ch. 31; that of oligarchy is in ch 32; that of licentious democracy or ochlocracy is in ch. 33. He concludes, accordingly, that these are not properly perversions, but fall altogether outside his definition of the state. In ch. 34 Scipio goes on to consider the three normal types of unmixed state in relation to his definition.

[97] Servius Sulpicius Galba (consul in 144 B. C.) was a powerful and ostentatious orator. Cicero asserts (*Brut.* 21. 82) that Galba's style was rough and archaic in comparison with that of his contemporaries, Laelius, Scipio, and Cato. See Duff: *Literary History of Rome* (1914), p. 258.

[98] Nonius, p. 262. 24. This is perhaps an allusion to Isocrates, forming part of a discussion of the Attic orators, introduced by the preceding sentence. See Cic. *de or.* 2. 3. 10; Christ-Schmid: *Gesch. d. gr. Lit.* 1 (1912), p. 565.

The bull would bellow with the groans of the men shut up inside it.[99]

XXXI. SCIPIO: . . . to restore. Who, therefore, could have called the government of Agrigentum the people's affair, that is, a commonwealth, at the time when all were oppressed by the cruelty of a single man, when there was no common bond of law, and when there was no agreement regarding what is right and no social union such as constitutes a people? This same condition existed at Syracuse. It was a famous city, called by Timaeus[100] at once the greatest of Greek cities and the most beautiful city in the world. Its citadel deserved to be visited by travelers, and its harbors extended to the very center of the city and bathed the walls of the houses.[101] Nevertheless, [neither these wonders nor] its broad streets, its porticoes, its temples, and its walls, availed in any way to make it a commonwealth, so long as Dionysius was its master. For there was nothing that was the people's affair, and the people themselves were the possession of a single man. Hence, where there is a tyrant, we must not say, as I said yesterday, that there is a perverted commonwealth, but, as reason now obliges us to conclude, that there is clearly no commonwealth at all[102]

XXXII. LAELIUS: You state your case plainly, for I see now where the argument leads.

SCIPIO: You see likewise, then, that a government which is altogether in the hands of an oligarchy cannot properly be called a commonwealth.

LAELIUS: I concur fully in that conclusion.

SCIPIO: And you are certainly right. What, I ask, was the

---

[99] Schol. Juvenal: *sat.* 6. 486. This is a reference to Phalaris, tyrant of Agrigentum; see Cic. *de rep.* 1. 28, above, and note. The first word (*reportare*) of the next chapter is perhaps part of an account of the restoration of the famous bull to the Agrigentines by Scipio in 146 B. C., after he had captured it from the Carthaginians; see Cic. *act. sec. c. Verrem*, 4. 33. 73.

[100] Timaeus of Tauromenium (c. 345—c. 250 B. C.) was the author of a history of Sicily; see Christ-Schmid: *Gesch. d. gr. Lit.* 2 (1920), pp. 218 ff.

[101] For the topography of ancient Syracuse see Freeman: *History of Sicily*, 1 (1891), pp. 345 ff.

[102] Cf. Plato: *Laws*, 832 b-d.

affair of the Athenians when, at the close of their great war with Sparta, the city was ruled by the Thirty Tyrants in utter defiance of law? Did the ancient renown of the state, or the celebrated beauty of the city, its theater, its gymnasia, its porticoes, its splendid propylaea, its citadel, the marvelous creations of Phidias, or its magnificent harbor at Piraeus— did all these make it a commonwealth?

LAELIUS: By no means, for there was no affair of the people.

SCIPIO: Again, what was the case at Rome, when the decemvirs, in that notorious third year, allowed no appeal to the people from their decisions, because there was then no such thing as liberty?

LAELIUS: There was no affair of the people; on the contrary, the people took steps to recover their affair.

XXXIII. SCIPIO: I come now to the third kind of state [the democracy], in which there will perhaps appear to be certain difficulties for our theory. When it is said that all public acts are accomplished through the people and that everything falls within the people's power, when the masses inflict punishment on whomsoever they choose, and when they plunder, seize, keep, or squander whatever they wish—can you deny, Laelius, that there is then a commonwealth? For, surely, then everything belongs to the people, and we have defined the commonwealth as the people's affair.

LAELIUS: As a matter of fact, there is no form of state to which I should sooner deny the name of commonwealth than to one which is wholly in the hands of the masses. For if we decided that Syracuse was not a commonwealth, and that Agrigentum and Athens were not commonwealths when they were subject to tyrants, and that Rome was not a commonwealth when it was subject to the decemvirs, I do not see why the word commonwealth is any more appropriate for a city enslaved by a mob. For in the first place, as I see the matter, a people does not exist unless, as you have excellently defined it, Scipio, the group is held together by a common agreement about law and right. But the mob that you describe is as tyrannous as if it were a single usurper; in one respect it is even worse, for there is nothing more odious than this monster which apes the appearance and usurps the name of a people. When the law[103] places the control of a madman's property in the hands of his relatives, because already his . . . ., it is not reasonable that . . . .

(The four inside leaves of the forty-first quaternion are missing)

XXXIV. SCIPIO: [The same reasons] which we used in the case of the monarchy may be given to show why [the aristocracy] is a commonwealth, or an affair of the people.[104]

SPURIUS MUMMIUS: The argument is even much stronger. For the king, since he is an individual, is much more like a master. But that form of government in which many good men control public affairs cannot be surpassed. But still I prefer even monarchy to democracy, since this third form of commonwealth, which you have still to treat, is the most defective of all.

XXXV. SCIPIO: I am aware, Spurius, of your rooted dislike of the popular form of government. And although it can be regarded more favorably than you are wont to regard it, still I agree that of the three [unmixed] forms of government none is less worthy of approval. However, I do not agree with you[105] that aristocrats are better than a king. For if it is wisdom that governs the commonwealth, what difference does it make whether this wisdom is found in one man or in several? But we are deceived by a certain fallacy in this mode of argument. For when aristocracy is called a government by the best men, it seems as if no other government can be better. For how can anything be supposed to be better than the best? On the other hand, when we speak of a king, the idea of an

---

[103] The law referred to is the Twelve Tables; see Girard: *Textes de droit romain* (1923), p. 14, tab. 5. 7 a; Bruns: *Fontes iuris Romani antiqui* (1909), pp. 23 f., tab. 5. 7 a; Gaius: *inst.* (ed. Poste), 1904, p. 116; Buckland: *Text-book of Roman Law* (1921), pp. 169 ff.

[104] In the preceding lacuna Scipio has gone on to the three good forms of unmixed constitution, showing that each is a commonwealth within the meaning of his definition. His account of monarchy is lost. The discussion of aristocracy is in ch. 34 and the first part of 35, with a short digression in the latter to justify his preference for monarchy, and the beginning of the discussion of moderate democracy is in the latter part of ch. 35.

[105] We read *tibi* for *aut tu* with all the editors except Ziegler.

unjust king, no less than that of a just one, presents itself to our minds. But the unjust king does not enter into the question when we are investigating royal government as such. If you will consider Romulus or Pompilius or Tullus as the typical king, you will perhaps not think so ill of monarchy.

MUMMIUS: What merit, then, do you leave to the popular form of government?

SCIPIO: Well, Spurius, I ask you: Do you not think that there is a commonwealth at Rhodes, where you and I were not long ago?[106]

MUMMIUS: I do indeed think that they have a commonwealth—and one not at all to be despised.

SCIPIO: Quite right. But, if you remember, all the citizens were successively commoners and senators. They followed a regular plan of rotation by which they determined in what months they should serve as commoners and in what months they should act as senators. Moreover, in both cases they received pay for their attendance, and both in the theater[107] and in the senate-house they all passed equally upon questions of life and death and upon all other matters. The power and competence of the senate were equal to the power of the masses. . . . .

(Of about forty quaternions which followed, all but
five leaves are missing)

FRAGMENTS OF BOOK III THAT CANNOT BE PLACED

1. Accordingly, there is something wayward in the human individual which either expands with pleasure or is subdued by trouble.[108]

---

[106] Scipio had been in Rhodes in 141 B. C., which he had visited while on a commission sent out to adjust differences among rulers in vassal states, and to repress the growth of piracy; see Cic. *de rep.* 6. 11, below; *acad. prior.* 2. 2. 5; Diodorus: 33. 28 a 1; Posidonius in Jacoby: *Die Fragmente der griechischen Historiker,* 2. a (1926), fr. 30. For the general topic of the Rhodian constitution see Gilbert: *Gr. Staatsalt.* 2 (1885), pp. 177 ff.; Greenidge: *Greek Constitutional History* (1914), pp. 218-219.

[107] That is, the meeting place of the *ekklesia,* or general assembly of citizens.

[108] Nonius, p. 301. 5. This fragment seems to refer to the irrational part of the soul (cf. *Tusc.* 2. 21. 47) and it may have formed part of Cicero's introduction to the third book.

2. But though they risk their souls, they see what they think they are going to do.[109]

3. The Phoenicians were the first who, by their trade and with their goods, brought to Greece greed and luxury and insatiable desire for all things.[110]

4. The name of the famous Sardanapalus was not nearly so monstrous as his vices.[111]

5. Unless someone wishes to transform all Athos into a monument. For what Athos or Olympus is so important. . ?[112]

6. *For I shall undertake in the appropriate place to show, according to the brief definitions of a commonwealth and of a people which Cicero himself puts into the mouth of Scipio, and also according to much corroborative evidence supplied by Cicero and those whom he represents as speaking in the same dialogue, that Rome never was such a commonwealth as he defines, because true justice never existed in it. But according to more plausible definitions, Rome was a commonwealth after some fashion of its own, and was better managed by the ancient Romans than by their descendants.*

Augustine: *de civ.* 2. 21.

---

[109] Nonius, p. 364. 7. We read *suum* for *seu* with Mercerus, and delete *sum* with Mueller.

[110] Nonius, p. 431. 11. For the part played by the Phoenicians in ancient commerce, see Bury: *History of Greece* (1916), pp. 76 ff.; Beloch: *Gr. Gesch.* 1. 1 (1924), p. 222; *Cambridge Ancient History*, 2 (1924), pp. 27 ff.; 378 ff.

[111] Schol. Juv. *sat.* 10. 362. Sardanapalus was a king of Assyria noted for his effeminacy; cf. Cic. *Tusc.* 5. 35. 101.

[112] Priscian: 6. 13. 70; ed. Hertz, p. 255. 9. Athos is the most easterly of three peninsulas extending south into the Aegean from Thrace.

BOOK IV

I. *Nevertheless, since body and soul have been mentioned, I shall undertake to expound the theory of both, in so far as the inadequacy of my understanding grasps them.*[1] *I regard it as particularly necessary to assume this task because, when Cicero, a man of unusual genius, attacked the question in the fourth book of his work on the Commonwealth, he compressed a wide range of subject matter within narrow limits and touched lightly upon certain main points. And yet, that he might not have any excuse for not treating the subject thoroughly, Cicero bore witness to the fact that he had lacked neither inclination nor interest in the topic. For in the first book of his "Laws," where he briefly alludes to this same subject, he says: "I believe that Scipio has dealt sufficiently with this question in the work which you have read."*[2]

Lactantius: *de opif. dei*, 1. 11-13.

And the mind both perceives the future and remembers the past.[3]

---

[1] This book probably had no prologue in which Cicero spoke in his own person. The general subject of the fourth book was education, but the remains are so fragmentary that it is not possible to reconstruct the argument or to determine the order in which the various topics were arranged. The most probable hypothesis is that the discussion of mind and body to which Lactantius refers was introductory to the treatment of education, and that Cicero followed Plato's lead in distinguishing the education of the mind from that of the body; see Plato: *Republic*, 376 e; see Introduction, pp. 66 f.

[2] The passage referred to is *de leg.* 1. 9. 27. The preceding and following paragraphs in the *Laws* probably indicate in a general way how Cicero treated the question of body and mind in this part of the *Commonwealth*. Man is the only rational animal, and his reason is akin to that which moves universal nature (cf. *de n. d.* 2. 21. 54 ff.), and makes him a fellow-citizen with the gods (cf. *de leg.* 1. 7. 22 ff.; *de rep.* 1. 13, above; Introduction, pp. 48 ff., above). Man, as the possessor of reason, is the only animal having the gift of language and therefore the capabilities of a moral and social life. The senses, the vaguely formed common concepts (*inchoatae intelligentiae*; see *de leg.* 1. 10. 30) which arise from sensuous experience, and the marvellously adapted human body are the servants of mind or reason.

[3] Nonius, p. 500. 9. This is probably a reference to the divine nature of the soul evidenced by its superiority to time; cf. Cic. *de rep.* 6. 24, below.

And if there is no one who would not rather die than be transformed into the shape of a beast, even though he were to retain the mind of a man, how much more wretched is it to possess the mind of a beast in the body of a man! It is more wretched, as it seems to me, in the same degree as the soul is nobler than the body.[4]

[Cicero said that] he did not think that the good of a ram and the good of Publius Africanus were the same.[5]

[Since], finally, [the earth] makes the shadow of night also by obscuring the sun—an apt device both for numbering the days and for giving remission from labor.[6]

And when in the autumn the earth has opened itself for the reception of fruits, and in winter [has closed to protect them, and in spring] has relaxed to let them germinate, and in summer has ripened them by softening or drying.[7]

When they put shepherds in charge of the flocks.[8]

---

[4] Lactantius: *inst.* 5. 11. 2. The fragment perhaps parallels Plato: *Republic*, 411 d-e, where the evil effects of an education too exclusively directed to bodily and military prowess are pointed out. But Cicero uses a similar expression (*de off.* 3. 20. 82) to describe the effects of vice on the soul. The mode of expression appears to have been used by the Stoics; see von Arnim: *Stoicorum veterum fragmenta*, 3 (1923), p. 189, no. 762.

[5] Augustine: *contra Iulianum*, 4. 12. 59; ed. Ben. 10, p. 612. The passage is similar to Augustine: *de civ.* 19. 3, which deals with the philosophy of Antiochus of Ascalon as reported by Varro. Since Antiochus was a teacher of Cicero as well as of Varro, it may be inferred that the thought expressed in this fragment comes from the same source. In any case, it is a typical Stoic taunt at the Epicureans (cf. Cic. *acad. post.* 1. 2. 6). It probably occurred in a passage distinguishing mind and body as the two constituent parts of human nature (cf. *Tusc.* 4. 5. 10), and praising mind as the divine element in man which sets him apart from all other creatures.

[6] Nonius, p. 234. 14. This fragment and the next were probably included in a description of nature as adapted to human well-being, a regular part of the Stoic proof of God's providential government of the world. Cicero probably referred to two motions of the sun, one which produces day and night, the other the regular rotation of the seasons; see *de n. d.* 2. 19. 49.

[7] Nonius, p. 343. 20. The text is manifestly corrupt. We have translated Quicherat's text which reads *ad con[servandas contraxerit, vere ad con]cipiendas*.

[8] Nonius, p. 159. 16. The fragment perhaps refers to the grouping of young men in Crete and at Sparta in "herds" (named *agelai* in Crete and *agelai* or *bouai* in Sparta); see Busolt: *Gr. Staatskunde*, 2 (1926), pp. 752 ff. for Crete; and pp. 695 ff. for Sparta. These organizations were devised to facilitate education and social discipline. There is a

II. SCIPIO: ....political influence;[9] how well arranged are the orders [of the citizens], and their groupings based on age or wealth, and the knights among whom the senate also is counted for purposes of voting. This advantageous arrangement too many persons now foolishly desire to overthrow. For they seek a new source of political patronage through the passage of a plebiscite whereby senators are deprived of their equestrian rank.[10]

III. Now consider how wisely all the other parts of the system were arranged to further the association of citizens in the pursuit of a happy and honorable life.[11] For the formation of such an association is the primary purpose which brings men together; and the commonwealth ought to secure to men, partly through its institutions and partly through its laws, that fundamental end of social life. In the first place, [our ancestors] did not desire that there should be a fixed system of education for free-born youth, defined by law or prescribed

---

fairly close parallel to Cicero in Plato: *Laws*, 666 e. The leaders of these "herds" were called *agoi* at Crete and *buagoi* at Sparta, and these terms may be represented by Cicero's word "shepherds" (*pastores*).

[9] At this point the Vatican palimpsest begins. Only five leaves are extant, two of which belong to the fourth book. The passage clearly refers to the excellence of ancient Roman manners and institutions (a topic which we know from *Tusc.* 4. 1. 1 was treated in *de rep.*), especially as they contrasted with the corruption prevailing in Cicero's own time; cf. Cic. *de rep.* 5. 1, below.

[10] This passage seems to be the only place in which the proposal is mentioned. It would appear that down to 129 B. C., the date of the dialogue, senators were grouped with knights for purposes of voting. At that time, a proposal was brought forward, probably at the instigation of Gaius Gracchus, that required anyone attaining membership in the senate to resign his equestrian status. There can be very little doubt that the measure was designed to create dissension between the senate and the equestrian order, for it was on this latter body that Gracchus relied in carrying out his policy of crushing the powers of the senate. On the meaning of the text, see Mommsen: *Röm. Staatsrecht*, 3. 1 (1887), pp. 505 ff.

[11] This passage closely resembles, in its implications, the famous saying of Aristotle, that the state comes into being for the sake of mere existence and continues in being for the sake of a good life; see Aristotle: *Politics*, 1252 b 27 ff.; 1329 b 27 ff. A belief in the higher ethical function of the state, as opposed to a merely utilitarian view, was an important issue between the Stoics and the Epicureans; see the extract from Lactantius in Cic. *de rep.* 1. 25, above; *de off.* 1. 44. 158. It is said by Cicero (*de leg.* 2. 5. 11) that the object of human legislation is to secure the end of an honorable and happy life.

by the state or made identical for all citizens. The Greeks, on the other hand, expended much labor in vain upon the subject of education; and this is the only point with respect to which our guest Polybius charges our ancestral customs with neglect.[12] For..........

(Either two or four leaves are missing)

[According to Cicero who says] that those who entered upon their period of military service were regularly assigned guardians by whom they are directed during their first year.[13]

Not only as at Sparta where boys learn to rob and steal.[14]

It was a reproach to young men if they had no lovers.[15]

IV. SCIPIO: [By the ancient Romans it was considered immodest for] a young man to be seen naked. Thus, certain

---

[12] Among the extant portions of Polybius there does not appear the criticism of Roman education to which Cicero alludes. Roman education, as Cicero says, was not controlled by the state; it was regarded as falling wholly within the sphere of family life. Children received their elementary education at home, either from their parents or sometimes from slaves, or in a private school. More advanced schools made their appearance about the time of the Second Punic War as a result of Greek influence. On Roman education see Marquardt: *Privatleben der Römer* (1886), pp. 80 ff.; Daremberg et Saglio: *Dictionnaire des antiquités grecques et romains*, s. v. *educatio;* Fowler: *Social Life at Rome* (1909), pp. 168 ff. If, as is probable, Scipio was the speaker of these lines, Cicero has appropriately put into his mouth a discussion of education, since it is known that Scipio was alarmed at some of the forms that education was taking in his day, and expressed his condemnation of them in no uncertain terms; see Macrobius: *sat.* 3. 14. 7; Greenidge: *History of Rome*, 1 (1904), p. 22.

[13] Servius: *ad Aen.* 5. 546. It is not at all certain that this paraphrase was derived from Cicero's *Commonwealth;* nor is it clear to what the fragment refers. A possible explanation is that Cicero is here, as below in the next chapter, alluding to the Athenian ephebic organization. A group of trainers, who might properly be named guardians (*custodes*), supervised the life and education of the Athenian ephebes during their first year; see Aristotle: *Const. of the Athenians*, 42. 2 ff.

[14] Nonius, p. 20. 12. See Plutarch: *Lycurgus*, 17. 3 ff., where it is implied that among the Spartans detection in stealing, and not stealing itself, was considered wrong.

[15] Servius: *ad Aen.* 10. 325. This is an allusion to the homosexual practices which prevailed throughout ancient Greece and especially in Crete and Sparta; in addition to Servius: *loc. cit.*, see Strabo: 483 b ff.; Plato: *Laws*, 636 b; 836 a ff.; *Republic*, 403 b, and *Symposium*, 181 d ff., in which passages Plato expresses his disapproval of the custom. Relationships between men were the only form of romantic attachment, with heights quite as well as depths, which were widely prevalent in the Greek world until the end of the fourth century B. C. See Ferguson: *Hellenistic Athens* (1911), pp. 71 ff., esp. p. 75 and note 4; Beloch: *Gr. Gesch.* 1. 1 (1924), pp. 407 ff.; Busolt: *Gr. Staatskunde*, 2 (1926), pp. 700 ff.

fundamental elements of modesty, if I may call them so, have come down from the distant past.[16] How ludicrous in truth is the exercise of naked young men on training fields! How trivial the military discipline of ephebes![17] How dissolute and unrestrained their fondling and love-making! I say nothing of the Eleans and the Thebans, among whom, in the loves of free-born young men, lust is actually allowed free rein.[18] The Spartans themselves, while permitting everything in the affairs of young men except actual debauchery, set up a very slight barrier indeed against that which they forbid, for they permit embracing and lying together with only a coverlet between.

LAELIUS: I perceive clearly, Scipio, that in respect to these Greek systems of education which you condemn, you prefer to oppose the practices of famous peoples rather than the views of your master Plato, whom you do not even mention, especially since[19]. . . . .

V. *Socrates' disciple, Plato, whom Cicero calls a god among philosophers,*[20] *was the only [pagan] thinker who so conducted his philosophical studies that he nearly reached the truth.*[21] *And yet because he knew not God, in many respects he missed*

---

[16] Cicero discussed gymnastic and military training as the education of the body. His reproach directed against the gymnasia was due to the Roman belief that evil passions are aroused by the sight of the naked body; see also *Tusc.* 4. 33. 70 (the verse quoted from Ennius); *de off.* 1. 35. 129; *de orat.* 2. 55. 224; Plutarch: *quaest. Rom.* 40. This attitude is in marked contrast with that of the Hellenic peoples, though Plato (*Republic*, 452 a ff.) remarks that the Greek practice of exercising naked came late in their history. He attributes the origin of the custom to the Cretans, while Thucydides (1. 6) attributes it to the Spartans. Plato, like Cicero, pointed out the tendency of the gymnasia and the common mess to foster homosexual practices; see *Laws*, 636 a ff.

[17] For the corps of Athenian ephebes, see Busolt: *Gr. Staatskunde*, 2 (1926), pp. 1188 ff.

[18] For the Eleans and the Thebans see Xenophon: *de rep. Lac.* 2. 12 ff.; Plato: *Symposium*, 182 b; Plutarch: *amatorius*, 761 d.

[19] This sentence is ambiguous both in Latin and in English. It may possibly have introduced a criticism of Plato by Laelius for his somewhat frank treatment of homosexual love in such dialogues as the *Symposium* and *Lysis*, but it is more probably a reference to Plato's strictures on the obscene aspects of relations between men in the *Laws* (636 a ff.; 836 a ff.).

[20] Cf. *de n. d.* 2. 12. 32; *ad Att.* 4. 16. 3.

[21] If the editors be correct in supposing that this passage from Lactantius is derived from Cicero's *Commonwealth*, Cicero must have offered

*the truth so completely that no one has made worse blunders.
Thus, in particular, in his political works he proposed that all
men should have all things in common. So far as property
is concerned, this might be borne, though it is inequitable. For
it is not right that anyone should be at a disadvantage when,
as the result of his own industry, he has more than another;
nor should anyone be favored when, as a result of his own
fault, he has less. Still, as I have said, communism in property
might be borne in one way or another. But shall wives also
be held in common, and children too? Shall there be no distinction of blood, no definite line of descent, no families or relationships by blood and marriage? Shall everything be pro-
miscuous and indiscriminate, as in herds of cattle? Shall there
be no continence in men or chastity in women? What con-
jugal love can exist between two persons between whom there
is no permanent and personal affection? Who will feel filial
piety when he does not know of whom he was born? Who
will love a son whom he believes to be another's? Plato actually opened[22] the senate-house to women and permitted them
to do military service and to hold civil and military offices.
How great will be the misfortune of that city in which women
hold the positions that belong to men!*

Lactantius: *epit.* 33 (38). 1-5.

And our master Plato goes even further than Lycurgus,
since he directs that everything shall be in common, in order
that no citizen may call anything his own private possession.[23]

---

a refutation of Plato's communism of property (*Republic*, 416 d ff.)
and of wives (449 ff.). It is not necessary to indicate in detail the
unfounded character of Lactantius', and also Cicero's (see the following
fragment from Nonius) attack on Plato. Plato's communism, for example, applied not to all citizens but only to the guardian class; and there
was a close supervision and restriction of the sexual relations between
men and women of this class.

[22] For *reservavit* (that is, "reserved") we read, with most of the
editors, *reseravit* (that is, "opened").

[23] Nonius, p. 362. 11. The meaning appears to be that Lycurgus provided that property only should be common, while Plato taught that
women also are to be possessed in common. At Sparta the citizens
owned their allotments of land, but the land was tilled by serfs and
the produce went to maintain the common tables. Other property also
was subject to common use. On Spartan communism see Busolt: *Gr.
Staatskunde*, 2 (1926), pp. 659 ff.; Xenophon: *de rep. Lac.* 6; Aristotle:
Politics, 1263 a 33 ff.

Even as [Plato] expels Homer, though crowned and anointed, from the city which he imagines, so I [would expel Plato].[24]

VI. The judgment of the censors exposed the condemned to practically no penalty except disgrace. Since, therefore, their pronouncements may only attach reproach to a name, such censure was called ignominy.[25]

First, the state is said to have trembled before the severity of the [censors].[26]

Nor indeed should an overseer be put in charge of the women, as is customary among the Greeks, but let there be a censor to teach husbands to govern their wives.[27]

---

[24] Nonius, p. 308. 38. The supplement is taken from Mai, who conjectures that Laelius thus reproaches Plato for his theory of communism. Because of the impiety of the stories told by the poets about the gods, and because poets in general stressed the emotions unduly, Plato (*Republic*, 386 a ff.; esp. 398 a ff.) excluded all poets from his ideal commonwealth except those writers whose works had a good moral influence.

[25] Nonius, p. 24. 5. The passage contains a play on the words *nomen* and *ignominia*. It seems that Cicero, in pointing out the excellence of Roman institutions, praises the censorship as a means of preserving the purity of morals, and contrasts it with other institutions established for a similar purpose in other states. The censors did not possess criminal jurisdiction in the ordinary sense, but because of their control of the census rolls, they could change a man from one tribe to another or degrade him in his civil status. For an account of their functions and competence, see Cic. *de leg.* 3. 3. 7; Bouché-Leclercq: *Manuel des inst. romaines* (1886), pp. 64 ff.; Mommsen: *Röm. Staatsrecht*, 2. 1 (1887), pp. 331 ff.; Greenidge: *Roman Public Life* (1911), pp. 216 ff.

[26] Nonius, p. 423. 4. The word *severitas* had a special application to the power of the censors to regulate morals; see Gellius: *noct. Att.* 4. 20. 1.

[27] Nonius, p. 499. 13. This is an allusion to the *gynaikonomoi*, who were established in Athens by Demetrius of Phalerum, Macedonian regent from 318-7 to 308-7 B. C., to curb license among women and in general to check all forms of sumptuary excess. It is true that the institution was a common one among the Greeks, being found at Samos, Syracuse, Gambreium, and Andania. For the office in Athens, see Cic. *de leg.* 2. 26. 66; Ferguson: *Hellenistic Athens* (1911), pp. 45 ff.; Gilbert: *Gr. Staatsalt.* 1 (1893), p. 178; Busolt: *Gr. Staatskunde*, 2 (1926), p. 929; for general references to the existence of such an office, see Aristotle: *Politics*, 1322 b 37 ff.; Newman: *Politics of Aristotle*, 1 (1887), pp. 194; 518; Gilbert: *op. cit.* 2 (1885), pp. 152; 255; 337. Cicero's criticism of the office probably expressed a preference for the ancient Roman custom of leaving such power (*patria potestas*) within the family in the hands of the *pater familias*. The censor's functions with respect to the behavior of women are not specifically mentioned in *de leg.* 3. 3. 7, where Cicero describes the competence of that official.

Thus the teaching of modesty has great influence: all women abstain from intoxicating liquor.[28]

And also, if a woman was of ill-repute, her relatives did not kiss her.[29]

Hence, boldness gets its name from asking, and wantonness from demanding, that is, from urging.[30]

VII. For I am not willing that the same people should be at once the ruler and the tax-gatherer of the world. But in the commonwealth, as well as on private estates, I regard thrift as the best source of income.[31]

For it seems to me that good faith gets its very name whenever what is promised is performed.[32]

In a citizen of high position and in a man of good birth flattery, display, and undue desire to please are marks of light-mindedness.[33]

Consider a little the work on the commonwealth from which you have imbibed the attitude proper to a patriotic citizen, namely, that good men place neither measure nor limit upon their devotion to their country. Consider and note, I beg you, how highly thrift and self-control are praised therein, together with loyalty to the marriage tie, and pure, honorable, and upright habits. Augustine: *epist.* 91. 3; *CSEL.* 34. 428. 21.

---

[28] Nonius, p. 5. 10. See Polybius: 6. 11. 4; Dionysius: *ant. Rom.* 2. 25. 6; Plutarch: *quaest. Rom.* 6; Gellius: *noct. Att.* 10. 23. 1, all of whom testify to the enforced sobriety of Roman women. In order to insure total abstinence on their part, it was provided that they should kiss all their own male relatives and all their husbands' male relatives up to second cousins each day on their first meeting. It is probable that Cicero derives this information from Cato's speech *Concerning Dowry*; see Gellius: *op. cit.* 10. 23. 4.

[29] Nonius, p. 306. 3.

[30] Nonius, p. 23. 17 and 21. Cicero derives *petulantia* from *petere* and *procacitas* from *procare*, i. e., *poscere*, suggesting perhaps that evil manners among women arise from avarice.

[31] Nonius, p. 24. 15. The expression, *optimum vectigal est parsimonia*, is a proverb; see Otto: *Sprichwörter* (1890), p. 266. It occurs also in Cic. *parad.* 6. 3. 49. Cicero doubtless enlarged upon the evils of luxury and extravagance and praised ancient Roman simplicity and frugality, as may be seen from the passage from Augustine below.

[32] Nonius, p. 24. 11. *Fides*, that is, comes from *fit*; for the same derivation see Cic. *de off.* 1. 7. 23.

[33] Nonius, p. 194. 26. We read, with Sigonius, *nimiam* for *meam*.

VIII.   I admire [in the law of the Twelve Tables] the preciseness both of its provisions and of its language. [The law] says, "If they disagree." Disagreement is the name given to a controversy between persons who still preserve their good will toward each other, and not to a quarrel between enemies. Therefore, the law considers that neighbors disagree with each other, but do not quarrel.[34]

[Men do not believe that] their interests end with their lives; hence the sanctity of burial is part of the pontifical law.[35]

[After the Battle of Arginusae, the Athenians] put to death [the generals], though they were innocent, because they left unburied the bodies which the violence of the storm did not allow them to recover from the sea.[36]

In this controversy I have taken sides not with the populace but with the aristocrats.[37]

It is not easy to resist a powerful people if you grant them no authority, or too little.[38]

---

[34] Nonius, p. 430. 29; *iurgium* from *iurgare* (disagree) and *lis* from *litigare* (quarrel). See Girard: *Textes de droit romain* (1923), p. 16 (tab. 7. 5). Probably Cicero commended the law, particularly the Twelve Tables, as material for education; cf. a similar provision in Plato: *Laws*, 811 d. That the law was learned by Roman boys somewhat as Christian children learn the catechism is clear from Cic. *de leg.* 2. 23. 59. A similar practice existed in Crete and elsewhere in the ancient world; see Busolt: *Gr. Staatskunde*, 2 (1926), p. 753.

[35] Nonius, p. 174. 7. Cicero mentions the care taken to prescribe burial rites as a proof of the belief in immortality; see *Tusc.* 1. 12. 27. Mai supplements the sentence above on the basis of this passage. The regulation of expenditure connected with funerals was a form of Roman sumptuary legislation prescribed by the Twelve Tables; see Cic. *de leg.* 2. 24. 60; Girard: *Textes de droit romain* (1923), p. 21, tab. 10. It is possible, therefore, that this fragment and the next were included in Cicero's praise of this aspect of Roman frugality.

[36] Nonius, p. 293. 41. This is undoubtedly a reference to the punishment inflicted by the Athenians upon the generals after the naval battle of Arginusae in 406 B. C. Though victorious, the generals failed to recover the bodies of the dead. See Xenophon: *Hellenica*, 1. 6; Grote: *History of Greece*, 7 (1869), pp. 414 ff.; Busolt: *Gr. Gesch.* 3. 2 (1904), pp. 1586 ff.; E. Meyer: *Gesch. des Alt.* 4 (1915), pp. 644 ff.; Beloch: *Gr. Gesch.* 2. 1 (1914), pp. 418 ff.

[37] Nonius, p. 519. 15.

[38] Priscian: 15. 4. 20; ed. Hertz, p. 76. 14. On its face this fragment appears to belong in a context where the need of granting some power to the people is pointed out, possibly in connection with the treatment of democracy at the end of Book 3 (cf. Cic. *de rep.* 2. 33). Priscian, however, expressly states that the fragment is found in the fourth book.

Would that I might have foretold the future for him truly and trustworthily and........[39]

IX. By their clamorous approval and applause,[40] the people mould the character of the poets according to their will—as if the public were some great and wise master whose praise is all-sufficient. But when poets are so highly extolled, what darkness they bring into the soul! What fears they incite! What passions they enkindle! They present debauchery and adultery in a pleasing manner; they rehearse varied forms of deception; they teach theft, robbery, and arson. Every example of evil which exists, or has existed, or can be imagined, they lay before the eyes of the illiterate rabble. No heavenly conflagration,[41] no flood, no earthquake has spread devastation among men comparable to the ruin which the poets have brought upon morality.

Cicero asserts that, even if the span of his life were to be doubled, he would not have time to read the lyric poets.[42]

Seneca: *epist.* 49. 5.

X. SCIPIO: Because they considered the stage and all theatrical art degrading, [the Romans] desired not only that this class of people should be ineligible to posts of honor which were open to other citizens, but also that the names of such persons should be erased from the tribal rolls by the censor.[43]

---

[39] Nonius, p. 469. 16.

[40] John of Salisbury: *policraticus* (ed. Webb.), pp. 655 d ff. We have substituted this quotation for the briefer paraphrase of the same passage by Augustine (*de civ.* 2. 14) which is printed by Ziegler. There seems to be no doubt that John gives a more extended extract from Cicero than Augustine, and it follows that he must have had access to a more complete version of the *Commonwealth* than the Vatican palimpsest presents. It is clear that Cicero followed the lead of Plato (*Republic*, 377 b ff.) in pointing out the evils in the state which are fostered by the poets. Cf. also Cic. *de n. d.* 1. 16. 42 ff.; *Tusc.* 2. 11. 27; 4. 32. 68 ff. This passage in the *Commonwealth* is partly identical with *Tusc.* 3. 2. 3.

[41] This is apparently a reference to the story of Phaethon; see Ovid: *metamorphoses*, 2. 31 ff.

[42] The ascription of this passage to the *Commonwealth* is not certain. Hense in his edition of Seneca's letters conjectures that it comes from Cicero's lost *Hortensius*.

[43] Augustine: *de civ.* 2. 13; similar passages in 2. 27 and 29. The Roman prejudice against the theatrical profession was real and expressed itself in legislation. Thus, by the *Lex Julia municipalis* (45 B. C.) an actor was debarred from holding any of the higher offices (sect. 123).

The opinion of the ancient Romans about the stage is shown by Cicero in his work on the Commonwealth, where Scipio says in the course of the discussion: Comedy could never have won the approval of audiences for the immoralities of its plots, unless social custom had tolerated a similar immorality. *In earlier times the Greeks maintained a consistent though erroneous view of the stage,[44] for the law itself granted to writers of comedy the privilege of referring by name to anyone they pleased. Accordingly, as Scipio says in the same work of Cicero:* Who is there that [comedy] has not meddled with, or rather, whom has it not aspersed? Whom has it spared?[45] Granted that it has pilloried vicious demogogues who were traitors to the commonwealth, such as Cleon, Cleophon, and Hyperbolus. This we may endure, though it is better that such citizens should be judged by the censor than by a poet. But after Pericles had wielded the chief civil and military

The *Lex Julia* (18 B. C.), passed by Augustus, prohibited marriage between a senator and an actress or the daughter of actors, and between the daughter of a senator and an actor or the son of actors (*dig.* 23. 2. 44, pr.). The *Lex Popia Poppaea* (8 A. D.) imposed certain disadvantages on freedmen who had been actors (*dig.* 38. 1. 37, pr.). In Welldon's edition of Augustine: *de civ.* (1924), 2, pp. 659 ff., there is an interesting summary of the attitude of the Church towards the stage.

[44] The view was consistent because, as Augustine (*de civ.* 2. 9 dʃ says, the Greeks believed that the gods desired the drama to be unrestrained.

[45] The reference is to the outspoken character of old Attic comedy, to which the philosopher Plato objected; see *Laws*, 817 b ff.; 935 c ff. Even the writers of Old Comedy were not allowed to assail the demos itself; see Pseud. Xen. *Ath. pol.* 2. 18. Cleon, the offensive but able leader of the Athenians after the death of Pericles (i. e., after 429 B. C.; see Beloch: *Gr. Gesch.* 2. 1, 1914, p. 314), was assailed by Aristophanes in the *Babylonians* (426 B. C.), the *Acharnians* (425), the *Knights* (424), and the *Wasps* (422). Cleophon, a financial leader who was the chief obstacle to peace with Sparta (see Beloch: *op. cit.* pp. 396 ff.), was attacked by the comic poet Plato (end of fifth century) in the *Cleophon* (405). Hyperbolus, the demagogue who succeeded Cleon (see Beloch: *op. cit.* pp. 346 ff.), was satirized by Plato in the *Hyperbolus* and by Eupolis (446—c. 411) in the *Maricas* (422). Cratinus (died between 425 and 421) is reputed to have been the first to introduce political satire on the stage. In the *Thracian Women* and the *Cheirones* he ridiculed Pericles. The best known example of public ridicule, the *Clouds* of Aristophanes (423), in which Socrates was the victim, is not mentioned by Cicero. In 440 B. C. and again in 416 the Athenians attempted to forbid the comic poets to satirize by name. The former decree appears to have fallen into desuetude, while the latter was repealed in 412. See Christ-Schmid: *Gesch. d. gr. Lit.* 1 (1912), p. 414 for Plato; pp. 412-413 for Eupolis; pp. 416 ff. for Aristophanes; pp. 409 ff. for Cratinus.

authority in his state for many years, it was as indecorous
for him to be traduced in verse and satirized[46] on the stage,
as it would have been if our poets Plautus and Naevius[47] had
presumed to abuse Publius and Gnaeus Scipio, or if Caecilius
had slandered Marcus Cato. *And a little later he adds,* On
the other hand, though our law of the Twelve Tables[48] had
established capital punishment for only a very few offenses,
it was deemed necessary that in this small number should be
included also the offense of making a pasquinade or composing
a song which was defamatory or libellous. It was an excellent
law. For our mode of life ought to be subjected to the decisions of magistrates and to the processes of law rather than
to the fancies of poets. Nor ought we to be subject to slander-
ous remarks, unless we can answer them and defend ourselves
by legal action.

*I have thought it advisable to make these quotations from
the fourth book of the Commonwealth, giving Cicero's own
language, except where I have omitted a few words or changed
them slightly for the sake of greater clearness. For the
passages have an important bearing upon the matter which I
am trying to explain, if I can. Cicero makes some further
remarks and then concludes by showing that* it seemed improper to the ancient Romans that any man, while he was yet
alive, should be either eulogized or satirized on the stage.[49]

---

[46] We read, with Halm, *exagitari* for *eos agi.*

[47] Naevius (c 270 - c.199 B. C.) got into difficulties by systematic vili-
fication of certain members of the ruling class at Rome; see Duff: *Literary History of Rome* (1914), pp. 126 ff. He was imprisoned and finally
exiled, a comparatively mild sentence since the law of the Twelve Tables
made personal libel a capital offense. Plautus (c. 254-184 B. C.) was the
chief of the Roman comic poets. His plays are largely a skilful adaptation of the middle and new Attic comedy, in which there were no personal
attacks; see Duff: *ibid.,* pp. 159 ff. Caecilius (c. 219-166) was a writer
of comedies, more urbane and finely wrought than those of Plautus, if
we may judge from tradition, but less interesting; see Duff: *ibid.,* pp.
201 ff.

[48] See Girard: *Textes de droit romain* (1923), p. 17 (tab. 8. 1); Bruns:
Fontes iuris Romani antiqui (1909), pp. 28 ff. (tab. 8. 1); Girard:
Manuel de droit romain (1924), pp. 419 ff.

[49] Augustine: *de civ.* 2. 9. We have translated the context from
Augustine, which Ziegler prints in the apparatus criticus.

XI. *Cicero says that comedy is an imitation of life, a mirror
of custom, and a representation of truth.*[50]

Donatus: *exc. de com.* ed. Wessner, p. 22. 19.

Aeschines the Athenian, a very eloquent man, though as a
youth he had appeared on the tragic stage, took an active part
in public affairs; and the Athenians frequently sent Aristodemus, who was also a tragic actor, to Philip as their ambassador
in the most important concerns of peace and war.[51]

XII. *For not every pleasure is blameworthy, nor is pleasure
the end of music. While pleasurable excitement is an incidental
element, the deliberate object of musical study is to direct the
soul towards excellence. This is a fact which has been unob-
served by many scholars and especially by the interlocutor who
harangues against music in Cicero's dialogue on the Commonwealth.*[52] *For I should not presume to assert that Cicero
expressed in that work his own feelings about music. No one
indeed could confidently affirm that he maligned and blamed
music as being an ignoble art. For in fact music is the science
which distinguishes excellence and worthlessness in the field
of harmony and rhythm; and it was Cicero who at that time
was filled with admiration for the actor Roscius, although he
was famous only for rhythmical effects which were ignoble
and base. Such, however, was Cicero's wonder that he declared that the gods had provided for Roscius' coming into
the world.*[53] *Now if it be said that Cicero expressed his real*

---

[50] This definition of comedy, according to Christ-Schmid (*Gesch d. gr.
Lit.* 2. 1, 1920, p. 45, n. 4), is derived from an epigram on Menander
written by Aristophanes of Byzantium.

[51] Augustine: *de civ.* 2. 11. The passage contrasts the esteem in which
actors were held in Greece with the contempt for them at Rome.
Aeschines (c. 389-314 B. C.) was the champion of the Macedonian interest
at Athens. His rival Demosthenes asserts that he had been an actor
(18. 209; 262), and the tradition is preserved by Plutarch (*Orators*,
840 a). Aristodemus was sent to treat with Philip on behalf of the
Athenians after the fall of Olynthus in 347 B. C. See Aeschines: 2.
15-16; Grote: *History of Greece*, 11 (1869), p. 177.

[52] That Cicero regarded music as an important element in a state may
be seen from *de leg.* 2. 15. 39; 3. 14. 32, where he approves Plato's
assertion (*Republic*, 424 c) that a change in musical style means a
change in the character of the state.

[53] No such expression occurs in the extant portion of Cicero's *pro
Rosc.* That Cicero greatly admired Roscius appears from *pro Arch.*
8. 17; *de div.* 1. 36. 79; *pro Quint.* 25. 78; *de leg.* 1. 4. 11; Macrobius:
sat. 3. 14. 11.

views in his discussion of the Commonwealth, while in his plea for Roscius he spoke to win his case, we may also reverse the argument. Nevertheless, we should go unchallenged if in our present inquiry we rejected the testimony of the orator instead of reconciling his statements. For when our concern is the discovery of truth or an impartial judgment, we cannot trust the evidence of a man who makes his argument rest upon flute music or upon some immediate purpose, and does not base his conclusions upon the true nature of music. I do not think that Cicero would blame the art of rhetoric because some orators accept bribes. Accordingly, even if some artists sing ignoble music because it pleases the vulgar, the blame does not attach to music itself. In fact, in the days of Numa and the kings who immediately succeeded him, when the Romans were still somewhat uncouth, the state instructed its people in music. Such is Cicero's own affirmation, for he says that music both cheered their private banquets and had its place in all their public religious rites.

Aristides Quint. *de musica*, 2, pp. 69-71, ed. Meibomius; p. 43. 38 ff., ed. Jahn.

Bracelets.[54]

---

[54] Priscian: *partit. 12 vers. Aen.* 1. 14; ed. Hertz, p. 462. 32.

BOOK V

I. *The Roman state, being in the condition which Sallust describes, could not properly be represented as a "corrupt and depraved" form of government, as Sallust calls it.*[1] *In fact, it was not a commonwealth at all, if we accept the theory set forth in [Cicero's] dialogue on the Commonwealth, in which the speakers were the great statesmen [of the Gracchan age]. Indeed, at the opening of Book V, Cicero himself, speaking not in the character of Scipio or of anyone else but in his own person, first quotes the verse of Ennius wherein the poet had declared that*

By ancient customs and by men the Roman state endures,

and then adds, this is indeed a verse which, by its brevity and truth, makes me feel that Ennius spoke as if he were an oracle. For neither distinguished men without a state thus endowed with a high standard of conduct, nor a high standard of conduct without distinguished men in positions of authority, could have either established or long maintained so great a commonwealth as ours and one of such extent and dominion. Before our time, therefore, our inherited standards themselves brought forward distinguished men, and eminent men cherished the ways and customs of our ancestors. But our own generation, after inheriting the commonwealth as if it were a painting, of unique excellence but fading with age, has not only failed to restore its original hues, but has not even troubled to preserve its outline and the last vestiges of its features. What, I ask, is left of those ancient customs by which,

---

[1] Sallust: *Cat.* 5. We translate the context from Augustine, which Ziegler prints in the apparatus criticus. Like the dialogues of the first and second days (the first in Books 1 and 2, the second in Books 3 and 4), the dialogue of the third day (Books 5 and 6) was preceded by an introduction in which Cicero writes in his own person. Augustine's excerpt comes from this introduction. When Cicero wrote (c. 54 B. C.) men felt that the Roman state had declined from its greatest days; see Cic. *in Cat.* 1. 1; Sallust: *Cat.* 5; *Iug.* 41; fr. 12 (ed. Kritz); Livy: *praef.* 9 ff. Book 5 of the *Commonwealth* dealt mainly with the character and training of the great statesman, who might restore the ancient health of his country.

as Ennius said, the Roman state endures? We see them so out of fashion and forgotten that they are no longer even known, much less cherished. And what shall I say of men? It is indeed the lack of distinguished men that has caused these rules of living to perish. This is an evil for which we must not only render an account, but which we must even answer for as if we were defendants on a capital charge. For it is by our defects of character and not by accident that we long since lost the substance of the commonwealth, though we still retain its name.   Augustine: *de civ.* 2. 21.

II. MANILIUS ?[2]: [They felt that there was no task of government more] becoming to a king than the pronounce- ment of justice; this included the interpretation of the law, which private citizens habitually sought from their kings.[3] For this reason lands, fields, and broad and fertile grazing places were set apart for the kings, to be cultivated without toil or labor on their part. In this way, therefore, it was intended that no concern for their private affairs should distract them from public interests. In fact, there was not a single arbitra- tor or judge in private station, and all legal business was transacted in the royal courts. I, at least, feel that Numa in particular followed the ancient custom of the kings of Greece. For our other kings, though they concerned themselves also with the duty of administering justice, mainly waged wars and developed the laws of war. But the long peace of Numa's reign was the mother of law and religious observance in our city. Numa also drew up statutes which, as you know, are still extant.[4] Now legislation is the special function of the

---

[2] Chapters 2-5 include the remaining three leaves of the Vatican palimpsest. The supplement at the beginning of ch. 2 is Mai's. He attributes the speech to Manilius as the representative of the law among the interlocutors; see Cic. *de rep.* 1. 13, above, and Introduction, p. 5. Mai's hypothesis is probably correct, that Scipio and Manilius debated the value of a knowledge of law as part of the statesman's equipment, Manilius holding that it was of first importance and Scipio that it was subordinate to his management of public affairs; see *de rep.* 5. 3, below.

[3] Manilius urges the example of the ancient kings of Greece and Rome to prove that the statesman is primarily a lawgiver; cf. the origin of monarchy as described by Plato: *Laws*, 681 a ff.; and the duties of the king in the heroic age mentioned by Aristotle: *Politics*, 1285 b 3 ff.

[4] Cf. Cic. *de rep.* 2. 14, above.

statesman, whose character we are considering.. . . . .

(Either two or four leaves are missing)

III. . . . . .but, nevertheless, as the wise owner of an estate needs experience in cultivation, building, and calculation. . . . .[5]

SCIPIO: [If the overseer of an estate is interested] in knowing the nature of roots and seeds, it will not displease you, will it?[6]

MANILIUS: Not at all, if any need for it shall arise.

SCIPIO: But you do not think, do you, that such an interest belongs properly to an overseer?

MANILIUS: By no means, since very frequently his duties have nothing to do with tilling the soil.

SCIPIO: Very well, then, as an overseer understands the nature of the soil and a steward knows how to write, but as both of them turn away from the delight in knowledge to the performance of useful tasks, so our governor, though of course he will be interested in understanding the provisions of the law and will undoubtedly perceive the sources from which they spring, will not permit his duties as a jurisconsult, his researches, and his writings to prevent him from being, as we may say, the steward of the commonwealth and in some sense its overseer. In the law of nature he must be perfectly versed, for without this no man can be just. In the civil law he must not be unversed, but in the latter field his knowledge should resemble the pilot's knowledge of astronomy or the doctor's of natural philosophy, which these men adapt to their own uses but never allow to be an obstacle in their own pro-

---

[5] Nonius, p. 497. 23. The analogy of government with the management of an estate occurs in Plato: *Statesman*, 259 c, and is rejected by Aristotle: *Politics*, 1252 a 7 ff.; 1258 a 19; see Newman's note on the last passage. Elsewhere, Cicero calls the magistrate a steward (*vilicus*) of the Roman people (*pro Planc.* 25. 62), but does not pursue the comparison. Logically, Cicero, like Aristotle, ought to hold that political rule is generically different from domestic authority; see *de rep.* 1. 25, above.

[6] We translate Mai's supplement. The sense of the passage that follows is not clear but seems to be that knowledge of the civil law is an incidental part of the statesman's equipment, but subordinate to the management of public affairs, as an overseer's knowledge of agriculture is merely part of managing an estate; see the preceding chapter, note 2.

fession.[7] Now our statesman will perceive this.........

(The number of missing leaves cannot be determined)

IV. SCIPIO: ....in states where the best citizens desire renown and glory, they shun disgrace and shame.[8] Fear of the punishment that is prescribed by law does not move them so deeply as the feeling of shame which nature has implanted in man in the form of a fear of deserved reproach. This feeling the wise governor has strengthened by his guidance of public opinion and has brought to a state of great effectiveness by custom and education, in order that shame, no less than fear, might restrain the citizens from wrong doing. The same idea applies, of course, to the love of praise, and might have been expanded and developed in more detail.

V. As regards private life and the practice of everyday living this plan has been further elaborated by giving a legal sanction to marriage,[9] by describing children [born in wedlock] as legitimate, and by declaring holy the shrines of the Penates and domestic Lares,[10] to the end that all citizens might enjoy both common and private advantages. Thus it was in-

---

[7] In the long account of the general's art given by Polybius (9. 12 ff.) it is stated (ch. 20) that there are certain subsidiary sciences, such as geometry and astronomy, which a general should know, not thoroughly, but in sufficient degree to enable him to conduct his campaigns.

[8] Cicero elsewhere attributes great importance to the sense of shame (*verecundia*) as a social virtue; see *de off.* 1. 27. 93 ff. Like Plato (*Laws*, 718 b ff.), he prefers to secure obedience to law by persuasion rather than by force; see *de leg.* 2. 6. 14. Like the Stoics, Cicero regards the elements of all the virtues as innate; and the statesman can impede or assist the growth of these native virtues by appropriate laws and institutions; see Arnold: *Roman Stoicism* (1911), pp. 302 ff.; Hicks: *Stoic and Epicurean* (1910), pp. 77 ff.

[9] According to Roman law, marriage was a legal relationship between two qualified persons of opposite sex (see Gaius: *inst.*, ed. Poste, 1904, 1. 56 ff., and commentary), entered into by a form of bilateral contract (*ibid.* p. 47), assumed voluntarily (*dig.* 35. 1. 15), symbolized by a formal escort of the bride to her husband's domicile (*deductio in domum*; see *ibid.* 23. 2. 5; Paulus: *sententiae*, 2. 19. 8; Marquardt: *Privatleben der Römer*, 1886, pp. 53 ff.), marked by *maritalis affectio* (*dig.* 24. 1. 3. 1; 24. 1. 32. 13), assumed to possess a sacred and enduring character (*ibid.* 23. 2. 1), and designed for the propagation of offspring (Justinian: *inst.* 1. 10 pr.; Livy: *epit.* 59; Greenidge: *History of Rome*, 1, 1904, p. 64).

[10] By this mention of *iustae nuptiae, legitimi liberi*, the Lares, and the Penates, Cicero emphasized the chief elements in Roman family life. It is probable that he contrasted such a system with the communistic

tended that a good life should be impossible except in a good state, and that nothing might be more conducive to happiness than a well-organized government.[11] For this reason it always seems very strange to me.... .....what [form of training] is so powerful..........

(The end of the palimpsest)

VI. SCIPIO: A pilot's aim is a successful voyage; a doctor's, health; a general's, victory. Similarly, the goal set before the ideal ruler of the commonwealth is the happiness of his citizens;[12] and he strives to make them secure in their resources, rich in wealth, great in renown, distinguished in virtue. This is the task—the greatest and noblest in human life—that I would have the governor carry through to completion.[13]

And do you not recall the passage even in [pagan] litera-

theory of Plato. The Penates were deities who presided over the larder; see Fowler: *Religious Experience of the Roman People* (1911), pp. 73 ff.; Wissowa: *Religion und Kultus der Römer* (1912), pp. 161 ff. The Lar—in the plural form, the Lares—was originally the spirit which presided over the plot of land, including the house, occupied by each *familia,* and which guarded the productive powers of the land. In the later Roman worship the *Lar familiaris* is essentially a household divinity.

[11] See Cic. *de rep.* 4. 3, above, and note; Newman: *Politics of Aristotle,* 1 (1887), p. 63; see also Aristotle: *Politics,* 1264 b 16 ff., where Aristotle, arguing against Plato, declares that in a happy state the citizens must be happy.

[12] Cf. the fragment on kingship attributed to Diotogenes the Pythagorean in Stobaeus: *florilegium,* 48. 61, where the following words occur: "The duty of the pilot is to bring his ship safely to port; the task of the charioteer is to keep his chariot upright; the doctor's aim is to cure the sick; and the function of the king or general is to save those who risk their lives in battle."

[13] Cic. *ad Att.* 8. 11. 1. On the importance of the statesman's art see Cic. *de rep.* 1. 22, above, and note. For a discussion of Cicero's conception of the ideal statesman and the rôle which he should play in the state, see Introduction, pp. 93 ff. It will be sufficient to note here the various passages in which Cicero describes that ruler, whom he calls *rector et gubernator civitatis* (2. 29), *rector* (5. 3; 6. 1; 8; 13), *moderator rei publicae* (5. 6; also introductory sentences of Cic. *ad Att.* 8. 11. 1), *princeps* (5. 7), *gubernator* (2. 29), and, it would appear, simply *civis* either with or without qualification (1. 2; 29; 5. 2; 6. 1)— all of these terms being apparently used as translations of the Greek word *politikos.* According to Richard Heinze ("Ciceros 'Staat' als politische Tendenzschrift," in *Hermes,* 59, 1924, pp. 92 ff.), Cicero coined the terms *rector* and *moderator rei publicae* for that very object.

ture which praises the governor of a state who considers, not
the whim, but the advantage of his people?[14]

Augustine: epist. 104. 7; CSEL. 34. 587. 24.

VII. *Hence, even Cicero, in the same work on the Commonwealth, could not conceal the fact [that the love of glory,
though itself a vice, may yet restrain men from worse vices].[15]
For, speaking about the education of a chief of the state, he
says that such a man must be* nurtured by glory, *and then he
declares that* his ancestors performed many extraordinary and
brilliant deeds because of their love for glory.

Augustine: de civ. 5. 13.

The chief of the state must be nurtured by glory; and the
commonwealth endures only so long as all men accord honor
to their chief.[16]

Then we should be permitted to seek the character of a
great man in excellence, activity, and energy, except in those
cases where a nature too passionate and wild has in some way
[led him astray].[17]

This virtue is called courage; it includes the quality of high-
mindedness and a lofty scorn of death and pain.[18]

---

[14] This is a sentence from a letter written by Augustine to Nectarius,
a pagan, in which he says that defects of character must be treated
solely with an eye to the advantage of the defective person. There is
nothing to prove that the sentence was written by Cicero except the
words *patriae rectorem.* We do not agree with Ziegler in regarding the
words *et ubi . . . laudant* as Cicero's.

[15] This fragment and the following have usually been taken to refer
to the education of the ideal ruler (*rector rei publicae*). It has been
pointed out, however, that the value here set upon glory is in contradic-
tion to the contempt for human fame expressed by Scipio in *de rep.*
1. 17, above, and 6. 21, below. Accordingly, Richard Heinze has con-
jectured that this fragment refers to the education of the aristocratic
class in the state and that it should be transferred to Book 4; see
"Ciceros 'Staat' als politische Tendenzschrift," *Hermes,* 59 (1924), p. 77,
n. 2, and the reply by R. Reitzenstein, *ibid.* p. 359.

[16] Petrus Pictaviensis (Peter of Poitiers): *ad calumn. Bibl. patr. Lugd.*
22, p. 824.

[17] Nonius, p. 233. 33. We read, following Lindsay's suggestion, *quae-
rere daretur* for *quaereretur.* The passage is clearly corrupt.

[18] Nonius, p. 201. 29. See Cic. *Tusc.* 2. 18. 43. This quality (*fortitudo*),
which is perhaps here mentioned as one of the essential elements of the
statesman, Cicero further defines as a rational quality of soul which
fearlessly obeys the divine law despite suffering; as the preservation of
calm judgment in enduring and repelling sufferings which appear ter-

VIII.   As Marcellus was fierce and eager to fight, as Maximus was circumspect and deliberate.[19]

Included in the whole world..........[20]

Because he could inflict the disagreeable whims of his old age on your families.[21]

IX.   As Spartan Menelaus possessed the gift of mellifluous speech.

Let him practice brevity of speech.[22]

SCIPIO: And since nothing in a state should be freer from corruption than the use of the ballot or the decision of judges, I do not see why a man who corrupts by money should deserve punishment, while one who corrupts by eloquence should actually win praise. I, at least, feel that a man who directs his eloquence to corrupt ends really does more harm than one who corrupts a judge by money, because, while no honest man can be seduced by money, he may be corrupted by a specious plea.[23]

After Scipio had said this, Mummius approving heartily ...., for he was animated by a feeling of aversion towards orators.[24]

Then the good seed would have been sown in an excellent field.[25]

---

rible; or as knowledge which maintains unperturbed judgment about experiences which may be horrible or otherwise but which should be disregarded; see *Tusc.* 4. 22. 50 ff.

[19] Nonius, p. 337. 34.

[20] Charisius: *gram. Lat.*, ed. Keil, 1. 139. 17.

[21] Nonius, p. 37. 23.

[22] Gellius: *noct. Att.* 12. 2. 7. These fragments are apparently advice to the ruler.

[23] Ammianus Marcellinus: 30. 4. 10. Plato (*Laws*, 937 e ff.) provides penalties for the misuse of eloquence in courts. Perhaps the context of this passage in Cicero was a contrast of the right use of eloquence by the high-minded statesman with the corrupt use of it by the mere politician.

[24] Nonius, p. 521. 12.

[25] *Comment. anon. on Verg. georg.* 1, init., in Bandin. catal. lat. bibl. Laur. 2. p. 348

BOOK VI

I. Accordingly, you desire a full description of this ruler's foresight, a term which is derived from foreseeing.[1]

In his treatise on government Cicero says that the governor of a commonwealth ought to be a man of consummate ability and learning. Thus, he must be wise, just, and self-controlled; and he must also be eloquent, in order to make clear his inmost thoughts by a ready flow of words, and thus to control the populace. Furthermore, he must understand law and know Greek literature. This latter point Cicero proves by the example of Cato, who in extreme old age devoted himself to the study of Greek and thereby showed what practical value that literature had.[2]

Manuscript commentary on Cic. *de invent.*
printed in Osann's edition of *de rep.*, p. 349.

Therefore, the statesman must so train himself that he may always be armed to meet emergencies which unsettle the constitution.[3]

And such a disagreement among the citizens is termed a

---

[1] Nonius, p. 42. 3. Cicero derives *prudentia* from *providendo;* see also *de div.* 1. 49. 111; *de leg.* 1. 23. 60. The sixth book, like Books 2 and 4, probably lacked an introduction in which Cicero spoke in his own person. The sixth book continued the account of the ideal statesman begun in Book 5, apparently emphasizing his function in times of civil strife; see *ad Att.* 7. 3. 2; *de off.* 1. 25. 85 ff.; E. Meyer: *Caesars Monarchie und das Principat des Pompejus* (1922), pp. 182 ff. The book concludes with the famous dream of Scipio in which Cicero emphasizes the divine character of the statesman by picturing the heavenly life that awaits him after death.

[2] E. Meyer (*Caesars Monarchie und das Principat des Pompejus*, 1922, p. 182, n. 5) supposes that this passage should be included in 5. 6, above, on account of its close relationship with the latter.

[3] Nonius, p. 256. 27. This and the four following fragments seem to deal with the causes and prevention of revolutions; see Cic. *de rep.* 1. 45; 2. 29, above. The subject formed a regular part of ancient political treatises, as Cicero himself remarked (*de fin.* 5. 4. 11) ; see Thucydides: 3. 82 ff.; Plato: *Republic*, 543 ff.; Aristotle: *Politics*, 1301 b 19 ff.; 1307 b 25 ff. Cicero's *rector rei publicae*, like Aristotle's statesman, is essentially a man who can recognize political change in its beginning and pilot the state into safety; see *de rep.* 1. 29; 2. 25; cf. Aristotle: *Politics*, 1308 a 27 ff.; 1309 b 35 ff.

breaking up [of political life] because the citizens break up into several factions.[4]

And indeed, in political strife, when character counts for more than numbers, I hold that citizens should be weighed according to their merits and not merely counted.[5]

Fleshly lusts are harsh masters for our minds, since they compel and command us to enter upon courses which never end. Because they can in no way be appeased or satisfied, there is no crime to which they do not drive those whom their enticements have ensnared.[6]

One who has repressed its violence and its notorious savagery when released from restraint.[7]

II. This [act] was the more notable because, though they were colleagues and hence equal in responsibility, they were so far from being held in equal disfavor that the affection felt for Gracchus even mitigated the unpopularity of Claudius.[8]

He put at the disposal of this group of aristocrats and leading citizens his gift of austere, solemn, and dignified eloquence[9]

So that, as he writes, each day a thousand men wearing cloaks dyed with purple went down into the forum.[10]

In the case of these men, as you recall, a crowd of poor people gathered, and the funeral procession was quickly fitted out by means of the money contributed.[11]

[4] Nonius, p. 25. 3; Servius: *ad Aen.* 1. 149. Cicero derives *seditio* from *seorsum ire.*

[5] Nonius, p. 519. 17.

[6] Nonius, p. 424. 31.

[7] Nonius, p. 492. 1. The subject is not expressed; the passage may refer to the repression of lust by reason or the repression of sedition by the statesman.

[8] Gellius: *noct. Att.* 7. 16. 11; Nonius, p. 290. 15. The fragment refers to the trial of the censors Tiberius Sempronius Gracchus, father of the tribunes, and Gaius Claudius Pulcher in 169 B.C. Gracchus was believed to have secured the acquittal of Claudius by asserting that he would accompany Claudius into exile, if the latter were convicted while he himself were acquitted. See Livy: 43. 14 ff.; Heitland: *Roman Republic* (1909), sect. 631.

[9] Nonius, p. 409. 31. The text is hopelessly corrupt; we give a paraphrase of its apparent meaning.

[10] Nonius, p. 501. 27.

[11] Nonius, p. 517. 35. Possibly this refers to the funerals of Publius Valerius Publicola, Agrippa Menenius, and Quintus Fabius Rullianus.

For our ancestors desired the marriage-tie to be strong and lasting.[12]

The speech of Laelius, with which you are all familiar, [shows] how welcome to the deathless gods are the sacred bowls of the pontiffs and, to use his own expression, the Samian sacrificial cups.[13]

III. *When Cicero wrote on the Commonwealth, he followed Plato and even used the passage of [the "Republic"] which describes the return to life of Er the Pamphylian.*[14] *According to [Plato as reported by] Cicero,* Er came to life after he had been placed on the funeral pyre and revealed many secrets about the world below. *Unlike Plato, however, Cicero did not invent an incredible fiction, but used the plausible device of a cleverly constructed dream. In this way he neatly suggests that* accounts of heaven and the immortality of the soul are not[15] the fancies of dreaming philosophers or incredible myths, such as the Epicureans ridicule, but are tentative conclusions drawn by wise men. *Cicero introduces into his work the elder Scipio, who conquered Carthage and thus won for his family the cognomen Africanus, and makes him warn the younger Scipio, who was the son of Paulus, that he would be exposed to perils at the hands of his kindred, and that his life, constrained to its end by the fatal influence of number, was now*

These men were poor and money was voluntarily subscribed by the people to provide appropriate burial ceremonies. See Livy: 2. 16; 33; Apuleius: *apol.* 18.

[12] Nonius, p. 512. 27; Priscian: *gram. Lat.*, ed. Keil, 3. 70. 11. On Roman marriage see Cic. *de rep.* 5. 5, above, and note. In confirmation of Cicero's statement, note the tradition that there were no divorces in Rome before 231 B. C.; see Valerius Maximus: 2. 1. 4; Gellius: *noct. Att.* 4. 3. 2; 17. 21. 44; Heitland: *Roman Republic* (1909), sect. 261.

[13] Nonius, p. 398. 26. Cicero refers to the famous speech (called *aureola oratiuncula* in Cic. *de n. d.* 3. 17. 43; see also *ibid.* 3. 2. 5) delivered by Laelius in 145 B. C. opposing the proposal of Gaius Licinius Crassus to change the mode of selecting the augurs from cooption by the college to election by the people. The fragment perhaps formed part of a passage pointing out the statesman's duty to maintain religion in the state. Cf. Cic. *de n. d.* 1. 2. 3 ff., where he expresses the opinion that justice and human society could not survive without religion. Though Cicero was a skeptic, he was unwilling to submit fundamental moral and religious beliefs to skeptical criticism; see *de leg.* 1. 13. 29.

[14] The vision of Er is in Plato: *Republic*, 614 b ff.

[15] We read, with Barth, *nec* for *haec.*

approaching its appointed goal. Cicero asserts, moreover, that in the fifty-sixth year of Scipio's life, when the two perfect numbers combine,[16] he will restore his liberated soul to heaven whence he received it. For the essence of mind and soul, according to Cicero, is immortal; and for those who have deserved well of the state and have preserved their country there is reserved a bright and shining abode in the Milky Way.[17] Favonius Eulogius (ed. Holder), p. 1. 5.

IV. *Because of great brilliance of style and because of certain truths that he perceived, some of the Christian admirers of Plato declare that his views were not unlike the Christian belief, even in respect to the resurrection of the dead. Plato's opinion on this subject is alluded to by Cicero in his work on the Commonwealth, but he states that* Plato spoke figuratively and did not claim that his story was true. *For Plato does represent a man as having arisen from the dead and as having made certain disclosures which agreed with the views propounded in Plato's dialogues.* Augustine: de civ. 22. 28.

V. *It is in the following respect, however, that Cicero has imitated Plato most closely. For at the end of the "Republic" Plato introduces the story of one who was restored to life after he had apparently died. This man is made to reveal the condition of souls that have put off their bodies. To this Plato adds a not unprofitable picture of the spheres and planets. Similarly, in Cicero's work Scipio gives an account of the world which is not unlike Plato's in its meaning and which Scipio had learned in a dream.*

Macrobius: *in somn. Scip.* 1. 1. 2.

VI. *The arrangement which Cicero followed testifies no less to his discernment than to his ability. After his dialogue had treated every aspect of a commonwealth, both at rest and in action, and in every case had awarded the palm to justice, Cicero put at the very climax of the completed work an account of the blessed abodes of immortal souls and the secrets of the*

---

[16] For the significance of these numbers, see 6. 12, below, and note.
[17] Cf. Cic. *de rep.* 6. 13; 16; 24.

heavenly regions. Thus he showed where those are destined to go, or better, to return, who have wisely, justly, courageously, and temperately governed a commonwealth. In Plato these secrets are revealed by a man named Er, a Pamphylian by race and a soldier by profession. To all appearances he had died from wounds received in battle, but on the twelfth day after his supposed death, when he was to receive the honors of the funeral pyre along with the others who had died at the same time, it turned out that he had either retained his soul or received it back. For he unexpectedly took the witness stand, as it were, and reported to the human race all that he had done and seen in the days spent between this life and the life to come. Although Cicero, as cognizant of the truth himself, regretted that ignorant persons ridiculed Plato's myth, he took warning from an instance of stupid criticism and preferred that the narrator of his myth should be awakened from sleep rather than arise from the dead.

VII. *And before we consider the words of the Dream, we must explain what sort of men it was, as Cicero asserts, that ridiculed Plato's myth, but caused Cicero no fear for a similar ridicule of the dream of Scipio. Certainly his remarks are meant to refer not to the ignorant rabble, but rather to a group of men who are ignorant of the truth, though they pride themselves on their learning. For though they have studied these doctrines, they are moved to refute them. Accordingly, we shall mention those who, as Cicero reports, have indulged in foolish criticism of so great a philosopher, and especially the one who actually left a written indictment of him . . . The whole Epicurean School, which is itself as far from the truth as it is ready to ridicule whatever it does not understand, derided Plato's sacred work and the most revered secrets of nature. Colotes in particular,[18] who was rather well known among the pupils of Epicurus and had a name for loquacity, actually incorporated in a book his bitter and captious criticisms of Plato. We must omit all his unjust charges which*

---

[18] Colotes of Lampsacus was a pupil of Epicurus. His writings appear to have been directed especially against Plato. For references see Zeller: *Phil. d. Griech.* 3. 1 (1923), p. 380, n. 3.

have no bearing upon our present topic, the Dream, and address ourselves to those slanders which, if not disproved, will be a reproach to Cicero as well as to Plato. Colotes alleges that a philosopher ought not to have resorted to myths, since no form of fiction befits teachers of the truth. Why, he asks, if you desired to impart to us an idea of heaven and the destiny of souls, did you not do so by introducing the matter in a plain and direct way? Why, in fact, have a far-fetched dramatic character, a strange and carefully devised incident, and a stage prearranged to fit a preposterous fiction polluted with a lie the very portals of the search for truth? Since these queries raised about the vision of Er in Plato impugn also the dream of our slumbering Africanus . . . , let us meet Colotes' pressing questions and refute his vain arguments. Let our object be to disprove this one false accusation, and thus enable the achievements of both these writers to retain without blemish the reputation they deserve. Macrobius: *in somn. Scip.* 1. 1. 8 to 1. 2. 5.

VIII. *For Scipio himself was moved by the following circumstance to relate the dream upon which, he asserted, he had long deliberated in silence. Laelius was complaining that no statues had been publicly reared to Nasica to repay him for having caused the death of the tyrant [Gracchus]. After some other remarks Scipio replied as follows*: Though wise men find a generous recompense for virtue in the mere consciousness of deeds well done, yet their godlike excellence yearns for a more lasting and a more living reward than statues held in place by leaden clamps and triumphs adorned with their fading bays.

LAELIUS: What, I ask, are the rewards you mean?

SCIPIO: Since we have been keeping holiday for three days, allow me—*continuing with the other remarks by which he led up to the account of his dream. In this narration he explained that the rewards of a more lasting and more living character were those which he had himself seen reserved in heaven for distinguished governors of states.*

Macrobius: *in somn. Scip.* 1. 4. 2 ff.

THE DREAM OF SCIPIO

IX. After my arrival in Africa—where, as you know, I served under Manius Manilius as military tribune of the fourth legion[19]—my first desire was to meet King Masinissa,[20] who, for very good reasons, was a close friend of our family. When I met him, the aged prince embraced me and burst into tears. After a brief space he looked up into the sky and said: "To thee, O mighty Sun, and to you, ye other dwellers in heaven, I give thanks because, ere I depart this life, I behold in my kingdom and within this palace Publius Cornelius Scipio whose very name gives me new life. So constantly does my heart muse on the memory of his grandfather, that excellent man and invincible general." Then I questioned him about his kingdom, and he asked me about the condition of our commonwealth; and we spent the day together in lengthy conversation.

X. I was then entertained with princely splendor, and we prolonged our discussion late into the night. For the venerable man spoke of nothing except Africanus, and recalled not only all that he had done but even all that he had said. I was exhausted both by my journey and by the lateness of the hour. Accordingly, when we separated to retire, a deeper sleep than usual took me in its embrace. What ensued had its origin, I suppose, in the matter of our conversation. For quite regularly the subjects of our thought and discourse suggest our dreams, as Ennius writes that he dreamt of Homer, who no doubt was frequently the theme of his waking thought and conversation.[21] Thus it happened that Africanus appeared

---

[19] Manilius was consul in 149 B.C.; see Introduction, p. 5, above. At the time of this dream Scipio was about thirty-five years old. Each Roman legion was commanded by six *tribuni militum*, who at this time were elected by the people; see Bouché-Leclercq: *Manuel des inst. romaines* (1886), pp. 282 ff.

[20] Masinissa was the ally of Scipio Africanus the Elder in the campaign against Carthage in 204 B.C., and was made King of Numidia by the terms of the peace treaty of 201 B.C. A war between Masinissa and Carthage in 151 was the pretext for the Third Punic War. Masinissa died, at a very advanced age, before the capture of Carthage by Scipio in 146; see Sallust: *Iug.* 5. 4 ff.

[21] For the story that Homer appeared in a dream to Ennius, "shedding salt tears" and expounding the mysteries of the world below, see Lucre-

to me, in a form which was more familiar from his death mask
than from the man himself.[22] When I recognized him, I confess that I was stricken with fear. But he said, "Be calm,
Scipio; banish your fears, and inscribe my words in your
memory.

XI. "Do you see that city?" From a lofty station, bright
and glittering and filled with stars, he pointed out Carthage.
"Do you see that city which I forced to obey the Roman people,
but which now begins anew those ancient wars and cannot be
at peace? Although you who now come to besiege it are as
yet hardly a soldier, in three years you will be consul and will
overthrow it, and the cognomen which now you inherit from
me you will then have won for yourself by your own achievements. After you have destroyed Carthage, celebrated your
triumph, been censor, and traveled on an embassy through
Egypt, Syria, Asia, and Greece, a second time you will be
chosen consul, though absent from Rome, and by destroying
Numantia you will bring to a close Rome's greatest war.[23]
But when you have been borne to the Capitol in your triumphal
chariot, you will find the commonwealth thrown into utter confusion by the designs of my grandson.[24]

XII. "Then, Africanus, you must show to your country
the light of your courage, your character, and your wisdom.
But I see, as it were, the course of your destiny then becoming
uncertain. For when your life has passed through eight times

---

tius: 1. 120 ff.; Cic. acad. 2. 16. 51. For this explanation of dreams, see
Cic. de div. 2. 62. 128, and Pease's commentary.
[22] It was the custom of aristocratic Romans to decorate the central
hall of the house with wax masks (imagines) of deceased members of the
family; see Polybius: 6. 53. 4 ff.; Pliny: hist. nat. 35. 2. 6; Seneca:
de ben. 3. 28. 2; Marquardt: Privatleben der Römer (1886), pp. 240 ff.
Since the elder Africanus had died when Scipio was only about two years
old, he would naturally be known only from his death mask.
[23] Scipio was consul in 147 B. C., when he destroyed Carthage, and
again in 134. Election in the absence of the candidate was considered an
unusual honor. He was censor in 142. The embassy mentioned was sent
out in 141; see Cic. de rep. 3. 35, above, and note. The conquest of
Numantia was completed in 133 (see 1. 11, above, and note) and the
second triumph was in 132. Why Cicero should have considered the
struggle with Numantia "Rome's greatest war" is not clear.
[24] This refers to the attempted reforms of Tiberius Gracchus (133
B. C.), who was a grandson of the elder Scipio by his daughter Cornelia.

seven yearly revolutions of the sun, and when these two numbers, seven and eight[25]—each of which is considered perfect for a special reason—have by their natural cycle completed the span allotted you by destiny, then to you alone, because of your renown, the whole state will turn. On you the senate, all patriotic citizens, the allies, and the Latins will fix their eyes. On you alone the safety of the state will rest. In a word, you must be dictator and must set the state in order—if only you escape the godless hands of your kindred."[26]

At an exclamation from Laelius and at the deeper groans of the others, Scipio gently smiled. "Hush," said he, "pray, do not break my slumber. Hear yet a little longer what remains for me to tell."

XIII. "Yet, Africanus, that you may be more zealous in guarding your country, be assured of this: All men who have saved or benefited their native land, or have enhanced its

---

[25] A number mysticism, particularly with reference to seven and nine, was widespread among the Greeks and very ancient. Thus the number seven played a part in the cult of Apollo long before the birth either of philosophy or arithmetical science; see Roscher: "Die Sieben- und Neunzahl im Kultus und Mythus der Griechen," *Abh. d. phil.-hist. Klasse d. kgl. säch. Gesell. d. Wiss.*, 24 (1904), no. 1. After the Pythagorean philosophers began a more or less scientific study of number, various apocryphal explanations were given of the mystical properties of numbers and an elaborate symbolism developed; on number symbolism among the Pythagoreans see Zeller: *Phil. d. Griech.* 1. 1 (1923), pp. 495 ff.; 551. Eng. trans., *Pre-Socratics*, 1 (1881), pp. 419 ff.; 475. Number mysticism in philosophy received a great impetus from Plato, who was much influenced by the Pythagoreans, and it ran riot in later neo-Pythagorean and neo-Platonic philosophy; see Burnet: *Greek Philosophy*, 1 (1914), pp. 312 ff.; Zeller: *op. cit.* 2. 1 (1922), pp. 679 ff.; 947 ff. (Eng. trans., *Plato and the Older Academy*, 1888, pp. 254 ff.; 517 ff.); 3. 2 (1923), pp. 138 ff.; 190; 757 ff. A great collection of fanciful explanations for the significance of the number eight will be found in Macrobius: *in somn. Scip.* 1. 5. 1-18; for the number seven, *ibid.* 1. 6. 1-83.

[26] Scipio Aemilianus died in 129 B. C., the year of the dialogue. His opposition to the Gracchan land commisson had made him exceedingly unpopular with the party of reform. Hence, Cicero is wrong in saying that the whole state turned to him as its champion. When Scipio died suddenly in the fullness of his powers at the age of fifty-six, there were persistent rumors of foul play. His family was implicated in these rumors not only through the connection of the Gracchi with their grandfather, the elder Africanus, but also through Scipio's wife Sempronia, the sister of the Gracchi. No investigation was made at the time and there is no conclusive evidence as to the cause of Scipio's death. See Heitland: *Roman Republic* (1909), sect. 714; Greenidge: *History of Rome*, 1 (1904), pp. 159 ff.

power, are assigned an especial place in heaven where they may enjoy a life of eternal bliss. For the supreme god who rules the entire universe finds nothing, at least among earthly objects, more pleasing than the societies and groups of men, united by law and right, which are called states.[27] The rulers and saviors of states set forth from that place and to that place return."

XIV. At these words I was greatly frightened, less by fear of death than by the thought of treachery at the hands of my kindred. Nevertheless, I asked Africanus whether he and my father Paulus and the others whom we supposed dead were still living. "In truth," he replied, "only those are alive who have escaped the bondage of the flesh as from a prison,[28] while that which you call life is in reality death. Do you not behold your father Paulus coming toward you?" When I saw him, I poured forth a flood of tears, but Paulus embraced me and bade me not to weep.

XV. As soon as I mastered my tears and regained the power of speech, I said, "O father most excellent and holy, since true life is here, as Africanus tells me, why, I ask you, do I linger upon earth? Why may I not hasten to come to you?" "That may not be," he replied, "for, until God, to whom belongs this whole world before your eyes, shall free you from the body's prison, you may not enter this place. For the human race was born subject to the condition that they should guard the sphere which you see in the center of the heavens and which is called the earth. To them souls were given, drawn from those eternal fires[29] which you name con-

---

[27] See Cic. *de rep.* 1. 25, above.

[28] The doctrine that the body is the prison or tomb or sentry-post of the soul is developed by Plato: *Phaedo*, 61 e; 62 b; see also *Cratylus*, 400 c; *Phaedrus*, 250 c; *Axiochus*, 365 e. It is commonly supposed, as Plato himself implies, that the doctrine was Pythagorean and connected with the Orphic mysteries. See Vergil: *Aen.* 6, 733; Cic. *Tusc.* 1. 30. 74; *de sen.* 20. 73; Athenaeus: *deipnosophistae*, 157 c; Macrobius: *in somn. Scip.* 1. 13. 9 ff.; Burnet: *Greek Philosophy*, 1 (1914), p. 31; *Early Greek Philosophy* (1908), pp. 85 ff.; Whittaker: *Macrobius* (1923), pp. 63 ff.

[29] The identification of the soul with fire was a Stoic doctrine; see von Arnim: *Stoicorum veterum fragmenta*, 4 (1924), index s. v. *psyche*. Cicero has no definite theory of the nature of the soul. He regards it as different from matter, at least from the grosser forms of matter, and as

stellations and stars. These heavenly bodies are round like spheres. They are quickened by divine intelligences[30] and complete their cycles and rotations with wonderful swiftness. For this reason, Publius, you and all loyal men must retain the soul in its fleshly prison, and unless he who has bestowed the soul upon you so commands, you must not abandon human life, lest you seem to have deserted the earthly tasks imposed by God.

XVI. "But even as your grandfather here before you, even as I who begot you, so do you, Scipio, cultivate justice and loyalty, which is a noble spirit when shown towards parents and kindred, but noblest when shown towards your country. Such a life is the way to heaven and to the company of those whose life on earth is done and who, released from the body, inhabit the region which you behold, and which, after the Greeks, you name the Milky Way."

The place was a glittering circle that shone with exceeding brilliance in the midst of fiery stars. As I gazed down from it all other objects seemed dazzling and wonderful. There were stars which we have never seen from this earth of ours, and all of them had magnitudes such as we have never supposed to exist. The smallest of them was situated most remote from the heaven [of the fixed stars] and nearest to the earth, and shone with borrowed light. Moreover, the stars greatly surpassed the earth in size, and now the earth itself appeared so small that I felt ashamed of our empire, by which we cover a point, as it were, upon its surface.

XVII. Since I was observing the earth more intently than aught else, Africanus said, "How long, I ask you, will your thoughts be fixed upon the earth? Do you not perceive the heavenly spaces into which you have come? The universe is

---

divine in its nature, but does not deny that it may perhaps be fire or air as the Stoics assert; see *Tusc.* 1. 25. 60; 1. 28. 70.

[30] Aristotle assigned a spirit or separate motive force to each sphere within the heaven of fixed stars, in order to explain their motion in a direction contrary to that of the outer sphere as described in chapter 17, below; see *Metaph.* 1073 a 26-b 1; *de caelo*, 279 a 18-22. Plato (*Timaeus*, 41 d) assigns a star to each created soul, and declares (*Laws*, 899 b) that the souls of the stars are divine.

formed of nine circles or spheres, as we should more properly call them. One of these is the heaven [of the fixed stars] ; it is on the exterior of the universe, embracing all the other orbs, and is the supreme god himself who constrains and includes the remaining spheres.[31] In it are placed the eternal courses of the rolling stars. Beneath this outer circle are the seven orbs which revolve in a direction opposite to that of the heavens. The outermost of these spheres belongs to the planet which men on earth call Saturn. The next is the luminary called Jupiter, benign and propitious to the human race, and next the ruddy star, feared by earth, which you call Mars. Below Mars comes the sun, which holds almost the mid-region [between the earth and the heavens] and is the leader, chief, and director of the other stars, and the mind which keeps the universe in balance. Such is his greatness that he encompasses and fills the whole world with his light. In the sun's train, like comrades, follow the spheres of Venus and Mercury.[32] The lowest globe carries the moon, which is kindled by the rays of the sun.[33] All below the moon is mortal and transitory, except the souls which the gods have bestowed on man, while all above the moon is immortal.[34] The earth,

---

[31] This seems to be a misinterpretation of Aristotle: *Physics*, 267 b 6-9. Others besides Cicero so understood the passage; see Heath: *Aristarchus of Samos* (1913), pp. 226 ff. For the correct interpretation of Aristotle, see Ross: *Aristotle* (1924), pp. 179 ff. As a skeptic, Cicero himself usually regards certainty about the nature of God as impossible (*de n. d.* 1. 21. 60 ff.). He sometimes asserts the spirituality of the force which moves the universe (*de rep.* 3. 22; *de leg.* 2. 4. 10), though he does not object to identifying God with fire or air, in the Stoic fashion, or with aether, as he supposes Aristotle to do (*Tusc.* 1. 26. 65). For practical reasons he holds strongly to a belief in divine providence (*Tusc.* 1. 49. 118; *de n. d.* 1. 2. 3; *de leg.* 1. 7. 21; 3. 1. 3). See Zeller: *Phil. d. Griech.* 3. 1 (1923), pp. 689 ff.; Eng. trans., *Eclecticism* (1883), pp. 167 ff.
[32] This passage suggests that Cicero may have been acquainted with the astronomical theories of Heraclides of Pontus; see Heath: *Aristarchus of Samos* (1913), pp. 255 ff. The *Commonwealth* is a "Heraclidean" dialogue, that is, the interlocutors belong to a past generation.
[33] Plato (*Timaeus*, 38 d) places the sun next above the moon and so below Venus and Mercury. This represents the view of the older Greek astronomers, while the order given by Cicero first appears in the second century B.C. in the Stoic Diogenes of Babylon; see Heath: *Aristarchus of Samos* (1913), pp. 107; 258 ff.
[34] The theory of the sublunar region as the place of the terrestrial elements and the theory of absolute weight will be found in Aristotle: *de caelo*, bks. 3 and 4, *passim*. Birth, death, and qualitative change

which occupies the ninth position, is the center of the universe. It does not move, it is the lowest of the spheres, and all heavy bodies are swept to it by gravity."[35]

XVIII. When I recovered from the astonishment with which I was gazing upon this spectacle, I asked, "What is this mighty yet delightful sound which fills my ears?" "That," he replied, "is the melody produced by the swift movement of the spheres themselves. It is blended from notes of different pitch, and while the intervals between them are unequal, their differences are marked with exact proportion, and by a blending of high with low notes various concordant effects are harmoniously achieved. Motions so vast cannot sweep on in silence. It is natural, furthermore, for one extremity to have a low pitch while the opposite has a high pitch. Accordingly, the heaven's outermost sphere, which carries the stars and which revolves more rapidly, moves with a high and lively tone. On the other hand, the lowest pitch is the moon's, which is the innermost of the spheres.[36] For the earth, which is the

belong only to the sublunar region. Many citations of similar passages will be found in Zeller: *Phil. d. Griech.* 2. 2 (1921), pp. 466 ff.; Eng. trans., *Aristotle and the Earlier Peripatetics*, 1 (1897), pp. 506 ff.; Ross: *Aristotle* (1924), pp. 98 ff.; Heath: *Aristarchus of Samos* (1913), pp. 227 ff.

[35] Cicero's account of the heavenly spheres cannot be regarded as serious scientific theory, even from the point of view of ancient astronomy. Modern historians of science have shown that the theory of concentric spheres originated in an attempt, brilliantly successful in view of the difficulties of the problem, to discover a geometrical analysis of the apparently irregular movements of the planets. The problem was proposed by Plato (*Laws*, 822 a; *Republic*, 529 a ff.; Simplicius on Aristotle's *de caelo*, 292 b 10, ed. Heib., p. 488. 20-24), and the first solution was offered by his pupil Eudoxus of Cnidus (c.408-c.355 B. C.). The theory was developed by Callippus of Cyzicus (c. 370 - c.300 B. C.) and modified, though not improved, by Aristotle. But it is manifestly impossible even to approach the problem by assuming only nine spheres or one to each planet. Eudoxus used twenty-six (omitting the daily rotation of the heavens), Callippus thirty-three, and Aristotle fifty-five. The theory was accepted perhaps as late as Archimedes (c. 287-212 B. C.) but was displaced in later astronomy by the more plausible theory of eccentric circles and epicycles, because it contradicted the observed fact that the planets vary their distances from the earth at different times. See Heath: *Aristarchus of Samos* (1913), pp. 190 ff.

[36] Cicero is following a Pythagorean source; see the summary in Aristotle: *de caelo*, 290 b 12-29 (Diels: *Vorsokratiker*, 1, 1912, p. 355, 15-32). The discovery that pitch depends on the length of a stretched string and that definite ratios correspond to the intervals used in tuning the lyre

ninth planet, [does not produce any tone, since it] remains
motionless and abides in one place, occupying the center of the
universe. The eight [other] cycles, however—two of which
[Mercury and Venus] move with the same velocity—produce
seven notes of different pitch, and the number seven is, in a
sense, the bond which holds the entire universe together. This
method of creating harmony scholars have imitated in vocal
and instrumental music, and have thus won for themselves
a return to this place, even as other men have done who, blessed
with pre-eminent ability, have devoted their lives on earth to
studying the ways of heaven. The sound which we hear has
filled and deafened man's ears, since no sense is more easily
blunted than hearing. Thus, the people who live near what
are called the cataracts of the Nile, where the river sweeps
down from high mountains, have lost the power of hearing
because of the roar of waters, and similarly the sound caused
by the swift revolution of the whole universe is so overwhelm-
ing that human ears are insensible to it. In the same way,
you cannot gaze directly at the sun; its rays overcome your
sight and vision."

XIX. Though I was filled with awe at the celestial har-
monies, I kept turning my eyes constantly towards the earth.
"I see," said Africanus, "that you still contemplate the abode
and home of man. If the earth appears insignificant to you—
as indeed it is—ever lift up your eyes to these heavenly realms
and despise the concerns of men. For what fame can you
win among men or what renown worthy of your striving?[37]
You perceive that the earth is peopled only in scattered and
restricted regions, and that even within the patches where

---

suggested that similar ratios might be found between the diameters of
the orbits of the planets. The idea was elaborated with various musical
analogies; Cicero is evidently thinking of the heptachord lyre. In giving
the higher notes to the outer spheres, he seems to agree with Plato in
the Vision of Er (*Republic*, 617 a ff.) ; note, however, the different interpretation of Plato in Adam: *Republic of Plato*, 2 (1921), p. 452. On the
harmony of the spheres see Zeller: *Phil. d. Griech*. 1. 1 (1923), pp. 537
ff.; Eng. trans., *Pre-Socratics*, 1 (1881), pp. 460 ff.; Heath: *Aristarchus
of Samos* (1913) pp. 105 ff.

[37] With this sentence compare a striking passage on the insignificance
of fame in Marcus Aurelius: *Reflections*, 4. 3. The contempt of fame
was a Stoic commonplace; cf. Cic. *de rep*. 1. 17, above.

men live—if I may use the word patches—there are interspersed great tracts of desert. You see not only that the inhabitants are so dissevered that nothing can be interchanged, but also that some live in the same longitude with you but in the opposite latitude, some in the same latitude but in the opposite longitude, and some are even diametrically on the opposite side of the earth. From such as these assuredly you can hope for no renown.

XX. "You perceive, moreover, that the earth is also adorned and encircled with what we may call girdles.[38] Two of these zones are exactly opposite to one another and, lying beneath the very poles of the heavens, are congealed with ice. On the other hand, the middle zone, which is the largest, is parched by the sun's heat. Two are habitable, and of these the southern zone, in which the inhabitants are your antipodes, touches you not at all. There remains, then, the northern zone in which you dwell. Consider how small a portion of it concerns you. For all the territory which you possess is narrow from north to south and, while broader from east to west, is in fact only a small island surrounded by the body of water which you on earth call either the Atlantic, or the Great Sea, or Oceanus. But though you call it great, you see how insignificant it is! Has your fame, or the fame of any of us, been able to spread beyond the lands which you know and possess, and to pass over the Caucasus, which you see here, or to cross the Ganges, there? Is there anyone in the other extremities of the earth, whether in the east, west, north, or south, who will hear your name? And when you leave out these regions, you see how little is the world in which your ambition strives to make a show. And how short-lived will be the speech even of those who speak our name!

XXI. "Even if the children of generations to come should desire to recount to their posterity the praise of our several achievements which they have heard from their fathers, the

---

[38] The conception of the zones is as old as the theory that the earth is spherical in form. In origin it was due to astronomical rather than geographical considerations. Both Pythagoras and Parmenides are credited with its first statement. See Heath: *Aristarchus of Samos* (1913), pp. 65 ff.

destruction of the earth by fire or flood—disasters bound to recur at fixed periods[39]—preclude our winning lasting, to say nothing of immortal, fame. Indeed,[40] what matters it if the men who come after you will have your name upon their lips when the men who lived before you never mentioned you? XXII. And yet the earlier generation was quite as numerous as the later and was certainly composed of better men. [What matters human fame], especially when [we consider that], even of the men who can hear our name, there is not one who can remember the events of a single year? For while men loosely define a year as the time necessary for a revolution of the sun—that is, of a single star—in reality a year can truly be said to have completed its course only when all the stars have returned to the original positions whence they set out, and when after a long interval they have brought back the same arrangement throughout the whole heavens.[41] In this cosmic year I do not dare to say how many generations of men are included. Once, when the soul of Romulus entered these heavenly regions, men thought that the sun disappeared and was blotted out. Only when the sun has again passed

---

[39] The theory that the earth is doomed to periodic conflagrations was part of the Stoic philosophy. The fires of the sun and other heavenly bodies are fed from the sea, with the result that ultimately the fiery element must absorb the others; see Cic. *de n. d.* 2. 45. 118. Sometimes periodic destructions of the world by flood also were assumed, as in the present passage. Each destruction begins a new period in which the world and all its parts are formed anew. See Zeller: *Phil. d. Griech.* 3. 1 (1923), pp. 155 ff.; Eng. trans., *Stoics, Epicureans, and Sceptics* (1892), pp. 165 ff.

[40] We have modified the punctuation given by Ziegler, beginning with the words *quid autem interest,* as follows: *quid autem interest ab iis qui postea nascentur sermonem fore de te—cum ab iis nullus fuerit qui ante nati sint, qui nec pauciores et certe meliores fuerunt viri—praesertim cum,* etc. The style is conversationally fluid, but it seems clear that the clause beginning with *praesertim cum* should be taken closely with *quid . . . interest.*

[41] The conception of the great or cosmic year probably originated with the Pythagoreans, from whom it was borrowed by Plato (*Timaeus,* 39 d). The latter fixes the period arbitrarily at ten thousand years. Tacitus states (*dial. de orat.* 16) that Cicero in some work said that the great year contains 12,954 ordinary years; here he makes it not less than 11,740 years. See Cic. *de n. d.* 2. 20. 51 ff., with Mayor's commentary; Stobaeus: *ecl.* 1. 264; Zeller: *Phil. d. Griech.* 1. 1 (1923), p. 535; 2. 1 (1922), p. 811; Eng. trans., *Pre-Socratics,* 1 (1881), pp. 458 ff.; *Plato and the older Academy* (1888), p. 382.

into eclipse in the same region of the sky and at the same time, and when all the planets and stars have likewise returned to their original positions, are you to understand that a year has passed. Of this year be assured that the twentieth part has not yet revolved.

XXIII. "If, then, you give up the hope of returning to this place where all blessings await great and distinguished men, how puerile is the renown conferred by man, lasting as it does for only a small portion of a single year! But if you wish to look on high and to contemplate this abode and eternal home, you will not yield to the flattery of the rabble or set your hopes upon the rewards that men may give. Excellence itself, by its own inherent charm, must draw you towards true glory. What others say about you must be their concern; nothing will prevent their talking. All that they may say, however, is confined to the narrow limits you perceive; it is never lasting in the case of any man, but is obscured when men die and is blotted out when posterity forgets."

XXIV. After he had spoken thus, I answered: "Since, Africanus, there is, as it were, a path which leads to heaven and which lies open to men who have earned their country's gratitude, I shall strive for so glorious a reward even more earnestly than I have. And yet from boyhood I have followed in my father's footsteps and in yours and have not tarnished your glory." "Strive earnestly," he replied, "and be assured that only this body of yours, and not your real self, is mortal. For you are not the mere physical form that you appear to be; but the real man is the soul and not that physical body which men can point to. Know, then, that your true nature is divine, if indeed it is a divine principle which lives, feels, remembers, and foresees, and which rules, guides, and activates the body beneath its sway, even as the supreme god directs the universe. And as the world, which is in part mortal, is stirred to motion by God Himself, who lives forever, so the frail body is quickened by an immortal soul.

XXV. "For whatever possesses the power of ceaseless

movement is eternal.[42] On the other hand, whatever imparts movement to other things and is itself set in motion by external objects must end its life when its movement ends. Accordingly, only that which moves with self-originating motion never ceases to be moved, because it is never abandoned by itself; and it is, moreover, the source and beginning of motion for all other things that move. Beginning has no source, since all things arise from beginning, while beginning itself can spring only from itself. For that which took its beginning from something else could not be a beginning. If, then, beginning is never born, neither does it ever die. For beginning, if destroyed, will never itself receive new life from another source, nor will it create anything else from itself, since all things must arise from a beginning. Thus, it follows that the beginning of movement is derived from that which moves with self-originating motion and which can neither be born nor die. Otherwise, the whole heaven and the universe would collapse and stand still and would never receive any impulse by which they might again be stirred to motion.

XXVI. "Since, therefore, it is clear that whatever is self-moving is eternal, who will deny that this power has been given to soul? For everything that is stirred to movement by external forces is lifeless, but whatever possesses life is moved by an inner and inherent impulse. And this impulse is the very essence and power of soul. If, then, soul be the only thing which is self-moving, assuredly it is not created but is eternal. Train it in the noblest ways! Now the noblest concerns of the soul have to do with the security of your country, and the soul which is employed and disciplined in such pursuits will fly more speedily to this abode, its natural home. This journey it will make the swifter, if it looks abroad, while still imprisoned in the flesh, and if, by meditating upon that which lies beyond it, it divorces itself as far as may be from the body. For the souls of men who have surrendered themselves to carnal delights, who have made themselves as it were

---

[42] The whole of ch. 25, and ch. 26 to the words "but is eternal," appear also in Cic. *Tusc.* 1. 23. 53-55. Cicero translates the passage from Plato: *Phaedrus*, 245 c ff.

slaves of the passions, and who have been prompted by lust to violate the laws of gods and men, wander about near the earth itself, after their escape from the body, and do not return hither until they have been driven about for many ages."

He departed; I awoke from sleep.

FRAGMENTS THAT CANNOT BE ASSIGNED TO THEIR BOOKS

1. And nature herself not only prompted but actually required that [to be done].[43]

2. Strive.[44]

3. They surpass.[45]

4. *This virtue is defined by Cicero in his rhetorical works as wisdom; but in another place, namely, in his work on the Commonwealth, it is called foresight.*[46]

   Victorinus: *Explan. in rhet. Cic.*, ed. Halm, p. 156.4.

5. It is a difficult matter to praise a boy, Fannius, for we must praise not what he has done but the promise that he shows.[47]

6. *In Ennius' work Africanus speaks as follows:*

   If it be right for anyone to mount to the regions of the gods,
   For me alone the great door of heaven stands open.

   Because, of course, he had utterly blotted out a large part of the human race. How great was the darkness in which you wandered, O Africanus, or rather, O poet, to imagine that men are allowed to mount to heaven through slaughter and bloodshed. To this vain opinion even Cicero gave his assent, for he

---

[43] Nonius, p. 321. 16. Mai gives the not improbable conjecture that this fragment belongs in the introduction to the first book and refers to the compulsion which nature places upon good men to take part in the service of the commonwealth; see Cic. *de rep.* 1. 1 (end), above.

[44] Diomedes: *gram. Lat.*, ed. Keil, 1. 339. 31.

[45] Diomedes: *gram Lat.* 1. 374. 17.

[46] This testimonium apparently deals with the peculiar excellence of the *rector rei publicae*, and refers either to Cic. *de rep.* 6. 1. (cf. the first fragment from Nonius) or possibly to 2. 42. The Latin words are *sapientia* and *prudentia*.

[47] Servius: *ad Aen.* 6. 875. Mai conjectures that the passage is an echo of Plato: *Phaedrus*, 279 a, and refers to Lucius Licinius Crassus, the orator (140-91 B. C.), who would have been about eleven years old at the supposed time of the dialogue, and who became the son-in-law of the interlocutor Quintus Mucius Scaevola.

says, It is really so, Africanus, for the same door opened to Hercules also.[48]

Lactantius: *inst.* 1. 18. 11 ff.

7. In fact
himself
Since his interruption stopped us short of the very goal.

To him no one, whether citizen or stranger, will be able to pay the price which his deeds merited.[49]

8. Those who win men's favor by feasts and banquets clearly show that they are wanting in true honor, which is derived from excellence and worth.[50]

9. Gently and quietly, not violently and impatiently, ought faith to be shaken.[51]

---

[48] See Ennius (Vahlen, 2nd ed.) : *var.* 23. The verses clearly refer to the elder Africanus. Mai supposes that Laelius is speaking in compliment to the interlocutor Africanus, and that the fragment belongs with the reference to Hercules in Cic. *de rep.* 3. 28, above. We have translated the context from Lactantius, which Ziegler prints in the apparatus criticus.

[49] Seneca: *epist.* 108. 32 ff. The last fragment is from Ennius (Vahlen 2nd ed.) : *var.* 19, and refers to Africanus the Elder.

[50] Anon. paradoxa koronne apud Bielowski, Pompeii Trogi frag. p. xv f.

[51] Cod. manuscr. n. 458, p. 82 bibl. Ossolinianae apud Bielowski, 1. 1. p. xvi.

INDEX

INDEX

Esquiline Hill, 160.
Etruria, 171, 199.
Etruscans, 159, 174.
Eudoxus of Cnidus, 119.
Euripides, 14.
Euxine Sea, 204.

Fabius Maximus, Quintus, 94, 105, 249.
Fabricius, Gaius, 105, 222.
Fame, Vanity of, 122 f., 264 f.
Family, 65 ff., 246 f.
Fannius Strabo, Gaius, 6, 116, 268.
Fasces, 170, 183.
Fasti, 189 f.
Ferguson, W. S., 19.
Fetial College, 74, 169, 207.
Flamens, 72, 167.
Flavius, Gnaeus, 189.
Furius Camillus, Marcus, 108.
Furius Philus, Lucius, 5, 115, 124, 126, 198, 215.

Galba, see Sulpicius.
Gallus, see Sulpicius.
Ganges, 264.
Gauls, 160, 204.
Gorgias, 13.
Gracchus, see Sempronius.
Greece, 108, 127, 143, 158, 163, 204, 228, 244, 257.
Greeks, 125, 143, 162, 164, 178, 179, 185, 232, 235, 260.
Gymnastic, 232 f.

Hannibal, 4.
Harmony, 54 f., 193; of the spheres, 262 f.
Heraclides of Pontus, 261.
Hercules, 166, 221, 269.
Herillus of Carthage, 19.
Hesiod, 163.
Homer, 141, 163, 235, 256.
Horatius Barbatus, Marcus, 183.
Hostilius Mancinus, Gaius, 5, 213.
Hyperbolus, 239.

Immortality of the soul, 266 f.
Injustice, advantages of, 200 ff.
Interrex, 82, 84, 165.
Iphigenia of Ennius (or Naevius), 124.
Isidore of Seville, 150.
Isocrates, 13, 199.
Italy, 115, 158, 159, 168, 199.
Ius gentium, 36.

Julius, Gaius (consul), 187.
Julius, Gaius (decemvir), 188.
Julius Caesar, Gaius, 3, 44, f., 220.
Julius Caesar Octavianus, Gaius, 4.
Julius, Proculus, 164.
Junius Brutus, Lucius, 178.
Junius Brutus, Marcus, 36.
Junius Congus, 152.
Justice, 53 f., 193 f., 195, 200 ff., 206 ff., 210 ff., 215 ff.

Kosmoi in Crete, 185.
Knights, 172, 174, 231.

Laelius, Gaius, 5, 116 f., 128, 190, 198, 252, 255, 258.
Laenas, see Popilius.
Larcius, Titus, 184.
Lares, 246.
Latin Holidays, 113.
Latin League, 126, 222.
Latium, 177, 199.
Law in the state, 52 f., 89 f., 136.
Law of nature, 22, 27, 30 ff., 35 ff., 48 f., 208, 215.
Legatus, 82.
Lepidus, see Aemilius.
Lex Acilia de repetundis, 90.
  Aternia Tarpeia, 187.
  Caecilia Didia, 90.
  Calpurnia, 33.
  Canuleia, 188.
  Julia Papiria, 187.
Leges Porciae, 183.
Lex Valeria, 183.
  Valeria Horatia, 183.
  Voconia, 205.
Liberty, 55 f., 134 f.
Licinius Crassus, Lucius, 268.
Licinius Crassus, Marcus (Triumvir), 44.
Licinius Crassus, Publius, 126, 206.
Lictors, 170, 184.
Luca, Conference of, 2, 44.
Luceres, 161, 171.
Lucilius, Gaius, 5, 35, 200, 208.
Lucretia, 178.
Lucretius, Spurius, 183.
Lucretius Carus, Titus, 130.
Lucretius Tricipitinus, 178.
Lucumo, 161.
Lycurgus, 34, 74, 154, 161, 163, 165 f., 176, 177, 179, 185, 205, 234.
Lysias, 13.

INDEX

Popular assemblies, 86 ff., 90 f.
Porcius Cato, Marcus (censor), 35, 105, 123, 154 f., 173, 201, 222, 240, 250.
Posidonius, 46.
Praetor, 80, 84.
Priesthoods, 71 f., 167.
Progress, 63 f.
Proletarii, 175.
Provocatio, 146.
Publilius, Gaius, 186.
Pydna, Battle of, 4, 35.
Pyrrhus, 105, 222.
Pythagoras, 115, 142, 168, 206.

Quinctius, Lucius, 190.
Quirinal Hill, 160, 164.
Quirinus, 164.

Reason, 143 f., 197, 215.
Religion, 68 ff.
Remus, 156.
Revolution, 250 f.
Rhamnes, 161, 171.
Rhodes, 135, 227.
Roman Games, 172.
Rome, foundation, 155 ff.; decay, 243 f.
Romulus, 121, 143, 155 ff., 162 ff., 170, 182, 221, 227, 265.
Roscius, 241 f.
Rutilius Rufus, Publius, 6, 113, 115.
Rutuli, 156.

Sabines, 160 f., 172, 199.
Salian priests, 167.
Sallustius Crispus, Gaius, 43, 243.
Samnites, 222.
Samnium, 199.
Sardanapalus, 228.
Scaevola, see Mucius.
Scipio, see Cornelius.
Scipionic Circle, 5, 28, 34 ff., 47.
Sempronia, 4.
Sempronius Gracchus, Gaius, 6, 41, 231.
Sempronius Gracchus, Tiberius (cos. 177, etc.), 251.
Sempronius Gracchus, Tiberius (tribune, 133), 4, 41, 47, 63, 113, 125 f., 179, 222, 257.
Sempronius Tuditanus, Gaius, 113.
Senate, 83 ff., 161, 172, 184, 186, 216, 231.
Senatus consultum, 85.
Seneca, see Annaeus.

Servilius Ahala, Gaius, 108.
Servian constitution, 174 f.
Servius Tullius, 143, 173 ff.
Sestius, Lucius, 188.
Seven Sages, 112.
Sicily, 115, 158.
Simonides, 163.
Skeptics, 16, 23 ff.
Smyrna, 113.
Socrates, 16, 108, 114 f., 155, 165, 180, 198, 233.
Solon, 24, 112, 154, 186.
Sophists, 15 f.
Sparta, 154, 176, 179 f.
Spartans, 120, 137, 204, 233.
Spheres, Harmony of, 262 f.
Statesman, Ideal, 45, 93 ff., 181, 245, 248 f., 250 f.
Stesichorus of Mataurus, 163.
Stoics, 18 ff., 27 ff.
Suessa Pometia, 177.
Sulpicius Galba, Servius, 201, 223.
Sulpicius Gallus, Gaius, 118 f., 120 f., 124.
Sulpicius Rufus, Servius, 36.
Sun-dogs, 114, 116.
Sybaris, 168.
Syracuse, 118, 224, 225.
Syria, 257.

Tarpeius, Spurius, 187.
Tarquinii (city), 171.
Tarquinii (family), 178, 182.
Tarquinius Collatinus, Lucius, 178, 182.
Tarquinius Priscus, Lucius, 171 ff., 173.
Tarquinius Superbus, Lucius, 143, 146, 168, 177 f., 181 f.
Tarquinius, Sextus, 178.
Tatius, Titus, 160 f.
Taurians, 204.
Terentius Afer, Publius, 5, 35.
Terentius Varro, Marcus, 46, 142, 230.
Thales, 112, 119, 121, 142.
Theater, 238, 239 f.
Thebans, 233.
Themistocles, 108.
Theopompus, King of Sparta, 185.
Theseus, 154.
Thirty Tyrants, 133, 225.
Thrace, 158.
Thucydides, 8, 40, 99, 159.
Timaeus of Locri, 115.
Timaeus of Tauromenium, 224.